Shakespeare's Mortal Men

Studies in Shakespeare

Robert F. Willson, Jr.
General Editor

Vol. 1

PETER LANG
New York • San Francisco • Bern • Baltimore
Frankfurt am Main • Berlin • Wien • Paris

Patricia L. Carlin

Shakespeare's Mortal Men

Overcoming Death in History,
Comedy and Tragedy

PETER LANG
New York • San Francisco • Bern • Baltimore
Frankfurt am Main • Berlin • Wien • Paris

Library of Congress Cataloging-in-Publication Data

Carlin, Patricia L.
 Shakespeare's mortal men : overcoming death in history,
comedy and tragedy / Patricia L. Carlin.
   p. cm. — (Studies in Shakespeare ; vol. 1)
 Includes bibliographical references.
 1. Shakespeare, William, 1564-1616—Criticism and interpretation.   2. Death in literature.   I. Title.   II. Series.
PR3069.D42C37   1993   822.3'3—dc20   92-8722
ISBN 0-8204-1563-4   CIP

Die Deutsche Bibliothek-CIP-Einheitsaufnahme

Carlin, Patricia L.:
Shakespeare's mortal men : overcoming death in history, comedy
and tragedy / Patricia L. Carlin.—New York; Berlin; Bern;
Frankfurt/M.; Paris; Wien: Lang, 1993
  (Studies in Shakespeare ; Vol. 1)
  ISBN 0-8204-1563-4
NE: GT

The drawing by Rembrandt on the front cover is reprinted
by the kind permission of Rijksmuseum-Stichting,
Amsterdam.

Cover Design by Jim Brisson.

The paper in this book meets the guidelines for permanence and
durability of the Committee on Production Guidelines for
Book Longevity of the Council on Library Resources.

© Peter Lang Publishing, Inc., New York 1993

All rights reserved.
Reprint or reproduction, even partially, in all forms such as
microfilm, xerography, microfiche, microcard, offset strictly
prohibited.

Printed in the United States of America.

Acknowledgement

My deepest thanks are owed to Alvin B. Kernan, whose work on the history plays helped to spark this study, and whose suggestions and encouragement proved invaluable at many stages of this work; to Lawrence Danson, for his reading of various versions of this work, and for his consistently insightful advice; and to Thomas P. Roche, whose approach influenced mine in ways direct and indirect. I also wish to thank Lillian Zawisha for all her assistance and her competent supervision during the typing and preparation of this manuscript.

Table of Contents

Introduction 1
                The *Quem Quaeritis* Drama: Paradigm of
                the Medieval-Renaissance Dramatic
                Tradition 6

Chapter One   **Overcoming Death in Medieval, and
                Tudor Morality, Drama**............................ 17
                Medieval Morality Drama........................... 18
                Corpus Christi Drama (Cycle Drama) 22
                Saints' Plays 30
                Kingship and the Communal Body
                    in Tudor Morality Drama 36
                The King's Two Bodies............................... 42

Chapter Two   The World of the Second History
                Tetralogy (*Richard II, Henry Four, Part
                One, Henry Four, Part Two, Henry Five*):
                "Miracles are Ceased".............................. 55
                Land 59
                Debt/Currency/Counterfeiting 62
                Law/Justice/Warfare 79
                Conclusion.. 93

Chapter Three   *Love's Labor's Lost*: Setting the
                Shakespearean Dramatic Task.................. 107
                Wordplay.. 110
                Literature 123
                Action 135
                Conclusion.. 142

Chapter Four	***Romeo and Juliet*: Death Confronted**......... 151	
	The Communal Body................................. 157	
	Romeo and Juliet... 186	
	Denouement.. 194	
	Conclusion.. 202	

Conclusion 219

Works Consulted... 225

Index 245

For Roy; for my mother Mignonne Ladin;
and for Jennifer and John

Introduction

As abstractions "life" and "death" are opposites, but in actual existence they are fused. Biologically, the body which is the source of life is the source of death; and whether we view ourselves as in the process of living or of dying depends simply on how we view the same existential reality. The death aspect of physical existence extends also to social existence, for whatever its form, the social body is always both sustaining of and inimical to the lives of its individual members.

At some point (a point often dramatized in Shakespeare's work) each person discovers his mortality, and the biological fact of death is henceforth a psychological fact as well, coloring all aspects of existence. The faculty which enables a person to imagine his own death is pressed into service to create strategies for dealing with the knowledge; and an ongoing task of both individual and communal psychic life is to assimilate the reality of death in a way which permits symbolic mastery of it. Individual ways of doing this will be aided by, and are to some extent inseparable from, the materials a particular culture offers—the historical element in individual constructions of reality.

Symbolic mastery over death, a central task of psychic life, is a chief task of Shakespearean drama as well; for death in its inclusive sense—the fusion of life and death in physical and mental experience—is the essential stimulus to which Shakespearean drama is a response.[1] In dealing with death Shakespeare continues, while altering, a long-standing dramatic tradition, for the drama which precedes his work is also centered on the overcoming of death; and the theater of both medieval and Renaissance England offered a powerful communal resource for dealing with mortality. The Shakespearean deployment of this resource is integrally related to contemporary cultural realities, theatrical and non-theatrical.

For a complex of reasons (discussed below), the problem of death presented itself to Englishmen of the period with increased urgency; and the breakdown of older ways of dealing with death gives rise, in Shakespearean drama, to new theatrical strategies, new ways of confronting, in order to master, the death aspect of physical and social life. Death is a problem for the living; and in histories, comedies and tragedies alike Shakespeare presents us with dynamic models of the problem—kinetic images of human beings grappling with mortality amid circumstances which are at once particular and universal as they create, or fail to create, means of mastering different forms of death.

Although the particular way the death aspect of existence is formulated varies from play to play, the underlying situation, stated abstractly, is always the same. Man is locked into a physical and social body, each of which is simultaneously life-sustaining and death-dealing (the inescapability of the social body is less obvious to us than to the Elizabethans, but it is equally a fact of human existence). In short, the key element in the Shakespearean formulation of mortality is the image of the body—the body of death which requires revivification, but which can never be wholly escaped.

Recently, psychologists and anthropologists have begun to explore the centrality of death in individual and communal psychic life. Robert Jay Lifton, for example, elaborates a psychology based on the search for symbolic death-transcendence, the "struggle for symbolic immortality."[2] This struggle is "central to the human project," for we "require symbolization of continuity—imaginative forms of transcending death—in order to confront genuinely the fact that we die."[3]

Ernest Becker, in *The Denial of Death*[4] and *Escape from Evil*,[5] also puts the denial of death at the heart of individual and communal psychic life (*Escape* stresses the role death-denial plays in the formation of cultures, and *Denial* is more concerned with its effects in individual life). However Lifton, in contrast to Becker, focuses not on the denial of death, but on the positive uses of the effort to place death in a symbolic perspective which allows imaginative transcendence of it. Lifton himself distinguishes his work from Becker's as follows:

"Absent in Becker is a sense of the full significance of symbolization, and especially of the symbolization of the life-process.... In his work a unitary life-death paradigm is not realized."[6]

Lifton's approach more accurately describes Shakespeare's way of working. Shakespeare characteristically strips away the fabric of fictions surrounding the fact of death, and exposes the fact in all its nakedness; but as the death aspect of life is confronted it is encompassed within a kinetic image (a dramatic action) which revalues it—an image of resurrection which is the image of the life-process itself.

Kenneth Burke's kinetic definition of literature best describes what a Shakespearean play actually does. For Burke, a given text is a form of symbolic action which serves a function for author and audience—or, in Burkean terminology, "*a strategy for encompassing a situation.*"[7] Applying this approach to Shakespeare, we would say that a given play constitutes a strategy designed to incorporate, in a way which affirmatively revalues, the basic Shakespearean (and human) situation of the oneness of life and death. That situation is represented differently in every play, and the dramatic strategy of any particular play is likewise unique. However, basic similarities between strategies yield the generic forms of history, comedy, tragedy.

For affirmation to be meaningful, death must be fully confronted. *Love's Labor's Lost* sets the task for Shakespearean drama in Rosaline's command to Berowne to force laughter from the sick, suffering and dying, and in his response, "To move wild laughter in the throat of death?/ It cannot be, it is impossible" (V.ii.853-54).[8] Death as the animating force of Shakespearean comedy is least obvious in the early plays, pearls concealing the irritant which produces them.[9] Death intrudes more insistently in the problem comedies, is openly confronted in the tragedies, and is assimilated with finality in the late comedies where the worst of human and natural destructiveness is incorporated into an ultimately affirmative pattern—Berowne's task successfully completed.

To summarize, it is my contention that the wish to deal with the death side of life gives rise in Shakespeare to individual dramatic strategies, and to generic strategies as well. Moreover, it is a shaping force behind Shakespeare's overall dramatic development. Shakespeare's work falls roughly into three periods. The first is characterized by history and comedy (although also including tragedy). The second comprises the bulk of the darker or "problem" comedies and the mature tragedies. The third and final stage consists of the late comedies now called romances (as Shakespeare's contemporaries did, I am including the romances under the general term "comedy"). However, by a fairly early stage of his career Shakespeare had explored the life/death oneness of existence in all three genres, and had done so in a way which exposed the essential concerns of his subsequent drama as well. To illustrate this, I will discuss four history plays, an early comedy, and an early tragedy.

I begin my discussion of Shakespeare by examining the later and better worked out of the two English history tetralogies: *Richard II*, *Henry IV*, parts one and two, and *Henry V*. In the course of these four plays many of the elements characteristic of Shakespearean comic and tragic strategies are deployed, only to be eliminated. The world at the end of the tetralogy—the law-bound, money-based, "beehive" world of *Henry V*—is in many respects a capsule version of contemporary English society; and it is the normative social world from which Shakespearean comedy and tragedy proceed and to which they return. It can offer collective immortality, continuance of the race or nation, but not individual immortality.

Shakespearean comedy and tragedy focus on the problem of individual mortality; and I discuss *Love's Labor's Lost*, which sets the task for both comedy and tragedy by exposing the inescapability of individual mortality, and the necessity of confronting that fact before a dramatic/psychological way of dealing with it can be achieved. The way of dealing with death which *Love's Labor's Lost* points to—but does not achieve—is that characteristic of Shakespearean comedy: individual pleasure and fulfillment in love and marriage, and communal renewal (and partial individual renewal) through children.

In even the most successful of Shakespearean comedies death is only deflected—put off to a future beyond the time and space the comedy encompasses; for if we followed the lovers in time, they would of course age and die, and children offer only partial compensation for individual death. Tragedy, in contrast, confronts death directly. Death is admitted to the playing space, and we see what mortal men counterpose to the fact of their mortality. I discuss *Romeo and Juliet*, an early tragedy which epitomizes the essentials of subsequent Shakespearean tragedy. All Shakespearean tragedy depends for its effect upon a full acknowledgement of death's ultimate inescapability (which is to say, on acknowledgement of the limits of comedy). But *Romeo and Juliet*, which begins in a comic, and shifts to a tragic, mode, actually dramatizes the fact that the starting point of tragedy is the exposure of the limits of comedy vis-à-vis death. To put it otherwise, what is implicit in later tragedies is in *Romeo and Juliet* the very material of which the tragedy is built. I conclude this work with a very brief indication of the applicability of my hypothesis to other Shakespearean comedies and tragedies.

It might be objected that the genesis of Shakespearean drama is traceable to, and at least partially accounted for by, specific features of the dramatic tradition Shakespeare inherited. However, the deep links between Shakespeare and his predecessors actually reinforce my point, for the preceding English drama, from its medieval origins to its Elizabethan fruition, is itself rooted in the impulse to overcome death. The central action of medieval drama is also the central action of Shakespearean drama—resurrection, the revivification of the body of death, by which I mean the overcoming of the death aspect of physical and social existence. Both medieval and Shakespearean drama envision man as not only locked into a physical body, but into a social or communal body as well. "For whoever he be, he [*i.e.*, any man] must live in the body of the Commonwealth, and in the body of the church."[10] However, the way that the social body is portrayed undergoes a profound change between the earlier and the later drama, and an understanding of the implication of that change for the problem of death is, I believe, central to an understanding of

Shakespeare's work, both of his individual plays and of his generic forms. Therefore, before discussing Shakespeare's work I will first examine the *Quem quaeritis* texts, a paradigm for the entire medieval-Renaissance tradition. In a separate chapter I will discuss the early morality plays, cycle plays and saint's plays, which repeat the *Quem quaeritis* action in more complex fashion; and Tudor morality drama, which transforms the action in ways which lead directly to Shakespeare's work. My point is not that the earlier drama influenced the later (although often it did).[11] Rather, I am concerned to trace the changing way in which the imagination comes to grips with the fact of mortality; for drama in medieval and early Tudor times enacts publicly the overthrow of death which preoccupies individual men, and which continues, in altered form, to hold the center of the Shakespearean stage.

The Quem Quaeritis Drama: Paradigm of the Medieval - Renaissance Dramatic Tradition

Medieval drama represents a separate, self-contained dramatic tradition entirely unrelated to classical precedent. Following a ban on public theater in the fifth century, Greek and Roman drama disappear as a living force.[12] Drama reappears, some five centuries later, in connection with Christian liturgical practice centering on the symbolic and ritual enactment of Christ's death and resurrection. And resurrection — victory over death — is also the subject of this earliest drama, the so-called *Quem quaeritis* plays.[13]

Quem quaeritis texts exist from the tenth century onward, in versions ranging from brief dialogues to extended plays.[14] However, all the texts, earlier and later, simpler and more elaborate, consist of the same essential action. The grieving Marys visit Christ's tomb where an angel asks them whom they seek. When they reply that they are seeking Jesus, an angel tell them Christ has risen.[15] However described — death to resurrection, loss to restoration, grief to joy — this action remains the core of the medieval- Renaissance dramatic tradition.

The *Quem quaeritis* drama originated as an embellishment of the Good Friday-Easter liturgy.[16] When we examine the liturgy associated with the earliest drama, we see that all elements repeat the central action of the *Quem quaeritis* plays, death and resurrection.[17] The Eucharistic climax of each Mass repeats the action of death and resurrection symbolically and also ritually (that is, literally—the sacrament was considered to offer literal access to Christ's immortal Body). The Easter liturgy traces the same action, reaching its nadir of suffering and death on Good Friday, when the rite for transforming the wafer and wine into Christ's life-giving Body ceased to be enacted,[18] and reversing itself in the Vigil Mass, the Mass of the Resurrection, the climax of the entire Easter liturgy.[19] And the numerous liturgical and extraliturgical ceremonies, such as the darkening of the church on Good Friday and its subsequent reillumination on Easter, all, like the Mass and the Easter liturgy, repeat and exemplify the action of death and resurrection. The movement of emotion which accompanies this action is inseparable from it, and the action is perhaps better expressed as suffering-and-death followed by joy-and-rebirth.[20]

Resurrection requires death as its prelude, both in the obvious sense and also psychologically. To experience the impact of resurrection, a congregation has first to feel the impact of death. The Good Friday portion of the liturgy was designed to express the sorrow and bitterness of death to the fullest[21] in order that the final defeat of death might be felt with corresponding intensity. In the drama which follows the same effect obtains. The degree to which death is acknowledged determines the power of the triumphant denouement.

The difference of effect on an audience between a liturgy or drama which stresses Resurrection (the joy-and-rebirth aspect of the action) and one which stresses Crucifixion (the suffering-and-death aspect) will of course be considerable.[22] However, the containing form is still one indivisible whole, an action presenting the death and resurrection of a single human body which is at the same time a divine and communal Body embracing all men. It is this whole which is enacted, in briefest possible form, in the *Quem quaeritis* drama.

The status of the *Quem quaeritis* plays as the earliest medieval drama; their formal influences on subsequent drama; and the absolute centrality of their action *vis-à-vis* the whole of the ensuing dramatic tradition, all establish for these texts a position as the seminal form for medieval drama.[23] Accordingly, it is worth examining one version closely. A good version for our purpose is the *Visitatio Sepulchri* contained in the *Regularis Concordia*, a tenth century manual prepared by Sts. Aethelwold and Dunstan for use by English Benedictine monks.[24] This *Visitatio Sepulchri* includes unusually full directions, enabling us to know with certainty how it was meant to be performed; and it is an English text, and therefore especially suitable for my discussion, which deals with the treatment of death in English medieval and Renaissance drama.

The *Regularis Visitatio*, performed on Easter morning, formed the climax of a sequence beginning on Good Friday with a pair of ceremonies, the *Adoratio* and the *Depositio*, which follow one another in the *Regularis Concordia*.[25] These ceremonies together represent the suffering-and-death aspect of the action.

In both ceremonies a cross substitutes for Christ's body.[26] In the *Adoratio* the cross, symbolizing the crucified Christ, is set up before the altar, with two deacons holding it upright; the deacons sing Christ's *improperia*, or reproaches, as the subdeacons and schola reply antiphonally. "The reproaches of the dying Christ are directed to clergy and congregation alike. The dramatic setting makes the death motif extremely powerful—for many, perhaps, close to unbearable."[27] In the second ceremony, the *Depositio*, directions are given for a "likeness of the sepulchre"[28] to be constructed upon the altar with a curtain placed around it. The deacons come forward, wrap the cross in a cloth (signifying the graveclothes), and lay the shrouded cross in the mock sepulchre "as if the body of our Lord Jesus Christ has been buried" (*"ac si Domini nostri Jhesu Christi corpore sepulto"*).[29]

The *Regularis Visitatio*, the climax of the sequence beginning with the *Adoratio* and *Depositio*, consists of a histrionic revelation of the Resurrection, being a dramatic presentation of the Marys' visit to Christ's sepulchre and the angel's announcement to them that Christ has risen.[30] It offers visual as well as verbal confirmation of the Resurrection, for its directions specify that the angel reveal the now-empty sepulchre, and that the women remove the "shroud" (the cloth in which the cross was wrapped) and display it before the congregation. The *Visitatio*, then, is the joyful culmination of a sequence of action beginning with suffering and death and ending in joy and renewal of life. This is so whether we consider the sequence as extending from the *Adoratio* and *Depositio* to the *Visitatio*, or whether we consider the *Visitatio* alone; for the *Visitatio* itself contains the whole act of suffering and death (the women grieving) changed to joy and renewal (the announcement of the Resurrection to the mourners).

Life and death, joy and sorrow are fused in this one action, both for the characters in the play and for the beholders who participate vicariously in their emotions. The Marys stand for mankind, the assembled congregation in particular and the faithful in general, to whom the news of the Resurrection is given, and who, like the Marys, experience a turn from initial grief at death to joy in the news of victory over death. That is, the action communicated is simultaneously external and internal (death with the accompanying emotion of sorrow, and rebirth with the accompanying emotion of joy). At the outset of this chapter I stated that the fusion of life and death as a fact simultaneously of physical and mental experience is the situation which generates Shakespearean drama. This situation also obtains here, at the very inception of the medieval-Renaissance dramatic tradition.

The impulse behind the *Visitatio* is the wish to represent dramatically an ultimately victorious confrontation with death (death being understood in the inclusive sense just described). This wish gives rise to a drama which encompasses death in order to transcend it. That is, the *Quem quaeritis* drama, like the Christian redemptive history it illustrates, works to incorporate the facts of suffering and death into an overall pattern which gives full weight to, but compels affirmative revaluation of, those facts. The action of death and resurrection originally abstracted from the events of Christian history and expressed in the liturgy ritually and symbolically is, in the *Quem quaeritis* drama, restored to the world of time and space—made fully dramatic. However, this highly stylized playlet is as little particularized as is compatible with any representation of life in the world of time. In contrast to later medieval drama, it avoids elaboration of action, dialogue, naturalistic detail—of any of the representational features which might evoke a sense of mundane existence, of the intractability of time and the flesh as we actually experience them. Rather, the curtain of the sepulchre is drawn easily aside to reveal the utter absence of the body—the empty tomb, the vacant graveclothes, the total banishment of dead, corruptible flesh.

It should be stressed that the action of the *Quem quaeritis* drama is not, finally, sequential. The parts of an action in time necessarily follow one another, but the action itself is a whole. In the overall pattern which climaxes in resurrection, suffering and death are not dispelled, but their significance must be entirely revalued. This is an important point for the understanding of subsequent drama, including Shakespeare's work. Although the action of death and resurrection unfolds sequentially, the revisionary potential of the whole towards its parts is always implicit. In Shakespearean drama the revisionary potential of the ending may be exploited positively, as, for example, in *The Winter's Tale* where the statue of the supposedly dead Hermione comes to life, causing both Leontes and the audience to favorably revise their sense of the preceding action; or it may be exploited negatively as, for example, in *King Lear*, where the action culminates in the living pietà of Lear holding Cordelia's body. If Cordelia, believed dead, lives, "It is a chance which does redeem all sorrows" (*King Lear*, V.iii.268); and as Lear commands the audience on-stage and off-stage to "Look . . . Look . . . Look . . . look" (V.iii.312-13), we half expect this pieta to end as did the original. But this body does not, and will not, rise; and the hope of "resurrection," aroused and then dashed, moves us to an even blacker valuation of the preceding events.

We should note that in both the *Quem quaeritis* drama and its Shakespearean variations, witnesses to the action exist in the plays, as well as in the audience: in the earlier drama, the three Marys and, by extension, the congregation; and in the later drama, the characters typically assembled at the denouement of a Shakespearean play and, by extension, the playhouse audience. The action of resurrection is completed only in the minds of the witnesses, who are moved to reassess the meaning of what they have seen.

The *Quem quaeritis* play, a paradigmatic form for ensuing drama, is a history play depicting death and resurrection. The drama which follows repeats that essential action, whether in longer or shorter, simpler or more complex form, whether played out in the guise of psychic history as in the moralities, or in the guise of external history as in the cycle and saints' plays. In short, the conquest of the body is at the heart of Christian redemptive history and of the drama which that history gives rise to. However, the development of medieval and Renaissance drama may be viewed as a series of increasingly less successful attempts to deny the reality of creatureliness—an illustration of the Freudian law of the return of the repressed. In the earliest drama the death aspect of the body is wholly overcome: the tomb is empty, the body vanished.[31] In later medieval drama the reality of bodily existence is brought forcefully before us as, for example, in the dramatic insistence on imagery of decomposition;[32] but the death-aspect of the flesh is still successfully encompassed by the action of resurrection. In Shakespearean drama the claims of the body are at last fully acknowledged, and new revivifying actions are required, new ways of encompassing and revaluing the death aspect of bodily-based life.

The struggle of the imagination to deal with the body may be summarized in three central dramatic images: the empty sepulchre of the earliest drama; the risen Lazarus of later medieval drama, in whom corruption and revivification of the flesh are simultaneously evident; and finally the failed resurrection plot of *Romeo and Juliet*, in which the witnesses assembled at the denouement see not an empty sepulchre but two forever-dead bodies. Shakespeare's dramatic resurrections occur on a plane other than the literal. Accordingly, they satisfy our sense of reality even as they fall short of our desire.

Notes

1 James L. Calderwood, *Shakespeare and the Denial of Death* (Amherst, Mass.: U. of Massachusetts Press, 1987), and Kirby Farrell, *Play, Death, and Heroism in Shakespeare* (Chapel Hill and London: The U. of North Carolina Press, 1989), also see the effort to deal with death as centrally important to Shakespeare's work. Calderwood discusses some specific strategies for denying death culled from a variety of plays. He also discusses in brief six tragedies—*Romeo and Juliet, Richard II, Hamlet, Othello, Macbeth, Coriolanus*—in relation to death denial. He then discusses *King Lear* at length, expanding his focus on death denial from the strategies within particular plays to the nature of theatrical experience, in particular, the experience of tragedy. Finally he considers the connection between Shakespeare's interest in symbolic immortality and the lasting power of his work. Kirby Farrell also sees the wish to master death as a shaping force of Shakespeare's work. Following Ernest Becker's broad definition of heroism—"heroism means not merely conventional roles but individual and cultural value systems. Heroism is whatever produces a conviction of importance and worth" (p. 41)—Farrell focuses on ways in which "Imagination generates heroism in order to master the prospect of its own annihilation" (p. 36). He relates forms of play death, heroism, and apotheosis in Shakespeare's work to social and psychological conditions in Shakespeare's England.

See also Susanne Langer, *Feeling and Form: A Theory of Art* (N.Y.: Charles Scribner's Sons, 1953). Langer sees art as arising from, and uniquely expressive of, the simultaneously biological and symbolic nature of human experience.

2 Robert Jay Lifton, *The Broken Connection: On Death and the Continuity of Life* (N.Y.: Simon and Schuster, 1979), p. 18.

3 Lifton, p. 17.

4 *The Denial of Death* (N.Y.: The Free Press, Macmillan Publishing Co., Inc., 1973).

5 *Escape From Evil* (N.Y.: The Free Press, Macmillan Publishing Co., Inc. 1975).

6 Lifton, p. 52n.

7 "The Philosophy of Literary Form," in *The Philosophy of Literary Form: Studies in Symbolic Action* (Berkeley and Los Angeles, Calif.: Univ. of Calif. Press, 1941; revised 1973), p. 109.

Introduction 13

8 *The Complete Signet Classic Shakespeare*, general ed. Sylvan Barnet (N.Y.: Harcourt Brace Jovanovich, Inc., 1963).

9 Marjorie Garber, "'Wild Laughter in the Throat of Death': Darker Purposes in Shakespearean Comedy," in *Shakespearean Comedy*, ed. Maurice Charney (N.Y.: New York Literary Forum, 1980), agrees that "Shakespearean comedy is really about death and dying" (p. 121). See also Calderwood: "... one could argue that the denial of death is central to the form of both tragedy and comedy" (*Shakespeare and the Denial of Death*, p. 103).

10 Archbishop Laud, in R. H. Tawney, *Religion and the Rise of Capitalism* (N.Y., 1926), p. 172, quoted in Lawrence Danson, *The Harmonies of the Merchant of Venice* (New Haven & London: Yale U. Press, 1978, p. 144).

11 For a detailed study of the profound links between Shakespeare's work and the popular theatrical tradition see Robert Weimann, *Shakespeare and the Popular Tradition in the Theater: Studies in the Social Dimension of Dramatic Form and Function*, ed. Robert Schwartz (Baltimore and London: The Johns Hopkins U. Press, 1978).

I do not discuss folk plays, which Shakespeare's work also draws on, partly for reasons of space, but also because folk drama and Christian drama merge at what for my purposes is the central point, the overcoming of death. Cf. Robert Potter, *The English Morality Play: Origins, History and Influence of a Dramatic Tradition* (London & Boston: Routledge & Kegan Paul Ltd., 1975), who remarks, "There are indications that at least the structure of the morality play (as distinct from its intellectual substance, which is medieval and Christian) can be traced to similar origins in fertility ritual. The link which connects morality play and ritual is a folk ritual drama known as the mummers' play. . . . Its central act, a battle of champions to the death, with a miraculous revival, reproduces the ritual battle of winter and summer, the rhythm of death and regeneration, the ritual burial of winter and the resurrection of life" (p.12).

12 There were during this period popular entertainments such as performances by wandering minstrels and jugglers. However, our information about these is indirect, as no texts survive. And if we were to postulate a connection between these and classical drama (for example, in the survival of an acting tradition) we would be "postulating the influence of a lost body of literature upon another body of literature, which is itself hypothetical." Rosemary Woolf, *The English Mystery Plays* (Berkeley and Los Angeles: U. of California Press, 1972), p. 32.

13 These plays were associated with monasteries in England and on the continent, where they were performed by and for the brothers in connection with monastic services.

14 The texts vary as to degree of elaboration, and their relative chronology is not established with precision. However, from our point of view

variation between texts and their exact chronology are both unimportant.

15 The term *"Visitatio,"* applied to certain of these texts, refers to the whole action (the *Visitatio Sepulchri*, Visit to the Sepulchre) of which the *Quem quaeritis* dialogue forms a part. The appellation *"Quem quaeritis"* derives from a fixed feature of the dialogue, the angel's opening question to the Marys, *"Quem quaeritis,"* "Whom do you seek?"

16 The *Quem quaeritis* play is always associated with the Easter liturgy, but exactly where in the liturgy it originated is in dispute. O.B. Hardison, Jr., *Christian Rite and Christian Drama in the Middle Ages: Essays in the Origin and Early History of Modern* Drama (Baltimore, Maryland: The Johns Hopkins Press, 1965), believes it was originally associated with the Vigil mass, the climax of the Good-Friday Easter liturgy, and later displaced. Other scholars disagree; and in surviving manuscripts the *Quem quaeritis* dialogue is found in other positions.

The *Quem quaeritis* texts exemplify the difficulty of establishing a precise dividing line between an inherently dramatic liturgy and drama itself. Some *Quem quaeritis* texts were merely tropes, embellishments to the liturgy intended for singing rather than for dramatic performance. Other texts may have been performed, or may have simply been sung, perhaps in procession. However, this need not concern us, for explicit directions in certain texts, including the one we shall examine (the *Visitatio Sepulchri* from the *Regularis Concordia*), make it clear beyond question that these, at least, were to be given a fully dramatic performance.

17 For detailed description of the Good Friday-Easter liturgy associated with the *Quem quaeritis* drama, see Hardison.

18 In earlier times Communion was entirely withheld on Good Friday. But by the ninth century Communion was offered with a host sanctified on, and reserved from, the previous day. See Woolf, *The English Mystery Plays*, p. 7. In either case the meaning is the same. The day which commemorates Christ's death is the day on which death momentarily triumphs, and the transformation through consecration of the lifeless material wafer into Christ's life-bestowing Body cannot be performed.

19 "The Church recognized the climactic nature of the Vigil Mass and placed it in the most splendid of all liturgical settings. Extraliturgical, representational, rememorative, and purely mimetic ceremonies are also used in greater profusion for this occasion than for any other of the year. Almost all of them involve death-rebirth symbolism, and several have associations linking them to the *Quem quaeritis* play—white robes, burial, and tomb-symbols, to name the most obvious." Hardison, pp. 162-63.

20 Medieval writers on the Mass and the Lent- to-Easter sequence habitually described it as a movement of emotion, "the transition from *tristia* to *gaudium*," from sorrow to joy. Hardison, p. 285.

21 See Hardison.

22 For example, the Mass of the ninth century stressed the Resurrection, whereas the Mass of the later Middle Ages stressed the Crucifixion. Hardison, p. 65. Hardison also notes that "the Mass . . . is joyful on Christmas and deeply somber on Passion Sunday, although the same comic structure is used on both occasions" (p. 292).

   The essential action of the liturgy—suffering and death turned to joy and renewal—remains the same for the Elizabethan liturgy, although of course there are differences between the Roman and the Reformed rites, as there are even between the services of the earlier and the later Middle Ages. For a comparison of the Roman Mass with the reformed English Communion Service as set forth in the First Prayer Book of 1549 (prepared under Cranmer's supervision), see Stephen A. Hurlbut, ed., *The Liturgy of the Church of England Before and After the Reformation* (Washington D.C.: The St. Albans Press, 1941).

23 *Quem quaeritis* texts existed in England and on the continent, but this work deals only with English drama, which in certain respects developed differently from its continental counterparts.

24 This manual has been edited and translated by Dom Thomas Symons (London, 1953). The edition is cited in Woolf, *English Mystery Plays*, p. 340, n.6.

25 Neither of these ceremonies is unique to the *Regularis*.

26 Certain evidence indicates that originally the Host, rather than the Cross, was "buried". For a discussion of this see Woolf, *The English Mystery Plays*, pp. 7-8; and Hardison, 136-38.

27 Hardison, p. 132.

28 The translation is David Bevington's from his edition and translation of the *Regularis "Depositio,"* in *Medieval Drama* (Boston: Houghton Mifflin Company, 1975), p. 16.

29 Bevington, p. 16.

30 For my discussion of the *Regularis "Visitatio,"* I have used David Bevington's edition, in *Medieval Drama*, pp. 27-28.

31 At the period in which the *Quem quaeritis* drama took shape, "the moment in the Resurrection story which in art was taken to symbolize the whole was the visit of the three Marys to the sepulchre, and in this scene the empty grave-clothes were always visually stressed; in iconography it was they, and not the risen Christ Himself, that demonstrated the truth of the Resurrection." Woolf, p. 8. That is, the proof of Resurrection is not the revivified body but the total absence of the body.

32 The three forms of later medieval drama I shall now examine—the Corpus Christi drama, moralities, and saints' plays—arose in England coincidentally with a widespread, obsessive interest not merely in death, but in bodily decomposition, the details of which were graphically portrayed in art and literature alike. Critics who discuss this phenomenon in relation to the drama include Theodore Spencer, *Death and Elizabethan Tragedy: A Study of Convention and Opinion in the Elizabethan Drama* (Harvard U. Press, 1936); Willard Farnham, *The Medieval Heritage of Elizabethan Tragedy* (Oxford, England: Basil Blackwell, 1936; rpt. 1963); Bernard Spivack, *Shakespeare and the Allegory of Evil: The History of a Metaphor in Relation to Shakespeare's Major Villains* (N.Y.: Columbia U. Press, 1958); Robert Potter, *The English Morality Play: Origins, History and Influence of a Dramatic Tradition* (London and Boston: Rutledge & Kegan Paul Ltd., 1975).

Chapter One

Overcoming Death in Medieval, and Tudor Morality, Drama

Medieval drama may be roughly divided into two periods, the first beginning with the *Quem quaeritis* drama and reaching its height in the twelfth century, and the second associated with the late fourteenth and fifteenth centuries and including the drama I shall now discuss—morality drama, Corpus Christi drama and saints' plays. Drama from both periods exemplifies the central action of death and resurrection. However, there are some broad characteristic differences between the earlier and later drama which may be summarized as follows. The earlier drama was mostly in Latin (although it included a sprinkling of drama in the vernacular); was performed by the clergy and closely tied to the cyclical church year; was usually performed in church; and was highly stylized and markedly formal. The later drama was written in the vernacular; was performed by laymen, outside the church; was performed at times in the church year which did not necessarily coincide with the events being commemorated in the drama; and was characterized by greater informality and more verisimilitude.[1] What these changes amount to is that the later drama enacts death and resurrection within an increasingly particularized, or historicized, dramatic world. The pattern of death and renewal is imposed upon a mass of dramatic particulars expressive of embodied life at particular times and places (*i.e.*, of historical existence); but those particulars, although they weigh against the pattern, are still successfully encompassed by it.

Medieval Morality Drama

Medieval morality drama, because of its extensive use of personified abstraction, is perhaps the least overtly "historical" of the three later medieval forms. However, the pattern of death and resurrection which is the object of mimesis in the morality has been abstracted from the events of Christian history; and it can easily be reclothed in historical particulars, which is what in fact occurs in the saints' plays.

The personified abstractions of morality drama figure forth the movements of human spiritual history. The movement of emotion made visible on the morality stage is no mere correlative to, it *is* the action of resurrection, occurring on a plane of reality superior to that of the physical, observable world; for in this drama human emotion, like human history, has eschatological implications.

Mankind's history is reduced in morality drama to the history of one character who is all men everywhere in time. In the saints' plays this character is given a local habitation and a name—St. Paul, Mary Magdalene. In the morality he is simply Mankind—the King of Life, Mankind, Everyman, as he is variously called in the dramas we shall examine. The history of this character recapitulates the universal history of cycle drama because every human being recapitulates the story of the race: fall into death and potential resurrection.[2] The history of this character—death and renewal—*is* his nature, for the essence of the Mankind character is subjection to death and the potential for transcending it; or, to restate this, a body of death, the mortal physical body and the complex of drives and appetites associated with it; and a body of life, the "lofly likeness of God" in man,[3] man's potential for union with the undying Body of Christ.

The earliest known morality, the *Pride of Life*, is incomplete;[4] but the Prologue, which offers a precis of the plot, makes it clear that the drama repeats the familiar action of death-transcendence—a combat between death and life in which death, temporarily victorious, is ultimately overthrown. The King of Life, the protagonist of the drama, is a king figure we encounter throughout medieval drama, a representation of human mortality who in spite of youth, strength, riches and power, must die. Like the cycle and saints' play rulers, the King boasts of possessing limitless power; and undeterred by the displeasing reminders of his Queen and Bishop that he is mortal, he issues a challenge to Death. Death appears as a character in the drama, fights with and kills the King. The action continues after death, as devils bear the King to hell; but through the intercession of the Virgin Mary the King narrowly averts his deserved fate and is received into eternal life.

The strategy of this play is as familiar as its action. The inescapability of death is stressed throughout: in the Queen's petition to the King to reform because he must die (" . . . though thou be kinge/ nede schalt have ende;/ death ourecomith al thinge");[5] in the Bishop's sermon to the King, which repeatedly insists on the fact of the King's and all men's mortality; and not least by the King himself, whose challenge to Death's might reminds us the more strongly of it. The terror of death is further evoked by the appearance of Death himself, personified. But as death is insisted upon, the solution is before us: the Queen and the Bishop insist upon death's inevitability *because* salvation is achievable. Death is confronted within the affirmative context of an action whose satisfying end — the overthrow of death — is known and potentially assured.[6]

The *Castle of Perseverance* is the morality play equivalent of a full-scale cycle drama. The play comprises over 3,640 lines; a cast of some 36 characters including angels, devils, a host of personified abstractions and God Himself; a cosmic setting including heaven and hell, this world and the next; and a plot which epitomizes all of redemptive history, as we follow Mankind (*Humanum Genus*) from birth through a series of falls and renewals to death and the final renewal, eternal life (a microcosm of human history: Creation through world history to Doomsday). Nevertheless, like the mammoth cycle dramas, this lengthy, elaborate drama repeats the same action as that seen in little in the *Quem quaeritis* plays: death and resurrection.

Resurrection is represented in this drama by the fate of the soul after death. The Mankind character dies about four-fifths of the way through the play, calling on Mercy; and his Soul (*Anima*) crawls from under his deathbed and continues the action. The Four Daughters of God — Truth, Righteousness, Peace and Mercy — debate the fate of the soul before God. Righteousness and Truth want man damned for his sins; Peace wants him saved, and wants the four daughters to be in accord; and Mercy pleads man's case to God. God declares for man, asserting that His nature mingles Truth, Righteousness and Peace, but above all, Mercy;[7] and the resurrection action is consummated in another, but dramatically visible world.

The allegory of The Four Daughters of God, a familiar medieval motif, expresses a theological problem: how to reconcile God's justice, by which man incurs the penalty of death, and His mercy, by which man undeservedly escapes death. However, the conflict between justice and mercy is the theological expression of an existential fact: the unyielding reality of death and our need for transcendence of it. All men are under a death sentence from which there is no appeal, for as physical beings we are subject to natural law, which condemns us to die. Mercy represents the affirming forces, variously embodied in the drama, through which we experience the possiblity of transcending our fate. Shakespeare's naturalistic and problematic versions of this extend to whole plays, and also to specific scenes — for example, Hal's deliverance of Falstaff into the hands of the Lord Chief Justice in *Henry IV, Part Two*; the trial scene in *Merchant of Venice*; the two judgement scenes in *Measure for Measure* (before Angelo, and before the Duke, Isabella pleading first for her brother's, then for Angelo's, life).

Everyman, the latest, perhaps best known of the three moralities, reveals the same concern with death we see in the earliest known morality, *The Pride of Life*. The urgency of our need for a solution to death is not diluted in this play (as it is in *The Castle of Perseverance*) by a large cast of characters, extensive elaboration of the central action or sheer length.[8]. The plot is simple and stark; and its simplicity exposes, with corresponding increase in affective power, the concern with death which powers all morality drama. Death is sent by God to Everyman, who must then prepare to die; and the movement of the play is simply Everyman's journey to his grave, into which he finally, and visibly, descends (the action calls for him to enter the grave on stage). The movement of the play is thus a metaphor for life in a body, for bodily existence is a progress toward death.

As Everyman approaches his destiny he is successively deserted by his companions, who together represent all worldly goods and attachments: Felawship, Kinrede and Cosyn, Goodes, Strength, Discrecion, Five Wittes [Senses], and Beaute. During the play Knowlege and Confession help to free Good Dedes, formerly bound by Everyman's sin, to accompany him. But at the final moment Knowlege too is powerless against death; and Good Dedes alone accompanies Everyman into the grave.

The resurrection phase of the play is confined to its last fourteen lines (not including the Epilogue), in which Knowlege comments that although Everyman has suffered the fate "we shall all endure,"[9] Good Dedes "shall make all sure";[10] and an angel then calls Everyman to eternal life, promising a similar end for all men who live well. Thus, more than 900 lines of the play deal with the coming of death, and only fourteen lines with its transcendence. However, the imminence of death is countered from the very beginning of the play by the possibility of salvation implicit in a scheme of action in which death is no mere natural fact, but a messenger direct from God.[11] And while the fourteen-line conclusion does not undo the sombre effect of this powerful play, its affirmation of victory over death is sufficient to enforce a different valuation of the whole.

"Ded [death] is my destenye," Mankind declares in *The Castle of Perseverance*.[12] In the medieval morality Mankind confronts his destiny within the context of an action which promises a different destiny—resurrection, the conquest of death for eternity.[13] Morality drama, then, like the *Quem quaeritis* drama, works to overcome death symbolically by incorporating it in a pattern of action which negates it. The reality of death is dramatized with a power and immediacy absent from the

Quem quaeritis plays. However, while the dramatic focus is on death rather than its overthrow, ultimate and literal victory over death is still assured.

Corpus Christi Drama (Cycle Drama)

The English Corpus Christi play, which had reached its fully developed form by the last quarter of the fourteenth century, is historical drama. Like much of the earlier drama, including the *Quem quaeritis* plays, the Corpus Christi drama was based on scriptural (*i.e.*, "historical") material augmented by extrascriptural tradition, both being filtered through the lens of patristic thought (the influence patristic thinking exerts is noticeable, for example, in the selection and treatment of episodes). With this in mind, we can describe the typical Corpus Christi play as consisting of episodes dramatizing scriptural or traditionally sanctioned extrascriptural material presented in more or less chronological order, which together form a comprehensive account of redemptive history from the Creation to the Last Judgement.

This drama was performed in connection with the Feast of Corpus Christi, a celebration instituted to honor the Eucharist; and it was known in England (although not on the continent) as "the plaie of Corpus Christi." Does the English name connote a merely adventitious association of Feast and play, or does some deeper connection exist between a celebration of the Eucharist and a drama setting forth redemptive history?[14] The answer becomes clearer when we understand that redemptive history—the Resurrection, and the many lesser resurrections in human history which foreshadow and repeat it—is the story of the union of perishable man with the Corpus Christi, the transfiguring, life-giving Body of Christ.

Essentially, the Corpus Christi had two meanings for Englishmen of the period: the Eucharist; and the Mystical Body, a concept deriving originally from Paul who speaks of the whole body of believing Christians dead, living and yet unborn as one body of which Christ is the head. "For as the body is one, and hath many members, and all the members of that one body, being many, are one body; so also is Christ" (I

Cor. 12:13). "And whether one member suffer, all the members suffer with it; or one member be honored, all the members rejoice with it: (I Cor. 12:26). "Now ye are the body of Christ" (I Cor. 12:27). ". . . him . . . which is the head, even Christ" (Eph. 4:15).[15]

The salient fact about the Corpus Christi from our point of view is that it is the life-giving Body, the means by which death is overcome. The universal Church was the institutional embodiment of the Mystical Body; and in the drama of the period the resurrection action is often mediated through the Church.[16]

"Who shall deliver me from the body of this death?" asks Paul (Rom. 7:24). The body of death is the corrupt physical body of fallen natural man; the passions associated with that body; and the death-dealing society natural man creates. Redemptive history is the story of the transformation of that body into the incorruptible Mystical Body; or, put otherwise, the record of the incorporative movement by which death-bound man becomes one with the never-dying Body of Christ. This life-bestowing action played out within time in the events of Christian history is enacted repeatedly in the time-transcendent sacrament of Communion, which both perpetuates and commemorates the renewing action. Corpus Christi drama celebrates the Corpus Christi in its various aspects: the Eucharist; the Mystical Body (the only true form of man and his society); and redemptive history, the story of that Body (that society) in time.

The Corpus Christi may be a theological idea, but it is also an image. As such, its importance for the drama cannot be overstated. The Corpus Christi—the transfiguring, life-bestowing Body—is the central image of medieval drama and, in variant form, the central image of Shakespearean drama as well. It is a kinetic image, identical with the action of resurrection, for the Body and its revivifying effects are one.

Although I have referred to Corpus Christi drama as comprehensive, the term is relative only. The material which comprises any of the four extant cycles[17] is sufficiently lengthy and inclusive to create in the audience a sense of comprehensiveness in scope and size. However, even of the New Testament matter, only certain episodes are dramatized; and of the mass of Old Testament material much more is omitted. Further, the cycles are not in complete agreement. Each of the full cycles contains episodes not found in some of the others. Nevertheless, certain episodes are common to all four of the full cycles, and it is these which we may consider to comprise the essential matter of a Corpus Christi play (the episodes are somewhat differently elaborated in the various cycles). Kolve has compiled a list of these episodes, as follows.

> The Fall of Lucifer
> The Creation and Fall of Man
> Cain and Abel
> Noah and the Flood
> Abraham and Isaac
> The Nativity (Annunciation to Jesus and the Doctors)
> The Raising of Lazarus (the only Ministry play staged by all cycles)
> The Passion (Conspiracy to Harrowing of Hell)
> The Resurrection (Setting of the Watch to the Ascension
> Doomsday[18]

Examining this list, we see that the events of the drama constitute elements of a single action of death-transcendence, the same action presented in brief form in the *Quem quaeritis* drama. At the heart of the drama are the *Quem quaeritis* events of Christ's death and Resurrection. From this center the drama extends backward to the fall into death which necessitates the Resurrection, and forward to the ultimate overthrow of death at the end of time (Doomsday). In between are the manifold events of human history, consisting of repetitions of the central saving action, including the events preceding the Resurrection which both lay the ground for and prefigure it, and the events subsequent to the Resurrection which reveal its continuing death-transcending effects. The story of Noah and the Flood, for example, and the story of Abraham and Isaac, each illustrate a confrontation with death which climaxes in a renewal; and each, while maintaining its own concrete historicity, also foreshadows the ultimate renewal, Christ's death and Resurrection.[19] Death and resurrection, then, is the heart of the design. All details express it, and to it all details are subordinate; but the sheer length of the drama, and the specificity with which particular episodes are dramatized, evoke in us a sense of mundane existence, temporal and embodied, which plays against the still triumphant pattern of death-transcendence.

Kolve, in asking why a cycle of plays celebrating Christian world history is appropriate to a feast celebrating the Eucharist, confirms my view of the Corpus Christi drama as an elaboration of the *Quem quaeritis* action. Kolve points out that the papal bull of 1264 which originally called for a feast honoring the Eucharist stressed that the celebration be joyful.[20] But the "Eucharist serves to recall both the Last Supper and the flesh and blood of Christ offered on the cross—events about which it is possible to rejoice only when they are related to man's fall, Christ's Resurrection, and the Last Judgment."[21] Therefore "the English Middle Ages played the whole story, from man's fall to the salvation of the blessed at the Judgement, to reveal the central episode—the Passion—as joyful in meaning."[22] In other words, a cycle play, like the history it presents, is a strategy for revealing as ultimately joyful the meaning of the death at its center—or, in our terms, an action encompassing death in such a way as to revalue it.

Two aspects of cycle drama warrant particular attention because they are especially relevant to Shakespearean drama: the figures in the drama who represent earthly rulers, secular and ecclesiastical; and the episodes depicting the raising of Lazarus.

Earthly rulers, chiefly but not exclusively kings, feature prominently in these plays (as also in moralities and saint's plays). They represent Mankind—all men everywhere in time; and like the King of Life in the earliest known morality, they are essentially death figures, representatives of our own mortality. The characters of a cycle play, as of medieval drama generally, fall always into one of two groups: the seed of Abel and the seed of Cain, the saved and the damned, those who embrace the Corpus Christi and those who spurn it. All men must die once; but those cut off from the saving action are inflictors of pain and death, doomed to eternal death themselves. This division of postlapsarian humanity governs the conception and treatment of kingship as well. All earthly rulers are kings of death, implicitly and explicitly contrasted to Christ, the Lord of Life, who alone has "conquered death."[23] "Good" earthly rulers, however, acknowledge their mortality, which in this drama is synonomous with acknowledging Christ's sovereignty, therefore with salvation. Wicked rulers, in contrast, reject Christ's kingship, falsely claiming unlimited power over life and death, and visiting death on those around them.

Herod is perhaps the best-known of the wicked tyrants;[24] and the Herod in the Wakefield cycle epitomizes all the wicked rulers in cycle drama, and in medieval drama generally. In a style characterized by inflated, often heavily alliterative language, he reacts to news of the Nativity with furious threats of death and injury to those who will not acknowledge his sovereignty, and with assertions of limitless power: ". . . I have all in wold: in me standys life and dede [death]."[25] Like all earthly kings, however, this Herod is a king of "dede" alone. He can order the slaughter of the Innocents, but he can neither confer life on others nor ensure against even his own death. His eventual end may be only implied, as in the Wakefield Herod, or may be actually shown, as in the N-Town Death of Herod. But in either case, his claims to limitless power are belied by his obvious mortality; and his boasts of omnipotence are unintentionally ironic, evoking in us only a heightened sense of his vulnerability to death.[26]

The Chester Octavian, a "good" earthly ruler, also equates ultimate sovereignty with power over death; but in exact contrast to Herod, he will not allow his followers to honor him as God, because he is only mortal—made of flesh and blood, thus bound to time and death.

> But follye yt were by manye a waye
> such soveraygntye for to assaye,
> syth I must dye I wotte not what day,
> to desyre such dignitye.
>
> For of all flesh, blood, and bonne
> made I am, borne of a womane;
> . . .

> and of my life moste parte is gone,
> age shewes him soe in mee.
>
> And godhead askes in all thinge
> time that hath noe begininge
> ne never shall have endinge;
> and none of this have I.[27]

Later this "good" ruler is vouchsafed a vision of the infant Christ, whose Lordship he immediately acknowledges.

In short, the key fact in the depiction of ruler figures is their mortality. Each ruler is Everyman, special only in that his exalted status points up with correspondingly greater force his ultimate vulnerability. Good rulers acknowledge their mortality, bad rulers claim exemption from it; but good and bad, all human rulers in medieval drama are kings of death whose preeminent function is to remind us that all men, even the greatest, must die. This conception and use of kingship carries over to Shakespeare's work; but a change in the social/psychological context of the drama modifies the meaning and effect of the conception, rendering it at once more powerful and more problematic (see below, pp. 36 to 45, and Chapter Two). In medieval drama the problem of the King's mortality is inseparable from the dramatized solution to it, Christ's sovereignty, rooted in power over death (that power being always the ultimate subject of the drama). In Shakespearean drama king figures as diverse in character and function as Richard the Second and Lear continue to assert a more-than-mortal status, and then discover, terribly, their own mortal vulnerability.[28] To this extent Shakespearean drama resembles medieval drama. But the Shakespearean revelation of the King's (and by extension, all men's) mortality is no longer synonymous with a solution to it. Instead, the revelation pushes the characters within a play, and the audience watching the play, to a search for new ways of dealing with death, ways compatible with the more naturalistic Shakespearean theater, and with the social/psychological/metaphysical world that newly naturalistic theater represents.[29]

The raising of Lazarus, the other element of cycle drama which is especially relevant to Shakespeare's work, figures prominently in the cycle plays. As Kolve notes, it is the only play of the ministry to be staged in all four cycles (it was considered to be an antetype of Christ's resurrection and the chief miracle of His ministry).[30] Obviously, the episode anticipates Christ's rising from the sepulchre; however, it is a merely human body which we see dead and raised, a fact which imposes greater strain on credulity and, concomitantly, increases the affective power of the successful outcome.

The rendition of the raising of Lazarus varies from cycle to cycle, but all dramatizations include three key elements: (1) Mary's and Martha's grief at their brother Lazarus's death, and their subsequent joy at his return; (2) the mention that Lazarus' body, buried four days, is so far decomposed as to stink (a hint contained in scripture but given prominence here);[31] and (3) the staging of the moment in which Christ calls forth the dead man, who rises from the sepulchre before the spectators' eyes.

The way in which this episode recapitulates the *Quem quaeritis* action is obvious.[32] The grief of Mary and Martha at their brother's death, like that of the Marys at Christ's sepulchre, epitomizes all human sorrow at loss through death; and their joy at his return completes the *Quem quaeritis* action of suffering and death turned to joy and rebirth.

The second and third elements of the Lazarus episode must be considered together, for the emphasis on the putrefaction of the four-days-buried corpse is integral to the overall dramatic strategy. The knowledge that we inhabit a literally corruptible body, a knowledge omnipresent in the human psyche but normally repressed, is brought fully to our consciousness by the stress on decomposition. But as it is confronted it is negated, for the risen Lazarus stands before us, living and whole.

The Wakefield version of the Raising of Lazarus well illustrates this. Lazarus rises from the tomb in his worm-eaten graveclothes, offering the audience a "mirroure"[33] of what they must come to. The mirror is both visual and verbal: Lazarus' mere appearance, living testimony to the corruptible flesh; and the sermon he delivers, a powerful evocation of death's terrors, drawing especial power from its numerous images of decomposition. This account, which holds its own with the strongest of the numerous medieval and Renaissance treatments of the subject, draws its strength from its vividly sensual quality—as if the corpse had been alive to feel its own decay.[34] However, it is the *risen* Lazarus who speaks; and the horrors of death are therefore controverted even as they are forcefully communicated.

We see, then, that the Lazarus episode recapitulates the strategy of the larger drama. Death at its worst is incorporated into an action which negates it, and the more strongly the drama evokes our horror of death, the more strongly do we react to its final overthrow. But while the whole action forces us to revalue death, it does not expunge the horror previously aroused. As death is literally essential to resurrection, so the negative emotions evoked are inseparable from, indeed actually essential to, the affirmative denouement (a similar effect obtains in Shakespearean drama, where the negatives incorporated and revalued by the dramatic action are integral to the affirmative effect of the whole).

The late-medieval insistence on the decay of the body, seen throughout cycle drama and at its height in the Lazarus episodes, bears witness to the increasing force with which the claims of the body are felt. Yet as the Lazarus episode demonstrates, that very force both threatens to overwhelm, and is inseparable from, the victorious denouement. The two are held in a symbiotic tension. The power of the resurrection scene derives from the dramatic insistence on bodily decomposition; but the more graphic the portrayal of fleshly corruptibility, the more the weight of that reality threatens to overwhelm our faith in its reversibility. The most powerful drama hovers on the brink of irrreversibility—of failure to enact resurrection—a point approached most closely in Shakespeare's work in *King Lear*.

In the resurrected Lazarus, death and the undoing of death are one: the corpse which is raised cannot be separated from the action of raising it. The risen Lazarus, the revivified body of death, is an icon for both medieval and Shakespearean drama; but the special task of Shakespearean drama is to provide a naturalized version of the revivifying action.

Saint's Plays

The term "saint" is applied to a confusingly wide variety of personages—"prophets, disciples, members of the Holy Family, eminent philosophers or scholars, martyrs, and the like."[35] But what these figures all have in common is simply incorporation with the Mystical Body, the society of saints (Augustine's phrase)—the whole body of believers past, present and yet to come, whose head is Christ. In fact, ". . . it is better to talk about the life of the saint than the lives of the saints, according to Gregory of Tours, 'because though there may be some difference in their merits and virtues, yet the life of one body nourished them all in the world.'"[36]

Any human being has the potential for sainthood, for incorporation with this immortal communal Body;[37] but the term is more often used for those who partake of that Body to an exceptional degree. Christ, who "wishes his people to gain eternal life through him," is "the greatest of the saints,"[38] the ultimate source of power over death; but human saints, through the performance of miracles and acts of conversion, may extend to others the power achieved through union with the Body of Christ.[39]

The essence of the miraculous is the power to set nature, thus death, aside. Since all miracles involve power over nature, all imply power over death, whether they are simply wonders, or whether they are miracles of actual healing and resurrection. An act of conversion is also an act of death-transcendence, for conversion is the conquest of spiritual, thus of physical, death (physical death being considered to be a literal consequence of sin). In short, conversion is simply another form of the miraculous, another version of the setting aside of nature, thus of death. Shakespearean drama retains the idea of spiritual conversion as a form of death-transcendence; but the equivalence of this with literal death-transcendence is by then in question, for the enactment of physical resurrection is banished from the naturalized Shakespearean stage.

The essential features of saints' plays, miracles and acts of conversion—both of which are acts of mastery over death—are usually (although not invariably) performed through the agency of a human saint. The reason that a human saint is not essential is that the real protagonist of this drama is the immortality-granting communal Body, the Corpus Christi; and the saint is merely the medium through which the death-transcending power of this Body is made manifest.[40] However, the mere fact that the human exemplar of the Mystical Body is accorded an "historical" existence brings us closer to the actual world, bound to time and death and stubbornly resistant to transfiguration. Moreover, the victories over death in the saints' plays take place not on the universalized stage of the morality drama, nor in the far-removed world of biblical history, but on a stage which purports to offer a version of actual historical experience. The cycle plays do contain extrascriptural material (some of it sanctioned by tradition, some of it simply dramatic elaboration); but they are still basically limited to biblical history. The saints' plays, in contrast, are free to impose the pattern of death and resurrection on a wide variety of "historical" matter ranging throughout time and space; and they are thus natural precursors of Tudor historical drama, which attempts to impose the death-and-resurrection pattern on the materials of actual English history.

Few fifteenth-century English saints', or conversion,[41] plays have survived (many were probably destroyed in the Reformation). Two, *Mary Magdalene* and *The Conversion of Saint Paul*, are contained in the Digby manuscript; the third, *The Play of the Sacrament*, is associated with Croxton.[42] These three plays differ from one another in various respects, and all may be to some extent atypical. However, all dramatize the death-conquering power of the Corpus Christi as manifest in miracles and acts of conversion.

The way in which *The Conversion of Saint Paul* dramatizes the power of the Corpus Christi is self-explanatory. The plan focuses on Paul's conversion from doubter to believer; from inflictor of death, doomed to eternal death, to transmitter of the saving action, saved himself.

In *The Play of the Sacrament* the Corpus Christi as Eucharist is the protagonist, and performs the work of conversions usually performed by a saint. This fact accords with my idea that the object of imitation in medieval drama is always the immortality-granting Corpus Christi, whether manifested in individual history (saints' lives), collective history, or the Eucharist.

In the play a merchant steals a consecrated wafer at the request of the Jews, who then subject it to treatment mimicking the Passion. They torture the Host, nail it to a post, and finally throw it into an oven. In an enactment of Resurrection the image of Christ bursts open the oven and addresses his torturers, who are immediately converted. The dramatic image is economic. The oven is a conflation of the sepulchre and hell, immediate death and eternal death. The torturers are natural man, the fallen body and spirit in every man which is revivified by the power of the Resurrection.

In the act of conversion, doubters are transformed into believers. As said above, characters in medieval drama are always classifiable as either doubters or believers, those who reject the saving action and those who embrace it. The doubters who are converted in the *Play of the Sacrament* are mainly Jews, who along with wicked rulers are the most frequently encountered doubters.[43] In terms of relevance to Shakespeare's work, doubters are the most significant characters in all of medieval drama. Doubters may be skeptics, plotters, or both at once. But whether exemplified in the Jews in the Croxton play who doubt Christ's real presence in the sacrament; the midwives in the Chester and N-Town cycles who doubt the Virgin Birth; or the Jews and wicked rulers of innumerable medieval dramas who deny or plot to conceal the Resurrection, what doubters doubt is always the same: that the laws of nature can be transcended, therefore that death can be overcome.

The Ripoll Resurrection play, a twelfth-century expansion of the *Visitatio*, is one of countless examples from both earlier and later medieval drama which clearly indicate the association of these figures with denial of Resurrection. Mary and an angel announce the Resurrection to the disciples, who respond as follows: "A single true Mary is more to be believed than the race of the deceitful Jews. We know Christ has truly risen from the dead."[44]

Doubters and believers may be dramatized as separate characters, but as the act of conversion demonstrates they are in reality two aspects of the same character, Mankind. Our fear that physical nature (thus death) cannot be transcended, the instinctive skepticism of even the most devout believer, is projected onto the doubter figures, who consequently form a dramatic locus of intensely focused audience emotion, including fascination, hatred, fear—fear that they are right, therefore that we must die. These figures exist in order to be refuted, and their refutation constitutes another version of the central action in which death is confronted in order to be overcome.

Doubters—skeptics and plotters who deny the transcendent—figure prominently in all three Shakespearean forms, running a gamut from Falstaff (history) to Jacques and Shylock (comedy) to Edmund and Hamlet (tragedy). The function of these figures remains unchanged: namely to assert that which the drama exists to confound. But the challenge they pose can no longer be unambiguously refuted: for Shakespearean drama, as opposed to earlier drama, no longer splits the life/death aspect of existence in two. The extent to which and way in which the doubter figures are refuted establishes the generic limits of a Shakespearean play.

The Digby *Mary Magdalene*, a late-fifteenth-century saints' play, provides a good conclusion to this discussion of medieval drama because it uses techniques from all three major medieval forms, revealing the way in which all the techniques are used to dramatize the same basic action: resurrection, the overcoming of the death aspect of existence through incorporation with the immortal Corpus Christi. In addition, the play exhibits those features of medieval drama most relevant to Shakespearean drama: preeminently, the resurrection action; but also, the enactment of Lazarus-like resurrection scenes, including the resurrection of Lazarus himself; the portrayal of earthly rulers as kings of death; and the inclusion of doubter figures (many of whom are rulers as well). Moreover, the play makes clear the relation of all of those features to the central action, mastery over mortality.

The play falls into two apparently very different parts. The first half centers loosely on scripture and makes use of cycle and morality drama techniques, whereas the second half centers on non-scriptural events attributed to Mary Magdalene and presented in the manner characteristic of medieval haigiography. The difference between the halves is sufficiently marked for some scholars to have thought the play was composed of two originally separate plays somewhat clumsily conjoined. However, this view arises from a consideration of dramatic means rather than ends. The entire play is designed to enact resurrection, victory over the death aspect of life, and to this end the techniques borrowed from all three forms of medieval drama are directed.

Marking the division between the two seemingly disparate halves of *Mary Madalene* is a *Visitatio*, in all essentials a replay of the resurrection drama first presented over five centuries earlier in the *Quem quaeritis* texts. Resurrection is therefore the literal as well as the figurative center of this play. Moreover, the movement of the whole drama recapitulates the death and renewal at its center. In the first part of the play Cyrus, lord of Magdalen Castle, dies suddenly, followed soon after by his son Lazarus. The deaths are accompanied by the lamentations of Mary and Martha for their father and brother, recalling the sorrow of the Marys at Christ's death. The drama closes with a version of resurrection, being a depiction of Mary's death and ascension to heaven as angel and priest rejoice. The drama thus recapitulates both the *Quem quaeritis* drama and the *Visitatio* at its own center as it moves from initial suffering and death to joy and the conquest of death.

In between the initial death and final resurrection are repeated miracles of resurrection: the Resurrection itself, pattern for and source of all other revivifications; the conversion of Mary Magdalene and the raising of Lazarus, performed by the incarnate Christ; and the life-bestowing miracles which follow the Resurrection, all performed by Saint Mary Magdalene, a human transmitter of the saving action.

In presenting the action of resurrection, this play makes use of features characteristic of all three forms of fourteenth- and fifteenth-century drama. The first half, loosely based on scripture, centers on two miracles of Christ's Ministry, the casting out of devils from Mary (her conversion), and the raising of Lazarus. To the extent that the drama presents scriptural history it is in the cycle-play tradition. However, the conversion of Mary is presented in two ways: a scripturally-based scene, reminiscent of cycle drama, in which Christ casts out the devils; and a section depicting Mary's fall and repentance in classic morality fashion, using personified abstractions to represent her spiritual state. The protagonist of this section may be Mary Magdalene rather than Mankind, but the familiar supporting cast of morality drama is present, including the World, Flesh and Devil presented as three kings with the Seven Deadly Sins as their followers; and a good and bad angel who struggle for Mary's soul. The play also, in the second half, makes use of the materials characteristic of saint's plays: sensational miracles and conversions performed by a particular saint; and the romantic improbabilities typical of the genre, including a long sea-voyage complete with tempest and climaxed by a reunion involving resurrection (this section invites comparison with *The Winter's Tale*). We see then that the play reveals clearly the essential similarity of all forms of medieval drama. Whether a play focuses on scriptural history, allegorical abstraction, or the history of a particular saint, its underlying object of imitation is the same: resurrection, the conquest of the death aspect of bodily-based life achieved through incorporation with an undying communal Body. This body is defined always in contrast to the body of death (any merely natural social or physical body).

The same contrast is expressed in the juxtaposition throughout the play of mortal rulers—Tiberius Caesar, Herod, Pilate, the King of Marseilles—and Christ the King, ruler of life and death. The earthly rulers rage in their familiar alliterative and bombastic style, boasting of limitless power and using the language of salvation ("grace", "blisse"); but their boasts rebound ironically, for they must all die, whether on stage like the "good" ruler Cyrus, struck down at the height of prosperity and power, or in an undramatized but inevitable future like the "bad" rulers Tiberius and Herod. Thus in this play (as in medieval drama generally), all earthly rulers, good and bad, are death figures who exist to evoke simultaneously human mortality and the solution to it, Christ's kingship. In the first half of the play the contrast between earthly and Divine kingship is direct, for Christ Himself is a character in the drama. This section reaches its climax with two resurrection scenes, the raising of Lazarus and the Resurrection itself, which provide the final comment on the limits of earthly kingship.

In the second half of the play the contrast between earthly rulers and the Corpus Christi is manifest in a human saint. Mary Magdalene is commanded to convert the pagan King of Marseilles, a raging Herod-like ruler who threatens Mary with torture and death. But while this earthly king can inflict death, he cannot create life even in his own wife, who is unable to conceive. Mary's miracles, in contrast, all involve the bestowal of life: she makes fertile the barren Queen; she converts the King and Queen of Marseilles; and finally, in a miracle of literal resurrection, she restores to life the dead Queen and preserves the life of the Queen's infant until mother and child, left for dead on a rock at sea, can be united with the converted King. These victories over death, achieved through the power of Christ the King, stand in direct contrast to earthly kings' impotence before death; and the unbridgeable gap between mortal ruler and Divine King is scrupulously preserved in this, as in all other, medieval drama.

Kingship and the Communal Body in Tudor Morality Drama

At the beginning of the sixteenth century the contrast we have traced throughout medieval drama between Christ the king and earthly rulers remains unchanged. Later in the century, however, a change occurs which is of the first importance for Shakespearean drama. Earthly and divine sovereignty, the natural body (physical and social) and the Body of Christ, are no longer portrayed in unalterable and mutually defining contrast, but are now shown as fused. The aura of divine authority is transferred to the institution of kingship and therefore to some degree to the mortal king himself; and concomitantly the Corpus Christi, the imperishable communal body, is increasingly identified with the secular nation-state (the king and his kingdom are used interchangeably in this drama because the king was considered to be both head of and one with the body politic, just as Christ was both head of and one with the Mystical Body). The result of this fusion of previously distinct conceptions is problematic: a king who claims quasi-divine infallibility, but whose Achilles' heel is his own mortality; or, formulated differently, a secular nation-state which demands the absolute allegiance formerly owed to God alone, but which can confer immortality only to the extent that its flesh-and-blood members can identify with the fleshless body England.

The change in the dramatic portrayal of kingship and society can be seen clearly by examining two morality plays, *Mundus et Infans* (1508), an anonymous morality, and John Bale's *Kynge Johan*, completed by 1536, revised in 1538 and again in Edward VI's reign, and finally rewritten in 1561.[45] It should be noted, however, that Tudor morality drama portrays the changed concept of kingship and society without, apparently, understanding its problematic implications. It is left for Shakespeare, who fully grasps those implications, to explore them in depth.

Mundus et Infans, while differing from earlier drama in certain respects,[46] maintains the distinction between earthly and divine sovereignty. *Kynge Johan*, in contrast, portrays them as fused. The protagonist of *Mundus et Infans*[47] is the universal Mankind figure of earlier drama, whose nature is composed of a body of death and a body of life, mortality and the potential for salvation. The names bestowed upon this figure is the course of the drama (Infans, Wanton, Lust and Lykyng, Manhode, Shame, Age, Repentance) indicate mental and physical stages through which the character passes as he recapitulates the resurrection plot of earlier drama: sin, repentance and salvation; or, spiritual death and resurrection (the spiritual resurrection to entail a literal resurrection at the end of time).

The first two speeches in the play suffice to demonstrate the essential similarity of this and earlier drama. At the opening of the play Mundus, King of the World, is in possession of the stage onto which the Mankind figure will make his entrance (that is, man is born into a world dominated by the powers that be, the forces of sin and death). Mundus opens the play with a speech whose style—inflated and heavily alliterative—and content—a boast of power so great that it is godlike ("Me thynketh I am a god of grace")[48]—place him unmistakably in the tradition of the wicked rulers of medieval drama. Immediately on the conclusion of Mundus' speech Infans enters, and his first words are "Cryst, our kynge."[49] The opening of the drama, then, sets up the contrast between kings of the world and Christ the King, who alone can vanquish death.

In the remainder of Infans' speech he expounds on his (and by implication all men's) origin, nature and destiny, which are entirely death-bound (we should note that this exposition of mortality is made in the context of Christ's already acknowledged kingship). Infans' speech insists repeatedly on the bodily basis of human existence, which is synonymous with vulnerability to death. His mother's body, source of physical life, nourished Infans for the "fourty wekes" of gestation (a fact twice repeated).[50] But for the entire period his mother feared death in childbirth, and at the moment of birth mother and child were in fact in great danger: "When I was rype from her to founde,/ In peryll of dethe we stode bothe two."[51] Once born, moreover, the child's own flesh means that his life is synonymous with a journey towards death.

> Now to seke dethe I must begyn,
> For to passe that strayte passage;
> For body and soule that shall then twynne
> And make a partynge of that maryage.[52]

The problem of death is the problem of the perishable body, the basis of human existence. The mother's and son's mortal bodies are implicitly contrasted to Christ's immortal Body which, unlike the mother's body, can guarantee life to those incorporate with it. Infans refers to his mother's "Flesshe and blode,"[53] his food during gestation. This flesh and blood sustained the child, but could not ensure his safety, in contrast to the Eucharist, the flesh and blood of the Divine Body which alone can confer immortality.

Mundus et Infans maintains the traditional distinction between mortal kings and the King of Life, between the perishable human body and the immortal Body of Christ. In Bale's *Kynge Johan*, in contrast, the distinction between the mortal and divine sovereign is deliberately blurred; and the point of this play is as much to demonstrate the inseparability of earthly and divine authority as the point of the earlier work was to demonstrate the absolute divide between them.[54]

Bale's play concerns the historical King John, an actual thirteenth-century English monarch,[55] who defies the Pope and is consequently poisoned by a monk. Not only is the central character historical; he is also surrounded by morality abstractions who are later given the names of actual historical personages (Sedition and Dissimulation, for example, are later called Stephen Langton and Simon of Swynsett).[56] Much is made of this by various critics, and Bale's play is frequently described as transitional between the morality and the true history play.[57] Irving Ribner expresses the traditional view.

> In *Kynge Johan* we can clearly see the history play emerging from the morality, for in it the two exist side by side. *Kynge Johan* is actually two plays at the same time, with the central titular figure holding the two together. On the one hand we have a political morality play . . . with Yngelond as the central figure. Simultaneously, however, we have a history play with King John as the central figure.[58]

However, from my point of view the mixture of morality ("religious") and history ("secular") elements is important not because it is transitional, but in itself; for that very mixture gives expression to a single, albeit inherently dualistic, conception which is central to much of Tudor, and to all of Shakespearean, drama. A few scenes from the play will illustrate that conception.

John's death is the climax of the play, for it forms simultaneously the nadir of the action and its turning point. Following John's death the rebellious characters Clergy, Nobility and Civil Order repent their treatment of John, and are forgiven—the resurrection phase of the total action of death-and-resurrection. The character resurrected however is not the king, but the nation England, represented by the three powers which compose the commonwealth.[59] To restate this, the protagonist of this play is not, as in earlier drama, the Corpus Christi, but the body politic, an entity in which the material natural body and the immaterial immortal Mystical Body are inseparably blent.

The way the action unfolds after John's death is significant. Verity induces Clergy, Nobility and Civil Order to repent their treatment of John, and then declares, "I doubt not but the Lorde wyll condescende/To forgyve yow all, so that ye mynde to amend.[60] Immediately upon this cue Imperial Majesty enters and the three figures kneel and ask his pardon.[61] The effect is to identify the figure of Imperial Majesty with God Himself. That is, the "Lorde" who forgives is both God and Imperial Majesty (earthly Kingship), who are no longer wholly to be distinguished. The point made by the mere timing of this scene is underlined in other ways as well. For example, Verity—Truth—is identified as God's own servant (Imperial Majesty refers to the character as "God's Verytye")[62] However, Verity also serves Imperial Majesty, hastening to obey his wishes; and the effect is once again to identify Imperial Majesty (not the King, but Kingship) with God.

Imperial Majesty, a figure new in drama, makes his appearance only after John's death (the king is dead, but Kingship never dies). This figure, modelled after the Mystical Body, is the body of Kingship, which is synonymous with the body politic and which never dies, in contradistinction to the merely mortal body of the individual king. In the play Imperial Majesty appears apart from the individual King John; but in actuality the two cannot be separated, for the body of Kingship requires the mortal body of the king to activate it. This point is clearly made within the play itself. Clergy defends Nobility's attack on John as justified because Nobility "speaketh not agaynst the crowne, but agaynst the man."[63] But Verity, who is Truth itself, promptly refutes the view that the two can be separated: "The crowne of itselfe without the man is nothynge."[64]

After Imperial Majesty bestows his forgiveness on his rebellious subjects, the point that earthly and divine sovereignty can no longer be wholly distinguished is further underlined in two long speeches, one by Verity, the other by Imperial Majesty. These speeches set forth the orthodox Tudor view of absolute monarchy, in language which clearly identifies God and His sovereign minister on earth: "He that condempneth a kynge, condempneth God, without dought."[65]

At the end of the play the kingdom is once again united under a God-representing King, whose relation to the body politic is precisely that of Christ's to the Mystical Body. In a secular version of Doomsday, Imperial Majesty forgives the repentant and sends the unrepentant—those who are hardened against him—to their justly deserved deaths. The three orders of his kingdom (who represent his subjects collectively, and also the three sources of power in the Kingdom other than royal power) vow to accept the King's absolute sovereignty; and the three orders are united as one, a single body with Imperial Majesty at its head. The stage directions call for "OMNES UNA" ("All As One") to proclaim their unity in diversity: "By the helpe of God yche one shall do hys functyon."[66] The political idea here represented is the familiar medieval idea of the community functioning as one body, an idea based upon the Pauline Corpus Christi and its subsequent elaboration by generations of medieval thinkers.[67] However, the king and the nation have replaced the Pope and the universal Church as the visible, institutional forms of the invisible, immortalizing Body.

The relation of this change to the myriad material and psychological circumstances we lump together under the term "Reformation" is obvious; and equally obvious is the fact that the single most relevant circumstance is the king's assumption of sovereignty over the English church, given final ratification in the Act of Supremacy of 1534. That Bale's polemical work is a direct response to historical circumstance cannot be doubted. Bale, a Protestant clergyman, was a strong supporter of Tudor absolutism in general, and of the king's claim to head the Church in particular; and his play clearly reflects his strongly partisan views, both in its general anti-Catholicism, and in its specific espousal of the Protestant stance ("And your Grace shall be the supreme head of the Churche," Clergy declares forthrightly.)[68] However, the way of thinking about kingship and the state which Bale's drama portrays enters the imagination of Catholic and Protestant alike, as can be seen by examining Nicholas Udall's *Respublica* (1553).[69] Udall's polemical Catholic counterpart to Bale's Protestant polemics, composed in the reign of the Catholic Queen Mary (during which time Bale was in exile), portrays the fall of England under the Protestant Tudors and her restoration to grace (resurrection) under Mary's rule. Nevertheless, the change evident in Bale's work stamps Udall's work as well, for the protagonist of *Respublica* — the corporate body both the audience and the characters within the play are to identify with — is not the Mystical Body, nor yet its incarnation in the universal Church, but rather the body politic, the English commonwealth.

We see, then, that in Catholic and Protestant drama alike, earthly sovereignty is invested with the aura of absolute power formerly associated only with God; and the undying communal body men experience themselves as inhabiting is identified primarily with England rather than with the communion of the universal Church. Or, to phrase this differently, the immaterial body capable of transcending the spatial and temporal limits imposed by the flesh is now inseparable in men's minds from that simultaneously material and immaterial entity, the English nation-state.

The King's Two Bodies

The Tudor fusion of the previously distinct Mystical Body and natural body dominates not only the dramatic imagination, but also the theoretically less fanciful legal imagination, compelling testimony to the centrality of the conception. That this is so may be seen by reference to Ernst Kantorowicz's work on the legal concept he dubs "The King's Two Bodies." To illustrate the two-body concept, Kantorowicz quotes liberally from records compiled by Edmund Plowden, a law apprentice of the Middle Temple, who summarized arguments and judgements made in the courts in Elizabeth's reign. Plowden's reports are of particular value because they provide clear statements of contemporary juristic views on kingship, and also because Plowden cites enough different lawyers and judges to make it certain that the tenet he describes was not an esoteric doctrine espoused by a comparative few, but was rather in the mainstream of contemporary juristic thought. Reduced to its essentials, the tenet is that the king has two bodies, one immortal and free of all defects associated with the fallible flesh, and the other mortal, subject to death and all infirmities of nature, mental and physical. Two citations from Plowden will suffice to illustrate this.

> For the King has in him two Bodies, *viz.*, a Body natural, and a Body politic. His Body natural (if it be considered in itself) is a Body mortal, subject to all Infirmities that come by Nature or Accident, to the Imbecility of Infancy or Old Age, and to the like Defects that happen to the natural Bodies of other People. But his Body politic is a Body that cannot be seen or handled, consisting of Policy and Government, and Constituted for the Direction of the People, and the Management of the public weal, and this Body is utterly void of Infancy, and old Age, and other natural Defects and Imbecilities, which the Body natural is subject to. . . .[70]

> The King has two Capacities, for he has two Bodies, the one whereof is a Body natural, consisting of natural Members as every other Man has, and in this he is subject to Passions and Death as other Men are; the other is a Body politic, and the Members thereof are his subjects, and he and his Subjects together compose the Corporation. . . and he is incorporated with them, and they with him, and he is the Head, and they are the Members, and he has the sole Government of them; and this Body is not subject to Passions as the other is, nor to Death, for as to this Body the King never dies . . . .[71]

Here clearly articulated are descriptions of the two bodies we have traced throughout medieval drama: the body which is synomomous with death—the vulnerable individual body and the complex of drives and appetites associated with it (the "Passions," in the language of the Tudor jurists); and the body which is life—the imperishable, immortality-granting Mystical Body, originally the Pauline Corpus Christi, now conceived of as a royal body of Kingship synomomous with the body politic (compare Bale's Imperial Majesty). These entities, distinct in medieval drama, are now conjoined—a single person or entity compounded of two bodies which can be neither wholly identified with one another nor wholly distinguished.

The inseparability of these bodies is explicitly formulated in Tudor juristic thought.

> to this natural Body is conjoined his [the king's] Body politic, which contains his royal Estate and Dignity. . . . So that he has a Body natural, adorned and invested with the Estate and Dignity royal; and he has not a Body natural distinct and divided by itself from the Office and Dignity royal, but a Body natural and a Body politic together indivisible; and these two Bodies are incorporated in one Person, and make one Body and not divers, that is the Body corporate in the Body natural, *et a contra* the Body natural in the Body corporate.[72]

In short, the king and the body politic, which he both is and is head of, is composed of a body of life and a body of death inseparably fused. As with the King, so with his subjects, each of whom is incorporate with that same dualistic body.

Kantorowicz reaches back into medieval political and legal theory in order to understand the antecedents of the two-body concept. Perhaps the most striking aspect of his discussion from our point of view is that in following the evolution of the two-body concept, he traces in legal/political thinking precisely the same development as we observed in the drama. First, the Pauline Corpus Christi—the life-giving Mystical Body and the ecclesiastical institution modelled after it, the universal Church—is kept clearly separate from, and in contrast to, the body of death (the natural body, and any merely secular political entity). Later, the idea of the Mystical Body is transferred to the secular state, resulting in what Kantorowicz calls the *corpus reipublicae mysticum* (mystical body of the republic), a development ending ultimately in the Tudor fusion of the Mystical and secular bodies, whereby the political entity and its head achieve an equivocal immortality function.[73]

In medieval drama the union of the Mystical and the natural bodies equals resurrection, the transfiguration of the natural body into the incorruptible entity it is not. An echo of this revivifying union is evident in the Tudor legal principle that the royal body of Kingship takes away the infirmities, mental and physical, of the king's individual body.

the Body natural and the Body politic are consolidated into one, and the Body politic wipes away every imperfection of the other Body, with which it is consolidated, and makes it to be another Degree than it should be if it were alone by itself . . . "[74]

But the weak link in the theory is the stubborn, untransformable reality of the king's mortal imperfection, which the Tudor fiction cannot dissolve.

In Shakespearean drama the fiction of quasi-divine Kingship stumbles against the *de facto* reality of the mortal king and his often lethally imperfect state. Shakespeare's histories, in particular his second history tetralogy, undo the Tudor structuring of reality, and in so doing expose anew the undispellable body of death at the heart of the fiction—the body which Shakespeare's own resurrection actions, his comedies and tragedies, are designed to encompass and revalue.

Any society is both nurturing and death-dealing; both sustaining of and inimical to the lives of its individual members. But the universal, timeless reality of the life/death aspects of the body and of human society are, in Shakespearean drama, couched in language reflective of, and peculiar to, a particular historical moment—language focused on the kinetic conception of the transfiguring Mystical Body and its Tudor variant, the Mystical Body of Kingship.

Notes

1 The thrust of recent scholarship is to stress the discontinuities rather than the continuities in the history of medieval drama; and most scholars agree that medieval drama is perhaps better thought of as a series of successive beginnings from common sources, rather than as a continuous whole in which later forms evolve directly from earlier ones.

2 Robert Potter, *The English Morality Play: Origins, History and Influence of a Dramatic Tradition* (London and Boston: Routledge & Kegan Paul Ltd., 1975), brings up and rejects the widespread view that the central action of morality drama is a psychomachia, or battle between the vices and virtues. In his view the central action is better described as "a sequence of innocence/fall/redemption." Potter, p. 8.

Potter places his emphasis on the overcoming of spiritual death. However, he confirms my view of medieval drama as a coherent whole centering around the dramatization of a single action: "If we grasp this idea of the morality play [*i.e.*, "a sequence of innocence/fall/redemption"], it is now possible to see the medieval religious drama as a totality in which the morality play performs the same ceremony in the microcosm of the individual life as that of the Corpus Christi cycle in the macrocosm of historical time." Potter, p. 8.

3 "The Castle of Perseverance," in *Medieval Drama*, ed. David Bevington (Boston: Houghton Mifflin Company, 1975), 1. 42. All subsequent references to this play are to this edition.

4 The date of composition cannot be established with certainty, but the play was found in the Account Roll, covering the years 1337-46, of a Dublin Priory.

5 "The Pride of Life," in *Tudor Interludes*, ed. Peter Happe (Harmondsworth, Middlesex, England: Penguin Books Ltd., 1972), 11. 203-05.

6 The salvation of the protagonist is a reliable convention in morality drama well into the sixteenth century.

7 The source of the allegory is Psalms 85:10: "Mercy and truth are met together; Righteousness and peace have kissed each other."

8 The play's economy and unrelieved sombreness are not typical of the medieval English morality, and the play may in fact be a translation of the Dutch *Elckerlijc* (although the Dutch version may equally well be a

Overcoming Death in Medieval, and Tudor Morality, Drama 47

translation of the English play). See Bevington's introduction to "Everyman," *Medieval Drama*, p. 939.

9 "Everyman," 1. 888.

10 "Everyman," 1. 889.

11 The same strategy is evident in the Elizabethan homilies intended for delivery in the time of the plague, in which the plague is represented as God's scourge for sinful man. See *Certaine Sermons or Homilies Appointed to be Read in Churches In the Time of Queen Elizabeth I (1547-1571)*, intro. Ellen Rickey and Thomas Stroup (Gainesville, Florida: Scholars' Facsimiles & Reprints, 1968).

12 1. 2844

13 Compare Potter: "In its original form . . . the morality play . . . moves to a rhythm even older and more fundamental than tragedy. It has the rhythm of the victory of life over death, the shape of enacted ritual" (p. 10). However, Potter's fundamental emphasis is on the morality as repentance drama; and he makes the above observation only when considering the origins of the morality.

14 For convincing, well-documented arguments demonstrating the connection between the meaning of the Feast of Corpus Christi and the meaning of the drama associated with it, see V. A. Kolve, *The Play Called Corpus Christi* (Stanford, Calif.: Stanford U. Press, (1966), especially pp. 42-50; and Jerome Taylor, "The Dramatic Structure of the Middle English Corpus Christi, or Cycle, Plays," *Medieval English Drama: Essays Critical and Contextual* (Chicago and London: The U. of Chicago Press, 1972).

For a discussion which emphasizes practical rather than conceptual factors in the association of Feast and play, see Rosemary Woolf, *The English Mystery Plays*, especially pp. 68-75.

15 These and all subsequent biblical quotations are taken from the so-called Bishop's Bible, the official bible of the Elizabethan Church (Ann Arbor, Michigan: University Microfilms, Inc.). I have used the Bishop's Bible because it is the version of scripture which Shakespeare would have known. There are no substantial differences between the way these verses appear in the Bishop's Bible and in the Vulgate, the Latin bible of the medieval Catholic Church.

16 ". . . we are bound to believe in one holy Church, Catholic and also Apostolic . . . without which there is neither salvation nor remission of sins . . ., which represents one mystical body, the head of which is Christ, and the head of Christ is God." From Pope Boniface's bull *Unam Sanctam*. Cited in Ernst Kantorowicz, *The King's Two Bodies: A Study in Medieval Political Theology* (Princeton U. Press, 1957), p. 164.

17 These are known as the York, Chester, Wakefield (Towneley) and N-Town (*Ludus Coventriae, Hegge*) cycles. A complete list of plays in the Beverley cycle survives, but not the cycle itself. There are in addition fragments of other plays, and a Cornish cycle. Records show the existence of Corpus Christi drama at other locations in England, but the plays have not come down. See Kolve, p. 36. The editions I have used in discussing the Corpus Christi drama are as follows: *The Chester Mystery Cycle*, I, ed. R. M. Lumiansky and David Mills, Early English Text Society, S.S.3 (London/N.Y./Toronto: Oxford U. Press, 1974); *The Wakefield Mystery Plays*, ed. Martial Rose (London: Evans Brothers Limited, 1961); *The York Plays*, ed. Richard Beadle [London: Edward Arnold (Publishers) Ltd., 1982].

18 Kolve, p. 51. Kolve checked this list against the list of episodes from the lost Beverley cycle.

19 The links between these lesser resurrections and the Resurrection itself are deliberate, evidence of the typological mode of thought in which Old Testament events, while maintaining their concrete historical reality, were considered also to foreshadow the New Testament events of Christ's life, death and Resurrection.

    A rich exegetical lore, including but not confined to typological interpretation, had grown up around all of the major and many of the minor events of scripture. For example, Noah's Ark was considered to be a type of the Church; and tradition conflated the wood of the Ark, the means of salvation from the universal destruction of the Flood, with the wood of the Cross, the means of final salvation from ultimate destruction. Typological principles helps to explain certain features of the cycles—for example, why some episodes are selected rather than others. But we need not explore this material in depth, for in the main it simply reinforces my point, since it too is built around elaborations of the central redemptive action.

20 "The bull of Urban IV stresses . . . the joy that the new feast is to occasion." Kolve, p. 45. Actually, however, the passage from the bull which Kolve cites stresses the mixed nature of the gift of the Eucharist, the inseparable mingling of sorrow and joy inherent in the occasion: ". . . *in ea et gaudemus pie lacrimantes et lacrimamus devote gaudentes, letas habendo lacrimas et letitiam lacrimantem;*" or, in Kolve's translation, " . . . on this occasion we both rejoice amid pious weeping and weep amid reverent rejoicing, joyful in our lamentation and woeful in our jubilation." Kolve, p 45 (Kolve does not italicize the Latin). That is, the occasion that prompts the feast, like that which prompts the drama associated with the feast, entails an inseparable mixture of joy and life and sorrow and death, the mixture which we have stated to be the generating situation of the medieval-Renaissance dramatic tradition as a whole.

21 Kolve, p. 48

22 Kolve, p. 49

23 The phrase in quotations is from the stage directions which conclude the *Regularis Visitatio*: ". . . the triumph of our king, in that he rose having conquered death;" " . . . *triumpho regis nostri, quod devicta morte surrexit . . .*," ed. and trans. David Bevington, *Medieval Drama*, p. 28.

24 Shakespeare refers to this figure, for example, the well-known reference in *Hamlet*, where an actor who rants noisily is described as one who "out-Herods Herod" (III.ii.14).

25 "Herod the Great," in *Medieval Drama*, 1. 92, p. 440. Whenever the cycle-play episode I quote from is contained in Bevington, my reference is to Bevington's easily accessible edition. Otherwise, the text I quote from is the edition cited in note 17.

26 In the N-Town "Death of Herod" his mortality is powerfully dramatized. A personified death appears at a feast and carries Herod off in the midst of his boast.

27 Chester "Nativity," 11. 317-332, p. 109.

28 Consider, for example, Richard's speech in prison, V.v.1 ff., or Lear's cry, "they told me I was every thing. 'Tis a lie, I am not ague-proof," IV.vi.104-5, as well as the entire train of events leading up to those recognitions.

29 Compare Marlowe's *Tamburlaine*. As with many of Shakespeare's Kings, Tamburlaine is unmistakably presented in the medieval wicked-ruler tradition—a death figure who boasts of limitless power, inflicts death on others, and finally dies himself at the height of his power and prosperity. But the Christian context of earlier drama is missing—the dramatized presentation of Christ's power which would enable us finally to evaluate Tamburlaine's life and death. This is why we find it difficult to locate Marlowe's point of view. The reader must decide what context to place the play in, for the text no longer supplies it. Moreover, in contrast to Shakespearean drama, the play does not proceed to construct other solutions to the hard fact of mortality—it simply exposes that fact.

30 Kolve, p. 51

31 John 11: 39.

32 The raising of Lazarus was considered to be a type of the Resurrection.

33 Bevington, "The Raising of Lazarus," 1. 120, p. 474.

34 This same technique yields equally powerful results in Shakespearean drama, where it occurs, in naturalized form, in various scenes of imagined death: for example in Juliet's imaginings of her awakening in

the charnel house; in Claudio's Lazarus-like envisioning of the afterlife ("to lie in cold obstruction and to rot," *Measure for Measure* III.i.118); and most powerfully, although least literally, in Lear's madness, his Lazarus-like experience of death and hell, from which he is raised to an even more terrible hell, knowledge of Cordelia's death.

35 Bevington, "Saints' Plays or Conversion Plays," *Medieval Drama*, p. 661.

36 David L. Jeffrey, "English Saints' Plays," in *Medieval Drama*, Stratford-upon-Avon Studies 16, ed. Neville Denny [London: Edward Arnold (Publishers) Ltd.], 1973, p. 72.

37 The point is that incorporation with the Mystical Body banishes the death aspect of bodily life—thus the belief that the saint's body does not decay after death. The *Legenda aurea* (*Golden Legend*), the medieval compendium of saints' lives compiled by Jacobus de Voragine, contains numerous accounts of saints whose bodies remain whole, sweet-smelling, clean, after their deaths. To give a more recent example, St. Bernadette's grave at Lourdes was opened periodically in order to demonstrate the incorruptibility of her remains, and so establish her sainthood.

38 The description of Christ as "the greatest of the saints" is from "The Service for Representing Adam," an Anglo-Norman play consisting of several episodes from scriptural history joined together (for this reason the play is often considered to be transitional between earlier drama, which characteristically consists of discrete episodes, and the comprehensive cycle drama). The lines, together with translation, are as follows.

> When the greatest of the saints appears—
> . . .
> By this greatest of saints, I mean Christ,
> He who wishes his people to gain eternal
>   life through him;
>
> Des sainz quant vendra toit li maires—
> . . .
> Co est Crist que li saint signifie,
> Qui vold par lui avront vie;

The quotation and translation are from David Bevington's edition of "The Service for Representing Adam," *Medieval Drama*, 11. 829, 833-34.

39 That power over death achieved through union with an immortality-granting body is central to the conception of sainthood is confirmed by examining medieval burial customs. In the early Middle Ages the preferred form of interment was burial *ad sanctos*, burial in a common grave in the vicinity of a saint's remains in hopes of sharing in his

death-transcending powers at the day of Resurrection. See Philippe Ariès, *Western Attitudes Toward Death*, trans. Patricia Ranum (Baltimore and London: The John Hopkins U. Press, 1974). Later in the Middle Ages, people stressed proximity to the the Eucharist rather than to a saint's remains. The preferred location for burial therefore was in the church, where Mass was celebrated; and the preferred location in the church was near the altar, "the table of the eucharistic sacrifice." Philippe Ariès, *The Hour of Our Death*, trans. Helen Weaver (N.Y.: Alfred A. Knopf, 1981), p. 72.

In practice, burial *ad sanctos* also meant burial in or near a church, since early churches were usually constructed around a saint's remains. But in either case, the underlying wish is the same: to secure protection against eternal death through proximity to the incorruptible Mystical Body, whether that Body manifests itself in human sainthood or in the Eucharistic rite.

40 It is for this reason also that medieval saints' lives all follow a similar pattern, and that not only the pattern, but even similar details, similar miracles and acts of conversion, are commonly attributed to saints from widely separated times and places.

41 David Bevington, *Medieval Drama*, uses these appellations interchangeably.

42 Bevington includes these three in his category "Saints' Plays or Conversion Plays." David Jeffrey allows only the two Digby plays, since the Croxton play does not deal with a human saint.

In discussing the three Saints' plays (the two Digby plays and the Croxton play), I have used David Bevington's editions in *Medieval Drama*.

43 The association of Jews and wicked rulers appears throughout medieval drama, as, for example, in the following lines from the Ripoll Resurrection play, a twelfth-century expansion of the Visitatio: "Iudeorum inuidia,/et principum perfidia," "the envy of the Jews,/and the treachery of princes!" The play and the translation are in Hardison, *Christian Rite and Christian Drama*, p. 241 and p. 302 respectively. The translation is Hardison's own; the text he uses is Karl Young's edition, in "Some Texts of Liturgical Plays," *PMLA*, XXIV (1909) 303-8; reprinted in *Drama of the Medieval Church*, 678-81 (Hardison's reference, p. 41n).

44 The translation is Hardison's, *Christian Rite and Christian Drama*, p. 304. The Latin lines, from Karl Young's edition, cited in Hardison, p. 244, are as follows: "*Credendum est magis soli Mariae ueraci quam Iudeorum turbe fallaci./ Scimus Christum surrexisse a mortuis vere.*"

45 The dates of composition and revision are from Irving Ribner, *The English History Play in the Age of Shakespeare* (Princeton, N.J.: Princeton U. Press, 1957), p. 37.

46 For example, the protagonist encounters his evil fate (in the form of illness, age, poverty) during his life, rather than, as in the earlier moralities, after death. For detailed discussion of the differences between earlier and later morality drama, see Bernard Spivack, *Shakespeare and the Allegory of Evil: The History of a Metaphor in Relation to Shakespeare's Villains* (N.Y.: Columbia U. Press, 1958); and Robert Potter, *The English Morality Play*.

47 For the discussion of *Mundus et Infans* I have used John Matthews Manly's edition, in *Specimens of the Pre-Shaksperean Drama*, I (1897; rpt. N.Y.: Dover Publications, Inc. 1967).

48 *Mundus*, 1. 20.

49 *Mundus*, 1. 25.

50 *Mundus*, 1. 32; 1. 40.

51 *Mundus*, 11. 34-5.

52 *Mundus*, 11. 36-39.

53 *Mundus*, 1. 33.

54 For my discussion of *Kynge Johan* I have used John Matthews Manly's edition, in *Specimens of the Pre-Shaksperean Drama*, I (1897; rpt. N.Y.: Dover Publications, Inc. 1967). Manley does not indicate the date of the version he uses, but in any case my point—that the play illustrates a changed conception of Kingship—is unaffected; and the date of Bale's final version being 1561, the change is in any event firmly established by the time Shakespeare is writing.

55 For an account of the historical King John see Peter Saccio, *Shakespeare's English Kings: History, Chronicle, and Drama* (N.Y.: Oxford U. Press, 1977). King John had been portrayed harshly by earlier Catholic chroniclers, including Polydore Vergil, whose work Bale refers to within the play; and Bale reverses this, portraying the king as a kind of martyr.

56 I have modernized the spelling of the characters' names, but not of the text.

57 See, for example, Bernard Spivack's discussion of the development of the Tudor morality, *Allegory of Evil*.

58 Ribner, *English History Play*, p. 37.

59 England, represented in the play by Clergy, Nobility and Civil Order (the three estates of the kingdom), is also represented by a figure England (Yngelond). This figure represents the commonwealth considered as a whole, as the conglomerate of subjects and land, rather than the commonwealth anatomized into its separate powers, or estates.

60 *Kynge Johan*, 1. 11. 2280-81.

61 Compare this to the conspirators in *Henry V* (II, ii) who ask not to escape the death penalty, but only for the king's forgiveness of their fault; a scene to be echoed in real life by Essex's similar plea to Queen Elizabeth after his arrest for treason.

62 *Kynge Johan*, 1. 2303.

63 *Kynge Johan*, 1. 2198.

64 *Kynge Johan*, 1. 2200.

65 *Kynge Johan*, 1. 2315.

66 *Kynge Johan*, 1. 2614.

67 For discussion of the medieval political and legal elaboration of the Pauline concept see Ernst Kantorowicz, *The King's Two Bodies: A Study in Medieval Political Theology* (Princeton, N.J.: Princeton U. Press, 1957).

68 *Kynge Johan*, 1. 2354.

69 For my discussion of *Respublica* I have used the text in *"Lost" Tudor Plays with Some Others*, ed. John S. Farmer (1907; facsimile rpt. N.Y.: Barnes & Noble, Inc., 1966).

70 Edmund Plowden, *Commentaries or Reports* (London, 1816), 212a, cited in Kantorowicz, *The King's Two Bodies*, p. 7.

71 Plowden, *Reports*, 177a, cited in Kantorowicz, *The King's Two Bodies*, p. 13.

72 Plowden, *Reports*, 213, cited in Kantorowicz, *The King's Two Bodies*, p. 9.

73 Kantorowicz summarizes his discussion of the evolution of the two-body concept as follows.

> The tenet . . . of the Tudor jurists definitely hangs upon the Pauline language and its later development: the change from the Pauline *corpus Christi* to the mediaeval *corpus ecclesiae mysticum*, thence to the *corpus reipublicae mysticum* . . . until finally . . . the slogan emerged saying that every abbot was a "mystical body" or a "body politic," and that accordingly the king, too, was, or had, a body politic which "never died." (Kantorowicz, p. 506)

74 Plowden, *Reports*, 238, cited in Kantorowicz, *The King's Two Bodies*, p. 11.

Chapter Two

The World of the Second History Tetralogy: "Miracles are Ceased"

The changed social-psychological reality expressed in the Tudor dramatic fusion of the Mystical Body and the body politic necessitates a different way of dealing with death. Medieval drama portrays the death and resurrection of a single human body which is also a divine and communal Body embracing all men. Tudor drama perpetuates (while altering) the medieval tradition, retaining the pattern of death and resurrection, but substituting for the central divine protagonist an entity at once material and immaterial, the English nation-state, for which semi-divine status is now claimed. The Mystical Body and the body politic, Christ the King and the earthly monarch, merge inseparably in this drama, reflecting the efficacy of the barrage of propaganda which followed Henry VIII's assumption of control over the English Church. The Shakespearean successors to this tradition include his two tetralogies on English history, the sequences from *1 Henry VI* to *Richard III*, and from *Richard II* to *Henry V*. Both tetralogies have as their protagonist the English nation, and both record the fall into death and eventual resurrection of the body politic. However, in contrast to the preceding dramatists, Shakespeare explores the inherent weakness in the new conception. The secular state cannot sustain its repeatedly made claim to semi-divine status because it fails precisely in the crucial point: the ability to confer power over death for the individual.

I will discuss the later and better worked out of the two English history sequences, the tetralogy comprising *Richard II*, *1* and *2 Henry IV*, and *Henry V*.[1] The four individual plays have their titular heroes, but the protagonist of the tetralogy as a whole is England: and together the plays trace the fall of the nation from the violated Edenic garden-world of *Richard II*, through deepening chaos, violence and near-dissolution in *1* and *2 Henry IV* (the death stage of the action), to the apparent resurrection of the body politic under its hero king Henry V.[2] The resurrection is only apparent, however, for the world at the end of the tetralogy, although it lays claim to divine sanction, is wholly secular: a pseudo-sacramental world which is in various major respects—military, legal, economic, political, philosophical-religious—a reflection of the actual Elizabethan world.[3]

At the time these plays were written feudal society was breaking up and the modern world, in many of its essentials, was forming.[4] Although the tetralogy ostensibly describes an earlier period (the reign of Richard II to that of Henry V), actually it offers a subtle and accurate picture of certain interrelated cultural changes occurring within Shakespeare's lifetime. In any period of change emergent social configurations co-exist with older ones;[5] and in the tetralogy, as in Elizabeth's England, two opposed forms of society compete: one sacramental and feudal, and the other secular, nationalistic and capitalistic. The first, historically older, form is envisioned as a society modelled after the Corpus Christi in which individuals are bound by love into a single hierarchically ordered whole, each in his pre-ordained place. The bonds which hold the society together are not the contracts of mutually self-interested parties, but mystical bonds, God-given structuring forms which, like those informing the living creation, prevent dissolution and death. The term "body politic" has thus a literal dimension: society is not merely analogous to, it is a living organism. The values of this older order, for which Richard, Gaunt and Carlisle are spokesmen in *Richard II*, include the following. The king is ordained by God. The land is not merely the sum of its material parts, but sacred and alive—a body with the king at its head, as Christ is the head of the Mystical Body. Words correspond to, and derive authority from, metaphysical truth, *the* Word. Truth is absolute and *a priori*. Social roles are predetermined by God

Himself, the creator and ultimate ratifier of the social order and its constitutent parts; and God intervenes directly in human history, rewarding the right and punishing breaches of the "natural" social order. Social structures are thus directly expressive of transcendental value, and for this reason the society contains inherently the possibility of death-transcendence.

The second, newer form of society is that of the secular nation-state whose members are united and restrained by merely human law which the strong impose on the weak—a world of individual ambition and Machiavellian *realpolitik*. The values of this order include the following. The king is he who seizes power and wields it effectively. Land, including England itself, is a commodity to be bought and sold. Men enforce the connection between words and reality by their will and actions, subject only to the limitations imposed by fact (although fact includes human opinion and belief). Value is *ad hoc* and relative, dependent upon an interplay of pragmatic forces—every virtue possessing its defects, every gain a loss. Men are held together not by an hierarchical network of obligation to their immediate social superiors, but by a cash nexus, and by the imposition of abstract, impersonal written law increasingly associated with obedience to a centralized authority. In this world individual lives, and the historical specificities which comprise the temporal circumstances of those lives, conform to no eternal and recurrent transcendent pattern. Men's wills, subject to the counterpointing forces of chance, circumstance and physical limit, determine their own and others' history; and the lives of individuals, circumscribed by death, pass away never to return. The fall into history is complete; and this body politic neither contains nor reflects the possibility of individual death-transcendence.[6]

In the opening and closing plays of the second tetralogy these two versions of reality dominate, respectively: in *Richard II*, Richard's theory of sacramental kingship, with the whole social and metaphysical reality which that implies; in *Henry V*, the self-validating secular nation-state, whose worth is measured by operative efficiency backed up by money and military might. It is therefore possible to view development in the tetralogy as diachronic (a reflection of the historical shift to a modern society), as we move from the feudal world of absolutes which initiates the tetralogy, through the chaos attendant on the period of transition, to the establishment of the new order at the close. But it is also possible to view the opening and closing plays as depictions of the same world differently described.[7] In the first play, for example, the Richard-Carlisle-Gaunt view of reality is undercut by Bolingbroke's success, which in itself makes a statement, and by Richard's own political actions (both new-order realities). And in the last play, power politics require legitimization in religious terms; and the new order is always spoken of as if it were the older order it has in fact supplanted.[8] In short, the world of *Richard II* and of *Henry V* may simply be the same world differently understood. But whether we view the difference between the two play worlds as reflecting actual chronological progression or merely a shift in viewpoint, it is still the case that the tetralogy reflects vast cultural changes then occurring;[9] and we can follow Shakespeare's embodiment of those changes by tracing the handling of three interrelated complexes of images and ideas: land; debt/currency/counterfeiting; and law/justice/warfare. The treatment of these, both locally and overall, is always the same. In each case one kind of value is translated into another: that which is sacred, absolute, priceless and individual (thus potentially transcendent of physical nature and death), is translated into that which is secular, relative, of fixed quantitative value and therefore exchangeable (finite, thus mortal). The process of translation both reveals and defines the true nature of the forces operating in dramatic and social worlds alike.

It should be stressed again that in Shakespeare's dramatic portrayal of social change, concrete social realities are inseparable from considerations of value. One cannot be reduced to the other, or given priority over it. The play world, like Elizabethan England, like twentieth-century America, is a moral/material construct whose institutions both create and express belief systems.

Land

In the opening play England is repeatedly described as of absolute value, a mystical entity not reducible to the sum of its parts. It is a green garden-world, life-sustaining and itself alive: an Edenic garden, as in Gaunt's sea-walled-garden speech (II.i.40-66), or the gardener's invocation of the well-tended garden which might have been (III.iv); and also a nurse, as in the "sweet soil," "My mother and my nurse" (I.iii), of Bolingbroke's farewell.[10]

The king is mystically connected with his land in a living relationship. When Richard stoops down to greet the earth on his return from Ireland, the physical gesture establishes and reinforces this literal yet mystical connection. This idea also lies behind Richard's assertion that the land will sicken in response to its king's sorrows, and in his dying assertion that Exton has "with the king's blood stained the king's own land" (V.v.110).

Opposed to Richard's words, however, are his actions, which reflect a contrasting, wholly secular reality. A chief source of the criticism directed against him, as Gaunt points out in the same sea-walled-garden speech, is that he has "leased" his country out "like to a tenement or pelting farm" (II.i.60). That is, he has treated the land not as a sacred entity to which he is tied in a live and mystical relationship, but as a thing to be bought and sold with an exact cash equivalent.

Those opposed and irreconcilable valuations of land appear throughout the tetralogy. The land-as-sacred concept is continually asserted verbally, but undercut everywhere at the level of action: for example, in the scene where the conspirators propose to divide England like the spoils of some great robbery (*1 Henry IV*); in the solid naturalism of the picture of rural England given in the scenes with Silence and Shallow (*2 Henry IV*); and in *Henry V*, where the king relies upon a dubious tangle of human law to claim by force of arms the "garden" world of France (V.ii.36).

This rather schizophrenic view of land—its supra-material valuation, versus the actual way it is acquired and used—

accurately reflects contemporary reality. Land was of central importance in the social, economic and political structures of the age. Landowners constituted a social elite: the greater the amount of land controlled, the higher one's rank. And for the overwhelming majority of Englishmen their place in society was determined by their relationship to land, in a hierarchy stretching from the landless poor (now a wage-earning class, displaced from their traditional roles by the termination of villeinage), to tenant farmers, through the lesser and greater gentry, to, at the very top, the great landed magnates whose power and wealth posed a potential challenge to the Crown itself.

There was at the time an emerging bourgeoisie, whose financial power and therefore influence was growing significantly. "By the seventeenth century some merchants were as rich as peers, though their fortunes were usually made in one lifetime.[11] And London, center of the new urban and commercial culture, was becoming an increasing influence on the rest of the country. But land remained the preeminent source not only of wealth, but of status. For land ownership constituted not only a source of income, but an entire way of life traditionally associated with a feudal-aristocratic complex of values. Newly-rich men—certain merchants, lawyers, and administrators in the royal service—would hasten to sink their profits into land, and far from challenging older ways, would immediately adopt the values and way of life traditionally associated with the landowning classes.

In earlier times, landowners resided on the estates they managed, and so had personal and long-standing relationships with their feudal dependents. Additionally, tenants had tended to discharge their feudal obligations through service, especially military service, rather than by cash payment. Prior to and during the 1590's, however, certain factors greatly affected traditional landlord-tenant relations. Chief among these was "an exceptionally rapid turnover of land."[12] This rapid turn-over would have resulted in, among other things, the exposure to view of the monetary basis of land ownership and, consequently, an erosion of belief in the "natural" basis of the social hierarchy.

For one thing, the availability of land allowed marked increase in social mobility. Although it was difficult to cross the line from the gentry to the peerage, it was relatively easy to enter the gentry from the bottom, as Shakespeare himself was to do through the purchase of Stratford real estate and the subsequent acquisition of a coat-of-arms. In addition, tenants would bear a different relationship to an owner who had acquired control over their land and livelihoods within their memories than they would to a landlord who had controlled the land through several generations, and whose established control, sanctioned by time and custom, could seem part of a natural order of things.

A further change in traditional landlord-tenant relations was caused by a rise in the number of absentee landlords, as peers, and eventually the gentry, flocked to the increasingly-felt attractions of London and the Court. And landlord-tenant relations were further eroded by the persistent inflation which caused landowners in need of ready cash to disrupt long-standing relationships with their tenants, forcing out freeholders and copyholders whenever possible, and converting long to short leases. "Increasing entry fines and racking rents seemed a revolutionary breach with custom: but it was the only means by which landowners could keep pace with rising prices."[13]

Thus, obligations of tenants to landlords were becoming less and less a matter of service (especially military service), and more and more a matter of cash payment. To what extent did financial considerations precede, to what extent follow, a change in values? Certainly, two competing ideals co-existed: the older aristocratic ideal of magnificent country living, including hospitality on a grand scale and the recognition of obligations toward one's tenants; and the new ideal of courtly magnificence in town, for which the tenants footed the bill. Equally certainly, the exodus to court was furthered because the financial benefits to be gained through royal favor constituted a lure few families could afford to ignore, especially in a period of rising inflation.

The Tudors exploited to the full both the landowners' hopes of profit and their desire for the newly fashionable life at court, as part of a long-term policy of reducing the power and independence of the feudal barons and converting them into royal dependents. The weakening of old landlord-tenant relationships could only contribute to royal security, since military service was a chief obligation of tenants under the older system, and every lord thus controlled a small army.

The 1590's—the period in which the history plays were written—marked a turning point between the older and newer forms of land use. "This decade saw the last of the age-old habit of regarding land not only as a source of money, but also as a means of obtaining military aid and outward signs of loyalty and esteem."[14] However, although feudal landlord-tenant relationships were rapidly being replaced by merely monetary obligations, and although the equivalency of land with cash was increasingly obvious, land ownership retained its unique prestige. Popular belief in the social and moral superiority land ownership conferred persisted among all classes. "Money was the means of acquiring and retaining status, but was not [thought to be] the essence of it.[15] Thus, a belief in the supra-material rights and obligations conferred by land ownership existed side by side with the now highly obvious fact that land was merely a commodity to be bought and sold, with clearly quantifiable monetary and exchange value, open to the highest bidder. At the most inclusive level—the land itself, the English nation—the question becomes whether, and in what way, England can be considered to constitute an entity greater than the sum of its material parts.

Debt/Currency/Counterfeiting

England was shifting from a land to a commercial economy. But this shift, even where understood, evoked enormous ambivalence, as centuries-old prejudices against commerce struggled against new realities. The relations between land and credit in this period well illustrate both the changing socio-economic reality, and contemporary ambivalence towards it. For example, the exigencies of estate management in this period of inflation led to a need for ready cash, which moneylenders were willing to supply. Earlier in the sixteenth century, there had been no convenient way to grant long-term loans. After 1572, however, a system was devised for extending long-term credit, which depended upon the use of land as security (and which therefore required the translation of land into a cash equivalent). Landowners did in fact make extensive use of the system in the following decades.[16] However, the advantages of the system for both borrower and lender were partially obscured by contemporary attitudes towards lending money at interest and towards borrowing. The former was traditionally viewed with disapproval and contempt, reflecting centuries of religious and legal sanctions; and the latter was looked upon with fear and horror. It was true that debt could lead to ruin, especially among the lower classes. Yet even among the larger landowners, for whom borrowing represented a convenience rather than a threat, fathers continued to warn sons of the dangers of borrowing, while consistently resorting to the practice themselves. And disapproval of money-lending in fact hindered the development of a much-needed system of credit throughout the sixteenth and well into the seventeenth century.

Shakespeare's handling of the shift to a commercial culture is inextricably involved with the problem of death in a way suggested by the very language of commerce, which invokes two opposed and competing realities. "Debt" and "redemption," for example, terms prevalent in the tetralogy, suggest the contemporary economic realities attendant on the nascent capitalism, including a heightened need for capital and an increased reliance on borrowing. On the other hand, these same terms evoke the Christian ordering of reality centered on the conquest of death: man's debt of death ("debt" and "death" were pronounced similarly)[17] incurred through Adam's sin; and the ultimate redemption, forgiveness, of that debt through Christ's self-sacrificial payment. Christian values are materially ineffective in the new money-based world; yet mastery of that world, though often necessary to stave off immediate death, cannot redeem the final debt, death itself.

The shift to a commercial culture, and the attendant shift in values, is expressed in the tetralogy by a complex of images revolving around bankruptcy, debt, redemption, counterfeiting and "passing current."[18] As with land, the shift is again from a world where absolute value, and thus the possibility of death-transcendence, is built into and expressed by the social system, to a wholly secular system which excludes that possibility, and is therefore associated with death.

The case for absolute, non-quantifiable value is made most explicitly in *Richard II*, often by the king himself (although by other characters as well, such as Carlisle and Gaunt). The king envisions heaven, and his own sacred status, as a kind of inexhaustible personal treasury upon which he can continue to draw. But in fact he is "bankrout" — of money, of moral credibility (II.i.257), and finally of "majesty" itself (IV.i.266). These moral and material elements are inseparable, in the play as in the larger reality the play represents. Again, it would be wrong to think of Elizabethan moral and religious views as mere grafting onto the facts — they are, on one level, the facts, something which is demonstrated over and over in the tetralogy, and also appreciated by modern historians.[19]

Puns on money — crowns, angels, royals, nobles (four coins of the period) — are frequent in the first three plays. This wordplay perfectly expresses the central opposition between the two fundamentally opposed realms of value already seen in connection with land: that which is non-material and priceless, versus that which can be reckoned up and exchanged for cash.

Perhaps the most striking instance in *Richard II* of wordplay on money occurs on Richard's return from Ireland when Carlisle and Aumerle enjoin him not to neglect the material means of maintaining his power. Carlisle points out that while heaven has power to keep Richard king, "The means that heavens yield must be embraced/And not neglected" (III.ii.30). Aumerle spells this out even more emphatically. Richard's response, which depends heavily upon puns on money, is a confident assertion that heaven will intervene directly on his behalf.

> For every man that Bolingbroke hath pressed
> To lift shrewd steel against our golden crown,
> God for his Richard hath in heavenly pay

> A glorious angel; then, if angels fight,
> Weak men must fall, for heaven still guards the right.
> (III.ii.58-62)

Richard's heavenly angels fail conspicuously to protect his crown against Bolingbroke's cash angels and crowns. Bolingbroke's angels equal armed fighting men who will be used to acquire the "golden crown"—the kingship itself, which is thus also precisely equatable with money.

Immediately after Richard's assertion that "heaven still guards the right," Salisbury enters with news of the Welsh army's fatally premature departure. Simply the timing of this points out, with ironic force, the fallacy of Richard's assumptions. Perhaps in another world right ensures victory, but on earth the angels of cold hard cash prevail.

In the last act Richard, alone and imprisoned, bewails his enormous losses. At this moment a groom enters and greets his former master with, "Hail, royal prince!" Richard responds, "Thanks, noble peer!/The cheapest of us is ten groats too dear" (V.v.67-8). "Royals", "nobles" and "groats" were three successively less valuable coins. Here, as in the "angels" speech, Richard puns on money, but in an exactly opposite way. Earlier, Richard asserted a priceless, metaphysical reality which would override and nullify the value and power of mere earthly currency. Here he devalues, ironically, all mere titles, with their implicit claim to register a non-quantitative intrinsic worth.

Richard has realized how bankrupt is the name of king without the military power, the wealth, and the validation by others which alone can convert the name of king into a substantial reality. Lacking money and material power to back them up, both king and groom are of precisely equal worth—that is, both worthless ("The cheapest of us is ten groats too dear").

Earlier in English history, peers were recognized as such either by letters of patent, or by being summoned to sessions of parliament. Noblemen who lost their wealth were simply dropped from the rolls of those invited to attend. But by Elizabeth's reign, "the legal definition hardened on the basis of an inalienable hereditary right.[20] Accordingly, there now existed "a potential discrepancy between wealth and title."[21] This potential materialized with a vengeance in Elizabeth's reign, during which a substantial portion of the Elizabethan aristocracy suffered sizable losses in both land and money, "as a result of which respect for their titles and their authority was diminished."[22] Thus, Richard's musings on the value of titles precisely reflect contemporary realities. On the one hand, the entire social system was based on distinctions of rank which were theoretically absolute, reflecting an innate, intangible and heritable superiority related to divine will. On the other hand, social conditions clearly revealed the *de facto* truth that impoverished peers were not measurably better off than their plebeian counterparts. Titles of nobility did confer many privileges, but these were not enough, in themselves, to restore lost fortunes. And certain of the privileges, such as immunity from arrest for debt, would only have exacerbated the growing disrespect for titles by emphasizing the lack of connection between moral worth and rank-based privileges.

The groom's visit to Richard dramatizes another, non-material value, although one which proceeds from man and not necessarily from God. The groom is moved by disinterested love and pity, a selfless love which resists translation into a cash equivalent. This value is dramatized for us—it exists before our eyes—but it does not necessarily correspond to any metaphysical reality. It does, however, point the way to the man-made resurrections of Shakespearean comedy and tragedy.

As we have seen, wordplay on money in *Richard II* tends to operate in a certain direction: the existence of absolute value is asserted, and immediately and pointedly contradicted. The realm of absolute value may exist, but the social order does not embody it in any literal way. In *1 Henry IV*, puns on money express a different, although related, concern. They constitute part of a complex of images centering on counterfeiting, debt and redemption, images which are discussed by virtually every character in the play including Hal, the King, Falstaff, Worcester, Hotspur and Douglas. This complex of imagery expresses the central issue of both *Henry*

IV plays, an issue integrally related to the problem of death. The king at the head of the realm is, on one level, a counterfeit king, who necessarily lacks the authority of the true king he had deposed and murdered—authority conferred only by lawful succession, and theoretically sanctioned by God. Yet by standards of simple efficiency, the true king's rule proved disastrous for his kingdom. He bankrupted the land, oppressed nobles and commons alike, and in the proposed confiscation of Bolingbroke's lawful inheritance, struck a fatal blow at the very principles by which he claimed his own authority.

Bolingbroke, in contrast, behaves like a good king, who could govern efficiently were he not plagued by the perpetual rebellions to which the conditions of his own ascent to power have given rise. Douglas unwittingly gives voice to this problem when after meeting a series of warriors dressed like the king, he meets Bolingbroke himself, and comments, "I fear thou art another counterfeit;/And yet, in faith, thou bearest thee like a king" (V.iv.34-5).

Is the civil disorder which plagues Bolingbroke's kingdom the just retribution for sin which Carlisle had foretold? Or is it the result of this very expectation in men's minds, coupled with the natural discontent of Bolingbroke's former allies? Because the action here (and in the tetralogy as a whole) is always fully accounted for at the level of human motivation, the question of Providential intervention in human history remains not only unanswered, but unanswerable.

Monetary imagery perfectly expresses the moral/material problem of finding an acceptable source of value. The king's stamped image on the currency of the realm symbolized the central power which backed that currency. In the older way of viewing things this power derived ultimately from God. But a usurper king lacks divine sanction, and a new kind of authority is required to make his reign acceptable—to make the counterfeit king "pass current". A consuming activity of the two *Henry IV* plays is the search for such an authority, and possible substitutes for the lost source of value are proposed by (among other characters) Hotspur, Glendower and Falstaff, each of whom offers his own version of redemption. These characters are anarchic individualists whose turbulent energies threaten the life of the body politic. Each represents an enduring psychic force, but also a concrete social force (Hotspur, Glendower and their ally Douglas represent respectively the great Northern semi-feudal families, the Welsh and the Scots, all perpetual sources of unrest and rebellion throughout Elizabeth's reign). These forces have both a life and a death side, but within the tetralogy all operate destructively, because no effective authority exists which can control them and direct them positively.

Hotspur's value is personal honor, gained by and expressed through prowess in arms. His solution to the times is redemption in battle, and like the other characters, he expresses this through the language of debt and payment, as he urges his father and uncle to revenge their shames.

> No, yet time serves wherein you may redeem
> Your banished honors and restore yourselves
> Into the good thoughts of the world again;
> Revenge the jeering and disdained contempt
> Of this proud king, who studies day and night
> To answer all the debt he owes to you
> Even with the bloody payment of your deaths.
>
> (I.iii.178-84)

If Hotspur represents something permanent in human nature—the love of aggression, in this case filtered through a chivalric code—he also represents a specific social type, the feudal aristocrat, whose preeminent value, like Hotspur's, was personal honor. Hotspur's portrait is in fact a kind of composite picture of that aristocracy, who constituted a military caste (as against the newer nobility, virtually all of whom had risen to prominence through non-military royal service). Stone describes this group as characterized by a fanatical concern for reputation, which they valued above all other things; extravagant generosity; a love for reckless gambling; a propensity for settling quarrels by violence; enormous arrogance; and extreme intemperance in word and deed, to a degree difficult for modern readers to grasp. Hotspur well fits that description. He is impulsive and touchy, quickly moved to intemperate rage at any treatment he considers less than his due (as when the King requests his prisoners). He values honor above all else. Even when dying, he regrets not his lost life, but "those proud titles thou hast won of me" (V.iv.78). He is reckless, wishing to rush into battle even at a disadvantage. He is also stubborn, arrogant, and difficult to restrain. And finally, he is generous. When Glendower argues about the "half-moon" of land, Hotspur is ready to battle his own ally for honor rather than to give in. But as soon as Glendower capitulates, Hotspur meets him freely: "I'll give thrice so much land/To any well-deserving friend" (III.i.136-37).

In Hotspur, then, Shakespeare epitomizes the very type of the medieval military aristocrat, with all his virtues—and his defects. Hotspur's courage, frankness, generosity—even his hotheadedness—show to advantage against his father's policy and vacillation, and seem even more attractive retrospectively compared to John's treachery against the rebels (*2 Henry IV*). But in spite of Hotspur's attractiveness, he is essentially destructive. In his quest for honor he can brook no "co-rival", and praises of Hal are unbearable to him: "No more, no more! Worse than the sun in March,/This praise doth nourish agues" (IV.i.110-11). He pushes aside his wife and calls for his horse, like a Hollywood movie cowboy, and for much the same reasons. Essentially, he rejects the arts of peace: poetry, courtesy, above all, romantic love, for which he would substitute armed violence.

> This is no world
> To play with mammets and to tilt with lips.
> We must have bloody noses and cracked crowns
> And pass them current too. Gods me, my horse!
>
> (II.iii.91-94)

Chivalric prowess, then, is the value Hotspur proposes to substitute for the lost values of the earlier age. But military adventuring stripped of the mystique of honor is, as Falstaff sees, equivalent simply to death. "I like not such grinning honor as Sir Walter hath. Give me life . . . ," Falstaff comments, looking on the body of Blunt slain in battle (*1 Henry IV*, V.iii.58-9). And Hotspur is, finally, a death worshipper, Bellona's bridegroom piling up human "sacrifices" "All hot and bleeding" at her altar—amassing corpses like so much coinage to swell the value of his reputation.[23]

Hotspur belongs to a transitional period between the old and new orders. If he contrasts favorably with Prince John, he contrasts unfavorably with Carlisle's portrait of Mowbray as the ideal Christian warrior.

> Many a time hath banish'd Norfolk fought
> For Jesu Christ in glorious Christian field,
> Streaming the ensign of the Christian cross
> Against black pagans, Turks, and Saracens,
> And, toil'd with works of war, retir'd himself
> To Italy, and there at Venice gave
> His body to that pleasant country's earth,
> And his pure soul unto his captain Christ,
> Under whose colors he had fought so long.
> (*Richard II*, IV.i.92-100)

In the Elizabethan view of the feudal system military prowess was, at least ideally, exercised selflessly, in the service of one's immediate and "natural" superior and thus, ultimately, in the service of God. But Hotspur fights selfishly, for personal glory, in contrast to the idealized portrait of Mowbray as Christ's soldier. Hotspur has retained the military proclivities of the feudal warrior, but cut loose from the form-giving ordering social structure which sanctified that aggression while directing it into socially useful, or at least neutral, form.

Of course, the feudal ideal was just that, an ideal or theory. In practice, in a system where power was vested primarily in persons rather than in laws, authority was as good or as bad as the person embodying it; and even in *Richard II* where the ideal is so often alluded to, it is seen only in the breach. Mowbray, for example, is described as Christ's soldier, but actually seen in Richard's service; and service to Richard, Mowbray's natural superior and a true, God-representing king, has already implicated Mowbray in murder even before the play begins.

Glendower is Hotspur's ally but also his opponent. He is associated with the related powers of art, love, magic, imagination — transforming illusions which, immaterial themselves, can nevertheless effect substantial change. These forces may be bent to the service of life, as happens in comedy (for example, *Midsummer Night's Dream*); or of death, as happens in tragedy (for example, in *Macbeth*). In the histories they are largely inoperative, and finally eliminated altogether.

What Glendower represents is seen most clearly in *1 Henry IV*, III.i; and it is Hotspur's abrasive skepticism in the scene which defines what Glendower embodies — magic, romantic love and art, none of which Hotspur values. Hotspur challenges Glendower's claim to magic (for example, 17ff. and 53ff.). He mocks the love between Mortimer and the Welsh princess, reducing it to mere sex ("Come, Kate, thou art perfect in lying down" 226); and he cannot hear the beauty of poetry or of music, claiming to prefer the cacophony of metal screeching on metal, or of a dog's howl, to either. However, the reality of all three — magic, love, art — are dramatized within the scene, made present to our senses. We hear the musicians whom Glendower claims to have summoned from "a thousand leagues . . . hence" (224). We see that for Mortimer and the Welsh princess, their love has a reality based on but transcending sexual attraction. And the quality of that love, acted out in dumb show by the lovers who can't otherwise communicate, is also powerfully communicated to us through art — through music, for example the Princess's Welsh song; and through Glendower's poetry (211-219), the lushest lines in the tetralogy, all the more effective because we hear nothing else like them. The dramatization of the powers associated with Glendower reminds us that they are real although insubstantial, at the same time that Hotspur's objections remind us of the qualified nature of their reality.

We may associate the realm Glendower conjures up with Sidney's ideal Golden World, or with Shakespeare's other enchanted regions, the forest of *A Midsummer Night's Dream* or the island in *The Tempest*. But in any case, the forces whose effects are made visible in this scene are glimpsed only briefly in the tetralogy, and always operate either unreliably or downright malevolently. As allies in the pitilessly actual world of battle, for example, the Welsh under Glendower are consistently unreliable. Frightened by ill omens, they desert Richard one day before his return to England, thus bringing about the very result they fear (*Richard II*); and they never arrive at the field in *1 Henry IV* (IV.i.124-26).

The Welsh are not only unreliable, they are actively destructive. Worcester, describing the aftermath of one of Glendower's victories, refers to the "beastly shameful transformation" the Welshwomen have wrought on the English dead (*1 Henry IV*, I.i.44) — an allusion to a suggestion in Holinshed that the Welshwomen castrated the enemy corpses. In a comic world the Glendower force can operate benignly, for example transforming, through the power of creative illusion, the animal fact of sexual attraction into human love. But in the world of history the Glendower force brings about only the perverse and lethal "transformation" of the mutilated corpses, a literal and figurative strike at the very source of human renewal.

Falstaff, who repeatedly voices his views on the debt/ redemption problem plaguing England, is the most important of the three individualists. Glendower is associated with a force which can transform the world to an earthly heaven or hell; but Falstaff is the world itself, that which is transformed. He is a representative of bodily life, and the physical world is, most immediately for us, the body and the drives and appetites associated with it. Because Falstaff is linked with the body, he is presented as simultaneously a source of life and of death. *1 Henry IV* emphasizes Falstaff's life side, and *2 Henry IV* his death side; but in both plays he is always both at once. Medieval drama, which splits apart the life/death aspect of existence, expresses the death aspect of life under the Christian catchall for death and sin, the tripartite scheme of the World, the Flesh and the Devil; and in the tetralogy Falstaff is repeatedly associated with all three.[24] But Falstaff perfectly sums up the change from medieval to Shakespearean drama. He is a direct descendant of the medieval doubter figures who doubt that the laws of nature (thus, that death) can be overcome; but unlike those earlier embodiments of death, he cannot be wholly rejected (neither can he be wholly accepted). Over and over, Falstaff calls attention, irrefutably, to the inescapable bodily reality which underlies all value, and life itself; and repeatedly, he engages that part of us which values life—pleasure and sheer survival—above all else. If Falstaff is a seamless blend of contradiction, including the ultimate contradiction of the oneness of life and death, that is because human existence is just such a blend; and the solution to the death side of life must include what Falstaff represents. Yet Falstaff's values, by themselves, are also inadequate against death.

1 Henry IV emphasizes the vitality of Falstaffian values, expressed by, and reaching a climax in, his battlefield "resurrection". Yet even in this play Falstaff's charm and abundant energies have a selfishly sinister and deathlike aspect, as when he tells us that he has led his soldiers into the line of fire, to mutilation and death (V.iii.35-38). In *2 Henry IV* Falstaff's dark side becomes more prominent. At his first appearance in the latter play Falstaff draws attention to his illness by a request to know the doctor's diagnosis of his urine; and this is only the first of many subsequent allusions linking Falstaff to age, illness, bodily decay, all the ills inherent in fleshly existence. Moreover, the destructive effect of Falstaffian values on social health is made equally clear—most so, perhaps, in the conscription scene, where Falstaff turns living men into commodities, sources of quick cash (still another version of the characteristic action of the tetralogy, where what is priceless and of infinite, irreplaceable value, is continually being translated into a cash equivalent).

Life is priceless, yet it is also assessable in terms of cash. Silence and Shallow's Beckett-like dialog of aging and death, interspersed with reminiscences of a roistering, vanished youth, is also punctuated with questions as to the going price for bullocks and ewes (*2 Henry IV*, III.ii). What is the value of these symbols of sexual fertility and physical life? As Silence tells us, the market value of "a score of good ewes" is precisely ten pounds (III.ii.52). Immediately after this the conscription scene follows, in which Bullcalf's market value is also precisely established: "four Harry ten shillings in French crowns"

(III.ii.228-29). The conscription system allows a price to be placed on human life. What, however, is the value to be placed on Feeble's appealingly plucky willingness to pay the debt/death owed to God? This is a value which transcends animal life. It both can and cannot be equated with cash, and, like the groom's visit in *Richard II*, it calls into question the other method of valuation so clearly at work in this play.

In Falstaff's insistence on the inescapability of bodily limits he is differentiated from Glendower, who claims to transcend them (through magic), and from Hotspur, who is contemptuous of them. Hotspur scorns all bodily limits including the ultimate limit, death: "die all, die merrily" (*1 Henry IV*, IV.i.134). Falstaff, in contrast, bases his values on bodily life, sheer physical existence. "To die is to be a counterfeit, for he is but the counterfeit of a man who hath not the life of a man" (IV, iv.115-17). The enacted image of the live Falstaff bearing away the dead Hotspur graphically expresses their relative strength. All secondary value rests on (though it is not reducible to) the life of the body, source and ground of any merely derivative abstractions.

What Falstaff represents is inseparable from the body, but not wholly reducible to it. If his pleasures include preeminently eating and drinking, they also include the intangibles of good fellowship; and if he exercises his wit in the service of material gain, he also does so for the sheer pleasure of it, as in the post-robbery dialogue with Hal where he multiplies adversaries far beyond what is needed to exculpate himself (*1 Henry IV*, II.iv.114 ff.). His witty and extravagant fictions are creations *ex nihilo*, and in his mock epic he manipulates the seemingly intractable reality of bodies and numbers—the material and the quantifiable—to his and our satisfaction, to achieve his significantly bloodless victory.

In our first sight of Falstaff he is dissociated from time, which is restated in terms of physical appetites. He inquires the time, and Hal replies, "What a devil hast thou to do with the time of the day? Unless hours were cups of sack, and minutes capons, and clocks the tongues of bawds, and dials the signs of leaping-houses, and the blessed sun himself a fair hot wench in flame-color'd taffeta" (*1 Henry IV*, I.ii.6-10). But in *2*

Henry IV, the world of time closes in. In his first appearance in *2 Henry IV* Falstaff successfully parries the demands of the Chief Justice. But as the play develops, Falstaff is seen as increasingly subject to the inexorable laws of nature and society which enforce limit, restraint and death; and at the end of the play he is led away to prison by his natural antagonist the Chief Justice, the very image of implacable Law.

Falstaff outlives the other individualists who threaten the social order (Hotspur dies in *1 Henry IV*, Glendower in *2 Henry IV*, and Falstaff only in *Henry V*). For this young-old man is linked to both the earliest (chronologically in human development) and the most basic of human drives, the individual's amoral pursuit of immediate pleasure and avoidance of pain, grounded in bodily reality; the infantile part of each individual which can be suppressed but never wholly exterminated, and which is renounced at one's peril because it is so closely connected to the survival instinct and to life itself.

As with Hotspur and Glendower, what Falstaff represents must be controlled or it becomes lethal; but total absence of the Falstaffian energies results in something differently but equally deathlike, the pleasureless world of *Henry V* presided over by a king who eschews all individual pleasure, and individuality itself, in favor of his public role.

Falstaff, Hotspur and Glendower differ markedly from one another, but each is associated, at least in part, with something non-utilitarian. Even the resolutely materialistic Falstaff lives also for the non-material pleasures of fellowship and wit. Hal, in contrast, exemplifies all that is pragmatic, functional, utilitarian.

This effective, but cold and calculating, king offers still another version of redemption, another way to make good the debt incurred by his father's actions; and it is his version, not Hotspur's, Glendower's or Falstaff's, which prevails. At the beginning of the play Hal states his intention to throw off his "loose behavior ... And pay the debt I never promised," thus "Redeeming time when men think least I will" (I.ii.212- 213, 221). This promise is eventually, like all of Hal's promises, scrupulously enacted.

In the middle of *1 Henry IV*, Hal defends himself against his father's criticism in a very characteristic way. He tells his father that he will "redeem" his spotted past "on Percy's head," and continues:

> ... the time will come
> That I shall make this northern youth exchange
> His glorious deeds for my indignities.
> Percy is but my factor, good my lord,
> To engross up glorious deeds on my behalf;
> And I will call him to so strict account
> That he shall render every glory up,
> Yea, even the slightest worship of his time,
> Or I will tear the reckoning from his heart.
> (III.ii.144-52)

The language of commerce which echoes throughout this passage—"exchange," "factor," "engross," "strict account," "render . . . up," "reckoning"—accords well with Hal's characteristic way of thinking. He recognizes no transcendent claims. Debts are promises to be paid off in actions. Honor, and all other non-material values, are commodities—not moral goods, but commercial goods, quantifiable, and therefore exchangeable.

Hal's definition of redemption is, in fact, a business definition, suitable to the bookkeeper mentality of this reliable yet calculating king: to buy back, to make material payment for. The Christian overtones of redemption—deliverance from spiritual and physical death—are wholly absent from Hal's conception of it.

Honor, for Hal, is a commodity in the many contemporary senses of the word: something associated with use, profit, advantage; with expediency; and with the common but somewhat disreputable practice whereby to obtain ready cash goods were bought on credit and sold back at a loss (usually to a usurer, who thus circumvented the laws prohibiting the taking of interest).[25] This last is precisely what happens in the tetralogy, and we can summarize the debt theme we have been tracing in detail in the following way.

Initially Richard had "leased out" England to obtain cash—one of the wrongs Bolingbroke and his allies intend to redress ("we shall .../Redeem from broking pawn the blemished crown" *Richard II*, II.i.291-93). But Bolingbroke plunges deeper into another kind of debt, even less susceptible of repayment. Bolingbroke's acquisition of the throne is essentially a business transaction conducted on credit. Allies flock to meet Bolingbroke on his return to England, and he promises to convert his "unfelt [*i.e.*, intangible, unsubstantial] thanks" into material reward, upon successfully claiming his inheritance (ostensibly his Lancaster inheritance, but in the event, England itself).

> Welcome, my lords, I wot your love pursues
> A banished traitor. All my treasury
> Is yet but unfelt thanks, which more enriched
> Shall be your love and labor's recompense.
> (II.ii.59-62)

Bolingbroke acknowledges the debt he incurs in accepting his allies' proffered "love" (their material aid), and promises repayment in kind. This constitutes an implicit acknowledgment of both Bolingbroke's and his allies' motives; a spur to his supporters to continue their efforts, in anticipation of the day when the resources of the royal Exchequer will enrich his own; and a forecast of the fate of all monetarily unprofitable values in a world where Bolingbroke is king.

Bolingbroke and his allies have reached an unspoken agreement as to the form repayment will take—cold cash, easily measured, therefore, presumably, easily repaid. But human greed defeats this calculation, and Bolingbroke dies still attempting, unsuccessfully, to discharge his debt. It is his son Hal who finally manages to "redeem ... the blemished crown"; but as with commodities, the transaction involves a certain loss, both material—money and lives—and intangible—the entire complex of transcendental values characteristic of the lost order and seen, even in *Richard II*, only in the breach. Gone forever is the assured conjunction of the earthly and heavenly worlds, and with it, the assured possibility of death-transcendence.

As Henry V, Hal finally provides what has been lacking in the realm—an acceptable source of authority. He is a counterfeit king whose operative excellence in the role allows him to "pass current" — to be accepted as a true king. With his success a new kind of value is established — operative, pragmatic value. His rule suffices to bind the fragmented parts of the social body back into a working whole, precisely as currency provides the bonds between men in a commercial society. For what binds Hal's kingdom together is not the divinely sanctioned hierarchical network of relations and obligations characteristic of a feudal society, with its natural and cosmic correspondences, but rather a system imposed from without, backed up by arms and cash. This new order strikingly resembles Marx's description of what replaced feudalism.

> The bourgeoisie, wherever it has got the upper hand, has put an end to all feudal, patriarchal, idyllic relations. It has pitilessly torn asunder the motley feudal ties that bound man to his "natural superior," and has left remaining no other nexus between man and man than naked self-interest, than callous "cash-payment." It has drowned the most heavenly ecstasies of religious fervour, of chivalrous enthusiasm, of philistine sentimentalism, in the icy water of egotistical calculations. It has resolved personal worth into exchange value....[26]

But Marx's elegiac tone is only partially appropriate to Shakespeare's overall vision. For as the tetralogy makes clear, the new order must be judged against what precedes it, the bloody chaos of *2 Henry IV*. Civil disorder in the play perpetually worsens, threatening the realm with extinction. All England is an armed camp. The color, good humour, larger-than-life quality of the earlier world of extravagant individualism is darkened and diminished, replaced by a black-and-white caricature world, increasingly empty and savagely parodic of its former self: Pistol's rant and John's treachery in place of the courage and honor of an older chivalry, and Falstaff's amusing appetites and warm good fellowship turned to a savage pike-and-dace cannibalism, as he gobbles up the Francis Feebles of the world.

This world is diseased and aged, dominated by a sick and dying king, Falstaff's perpetual laments at his age and illness, and the reminiscing voices of Silence and Shallow, mythologizing their long-vanished pasts with nostalgic accounts of youthful exploits which in fact never took place. These laments are analogous, on a personal and naturalistic level, to the lyric laments for the vanished Eden-England so prevalent in *Richard II*.

The Justices represent another (and diminished) generation which has itself grown and aged, and is now passing away. Each generation is successively further removed from myth and ideal, and increasingly closer to a harsh and secular reality: a kind of progression from Golden Age, to Bronze Age, to Iron Age.

Falstaff, a contemporary of Shallow's, was as a boy patronized by an already mature John of Gaunt, the figure we saw at the start of the tetralogy as immeasurably old and soon to die. John in turn was linked to the mythical king behind the whole tetralogy, Edward, who appears in *Richard II* only as the long-vanished idealized progenitor of the present defective reality.

Drama is by its very nature mimetic of time, and Shakespeare utilizes this fully in his tetralogy. In reading the plays we can turn back. But on the stage (as in life) the aged John of Gaunt appears briefly, invokes a still-further-removed past, and vanishes forever, to be resurrected only in the memories of another generation, itself now old and dying.

Cumulatively, then, those four plays render for us the sense of an irredeemably vanished world. The middle two plays represent not merely an interim of chaos before the eventual restoration of order, but a transition between two different things, one of which has passed away forever. The view of history as linear and never repeated rather than circular and endlessly repeated may be second nature to us, but it was at the time a new conception, stirring uneasily just below the surface of Elizabethan consciousness.[27] The acceptance of the newer concept of history, implicit in the debt theme, *is* the acknowledgment of the reality and permanence of death.

Law, Justice, Warfare

The restoration of a unified England under its hero-king Henry V is the resurrection phase of the total action of the tetralogy. However, the resurrection is, on one level, apparent only, for the state depicted in *Henry V* is not the earlier sacramental order it claims identity with, but a thoroughly secular nation state under the control of an absolute monarch.

Earlier in the history of the drama the community is presented as either a body of life (the Mystical Body) or a body of death (any merely secular community). The England of Henry V, in contrast, is presented in a thoroughly ambivalent way, as both positive and negative, a source of both life and of death. As king, Hal does succeed in ending civil warfare; but the bloody rebellions of the earlier plays are replaced by the equally bloody though official violence of foreign war, and the often lethal exactions of a harsh and impersonal justice, such as Bardolph's mutilation ("his nose ... executed," III.vi.111) and hanging. Moreover, the life-death doubleness of this state is not incidental, or capable of resolution. It is inherent in the very nature of the society, and represents a permanent and inescapable condition of existence within which individuals must operate (in this, the social body is precisely analogous to the physical body). At the heart of the depiction of this life-death social body is a certain conception of law.

Hal's ultimately successful imposition of order is integrally related to his use of law, a use which reflects actual conditions in Elizabeth's England. A centrally important feature of life in the sixteenth century was a continuing struggle for power between the Crown and the nobility; and the "greatest triumph of the Tudors was the ultimately successful assertion of a royal monopoly of violence both public and private, an achievement which profoundly altered not only the nature of politics, but also the quality of daily life."[28] The Tudors pursued their bid for power on a number of related fronts: economic, military, legal, religious and psychological. However, the preemption of the system of justice, and the promotion of litigation as a way to solve conflict, was one of the most important means by which the Tudors appropriated power. We are accustomed to considering warfare and legal trials as two quite distinct phenomena, but the gradual separation of these methods of settling conflict is a key factor in the emergence of a modern (as opposed to a feudal) society.

When at the end of *2 Henry IV* the newly kinged Hal submits himself and his realm to the authority of the Chief

Justice, he expresses the Tudor aim of "weaning the landed classes from their ancient habits of violence and subjecting them to the discipline of the law...."[29] Significantly, his assumption also marks the end of full-scale aristocratic uprisings in the plays.

The ascendancy of the Chief Justice, then, marks the success of the "royal monopoly of violence"—the arrogation of power to the Crown, achieved in good part through the imposition of centrally administered law. This process was both social and psychological: the subordination of powerful lords to a centralized royal authority, increasingly exercised through abstract law; and the internal acceptance of such authority, the subordination of individual desire to communal values.

Again, the play world reflects the real world. As noted in the discussion of Tudor morality drama, the fact that the monarch now headed the English Church affected the ways of thinking of Catholics and Protestants alike; and by Elizabeth's reign this was even truer. The entire English population, landless poor right up to and including the nobility, was "deeply affected by the heavy barrage of propaganda from pulpit and printing press on the subject of the necessity of loyalty to the sovereign. Elizabeth was extolled as God's Lieutenant on earth, and rebellion castigated as a grievous sin ...."[30] To some extent this reflected the fact that he who controls the block controls the definition of treason. But men did not simply succumb to superior power—they gradually internalized the State's teachings, and "By the end of the century rebellion was becoming not merely very chancy, but also very disreputable...."[31] Convicted traitors, to a man, "acknowledged themselves justly condemned to death for an offense against God and the King."[32] In *2 Henry IV*, Mowbray and Scroop protest their arrest for treason. But by *Henry V* all three of the discovered traitors accept their death and repent their sin, exactly as Essex was to do on the scaffold.

How are we meant to evaluate law and justice in Henry V's kingdom? Richard II opens with a ritual of trial by combat presided over by the King, who is head of an order at once sacred and secular (in fact, the distinction of the two realities is fundamentally a modern one). He is the earthly representative of divine power, and the law he exemplifies and administers is not merely man-made, but is both expressive of and ratified by God Himself. Moreover, Richard and his noblemen enact the process of justice directly, in their own persons. Just as feudal social obligations were matters of personal loyalty to overlords, so feudal justice existed in and through particular individuals. And trial by combat was not, in the view of the participants, a matter of might making right. It was believed that God intervened directly on behalf of justice, and victory therefore signified neither the triumph of the stronger nor the chances of war, but direct evidence from heaven of guilt or innocence. God alone (rather than chance, circumstance or human will) determined the outcome of human history, whether in individual conflicts or in the fate of nations.[33]

In contrast to *Richard II*, *Henry V* opens not with a ritual, sacramental judicial process, but with a scene depicting the political maneuvering of two churchmen devising strategies to retain money and power. Ostensibly, the secular power in this play still moves in accord with the laws of God. When the king contemplates war with France, he summons his Archbishop to pronounce "justly and religiously" (I.ii.10) on whether he "May ... with right and conscience" press his claim (I.ii.96). However, Canterbury's answer must be read in the light of the opening scene, where he and another churchman discussed ways to forestall the enactment of a law proposing to strip the church of wealth, and Canterbury revealed that he had already offered to finance the king's French venture with the obvious motive of retaining the king's support against passage of this law.

A similar plundering of the church had of course really taken place long before the writing of this play, largely through the passage in the 1530's of a series of acts mandating the dissolution of the monasteries, and declaring the king to be head of the English church. As Saccio points out, the key to the establishment of the predominance of the State over Church was a change in *legal* authority, as jurisdiction of such matters as wills and marriage was transferred from Rome to England. By the 1590's, the supremacy of the state was established both in law and in fact.[34] The tetralogy reflects a full understanding of the implications of a world where the secular authority is supreme.

In *Richard II*, Carlisle, spokesman for the church, offers the view of monarchy invented and promulgated by the Tudors, and passed off as a time-sanctioned theory of kingship. This view of monarchy involved the whole of what Tillyard refers to as the Elizabethan World-Picture: a great chain of being hierarchically arranged from lowest to highest, involving all of nature and supernature, the parts of which relate to one another analogically, both within levels and from level to level. It is a moral and sacramental order, established and sustained by God. In the Elizabethan understanding, this had been the view prevailing in medieval times.

In Bolingbroke's reign the church, represented by Scroop, espouses the "rebel" cause, a fact which both establishes and exposes the relativity of moral judgment in a world of usurper kings. In the final play the church, in the person of Canterbury, is back in the official fold. His language is the language of religion and morality, but it cloaks a concern for practical politics and temporal realities, rather than for the eternal verities. The key to the nature of law in Henry's kingdom, as well as to the relations between church and state, is the Salic Law speech, a preposterous farrago of dubious reasoning and even more dubious precedent, adduced to support the conclusion we know both Canterbury and Henry desire to reach. The form of the speech—a legal brief—expresses the political reality of the subjection of ecclesiastical authority to royal authority, and the philosophical/religious reality of the reduction of divine and eternal law to the musty imperfections of fallible and relative human law.

The king's appeals to know if his claim is "just" and "right"—his own reminders of the bloody consequences which will ensue if he is given permission to proceed—and Canterbury's confident assertions that the king can proceed without sin—all produce an effect opposite to that intended by the speakers, an insistent substratum of meaning which plays against the surface level. When Canterbury concludes "The sin upon my head, dread Sovereign!" (I.ii.97), we hear an underlying meaning, that a sin is (may be?) being committed. But this meaning can be heard only by negative implication, for in a world where the head of the church speaks the same language as his "dread sovereign," there are neither standards by which to question the secular authority nor words in which to put that question.

If in both church and state "the authority of the central power over all subjects was being made effective," "the agents of this royal nationalism" were the Justices of the Peace.[35] The Reformation had provided a system by which to exert royal administrative power, by making available to the J.P.'s the "ecclesiastical machinery of the parish," and thus "supplying what they had hitherto lacked, subordinate officers to carry out their commands. J.P.'s were appointed by the crown, and the dependents of great magnates were deliberately excluded from the commission of the peace."[36] Throughout the century the power of the J.P.'s increased enormously, in proportion to the decline in the power of the local peers (although at all periods J.P.'s were loathe to act against powerful local magnates). J.P.'s could punish or wink at infringements of the law, at their pleasure. For example, they were responsible for enforcing the laws concerning the poor, laws generally designed to ensure a continued supply of cheap labor. Being employers of wage-labor themselves, they generally enforced the laws in the manner best suited to their own interests.

The office of J.P. offered tremendous opportunities for enrichment, not only through self-interested administration of the law, but also through outright corruption. Not all J.P.'s took bribes, of course. But contemporaries valued the office precisely because it offered such scope for personal profit. And for victims of venal judicial decisions, like the unfortunate Clement Perkes in *2 Henry IV*, little recourse existed. In *Henry V* the profit motive is followed upward through the system of justice to the ultimate source of authority, the king/nation, from whose judgments there will also be no recourse.

J.P.'s also played a part in the shift of military control from the aristocracy to the Crown. For much of the sixteenth century "England was operating a dual military system, the one quasi-feudal and the other national."[37] Conscription, which was enforced through the J.P.'s, was therefore an especially important power, since it struck directly at the simultaneously useful and threatening ability of the peers to raise their own armies. However, the poor quality of the conscripts meant that for much of Elizabeth's reign she was forced also to rely on loyal peers.

In *Richard II* and *1* and *2 Henry IV*, the aristocratic rebels raise personal armies against the king. In contrast, the English army pictured in *Henry V* is basically a national army under the immediate control of the king. Shakespeare emphasizes the king's direct relationship with his common soldiers, rather than the chain of command which existed even in national armies—an expression of the growing control of the Crown over military power (in the earlier system, of course, soldiers would have responded primarily to the lord in whose service they were fighting).

The emphasis throughout *Henry V* on England as a nation-state—the constant appeals to patriotism—the welding of previously warring ethnic groups (Welsh, Scotch, Irish) into a single unit of Englishmen/fighting-men—all reflect a key feature of the ascendancy of royal power, a feature which was both cause and effect of that ascendancy: a new sense of national unity, and the growing belief that one owed one's loyalty primarily to the monarch and only secondarily to one's good lord. Significantly, however, the groups achieve national unity in the service of death—through the official violence of war.

Arrogation of power to the Crown is complete in the "beehive" world of *Henry V*, a world of order, but also of death, where those who do not serve the state are delivered "o'er to executors pale" (I.ii.203). What is the playwright's attitude toward this phenomenon, which accurately expresses conditions in his day?

Both in ideality and in reality, feudal justice was personal. Dealing with particular persons offered human satisfactions, but also great potential for abuse. Davy evokes both dimensions, although comically, when he pleads his friend's case by putting the claims of friendship and personal connection (old-order realities) before this representative of the impersonal new justice. Davy points out how long he has served Shallow, and declares with fervor that it's a hard world when a rogue can't gain favor through a friend: "I grant your worship that he is a knave, sir, but yet, God forbid, sir, but a knave should have some countenance at his friend's request" (*2 Henry IV*, V.i.43-5).

The argument surfaces again, in more troubling form, in Hal's rejection of Falstaff and his turning of his old friend over to the Chief Justice. We acknowledge the necessity of Hal's turning from his former ways; but Shakespeare, who was perfectly capable of making us feel this only as a regrettable necessity, has instead dramatized the scene in such a way as to evoke maximum ambivalence in us.

The imposition of harsh and impersonal justice, and the eradication of all personal feeling, seen in Falstaff's rejection, is complete in *Henry V*. The colorful and in their different ways appealing individualists of *1* and *2 Henry IV* are all defeated or dead: Hotspur, Glendower, Falstaff, the tavern mates; and characters in the play are increasingly presented in terms of their collective identities—stage Irishmen, Scotsmen, Welshmen, presided over by a king whose private self is wholly submerged in his public role. Even Hal's wooing of the French princess is a pseudo-love scene, since he loves not the princess, but the territory she represents: "I love France so well, that I will not part with a village of it—I will have it all mine. And, Kate, when France is mine and I am yours, then yours is France, and you are mine" (V.ii.178-882).

The extermination of individual desire, and of individuality itself, is part of a more pervasive lethalness; for Henry's kingdom, under the sway of evenhanded and implacable law, is ultimately a giant court of no appeal. The very term "justice" was, in one contemporary meaning, a synonym for the death penalty (*OED*); and from start to finish in the play the supremacy of the state is associated with the imposition of death, whether as the penalty for crime, or as slaughter in war.[38] But the point is not that the state is evil. On the contrary, it is as "good" as a state can be, in that it effectively serves the functions a body politic must serve within the fallen world. Under Hal, England preserves order within its borders, distributes justice impartially, and remains strong against its enemies outside; yet it is finally a merely human creation, impotent to prevent individual death and often an inflictor of it. The state's built-in limits are, moreover, inseparable from its political functioning, which often produces conflict between individual desire and communal good; between justice and love; between pragmatic goals necessary to preserve the life of the nation, and less tangible goals — pleasure, fellowship, love, personal feeling — without which individual life is not worth living.

The positive and negative aspects of the body politic — its life and death aspects — are reflected in the character of the king who heads it.[39] In medieval drama human kings are death figures who stand in implicit or explicit contrast to Christ the King, the source of life (see above, Chapter One). Human kings may be bad or good — wicked rulers, such as Herod, who boast of their omnipotence, inflict suffering and death, and often die themselves to provide a dramatic object lesson; or good rulers, such as the Chester Octavian, who acknowledge their own mortality while honoring Christ's sovereignty. But good or bad, the king-figure's function is the same: to embody human mortality in a way which points to the solution to it.

Richard II is a direct descendant of those medieval king figures. He is a murderer (his implication in Gloucester's death), and a despoiler of his land and subjects. He is boastful, claiming invincibility through the direct protection of heaven. Yet as Gaunt points out, Richard is king only of death. When Richard tells Gaunt he has "many years to live," Gaunt replies, "But not a minute, King, that thou canst give," and continues as follows:

> Shorten my days thou canst with sullen sorrow
> And pluck nights from me, but not lend a morrow;
> Thou canst help time to furrow me with age,
> But stop no wrinkle in his pilgrimage:
> Thy word is current with him for my death,
> But dead, thy kingdom cannot buy my breath.
> (Richard II.I.iii.225-31)

Richard can kill, but can neither preserve nor restore life. Richard is thus, like his dramatic predecessors, a death figure, a representation of human mortality. His claim to exemption from mortal limits is terribly belied by his fate; and his discovery of mortality, given explicit and powerful expression in the death-of-kings speech (III.ii.144-77), is also illustrated by the whole course of the play's action.

In these ways Shakespeare's treatment of Richard has clear affinities with preceding drama. But Richard operates in a fully historical world. Moreover, as in Tudor morality drama, the established social structure now backs up Richard's claim to quasi-divine status, which reinforces the impact of the discovery that his claim is false (compare Carlisle, who insists upon Richard's quasi-divine status, to the Bishop in the *Pride of Life*, who earnestly endeavors to bring home to the king-figure the fact of his mortal limits). And most importantly, Richard's death does not function ultimately as a confirmation of immortality. Richard's penultimate moment of truth—his monologue when imprisoned at Pomfret Castle—points not to Christ and a transcendent world, but to the secular world in which Richard discovered himself to be living. And the aftermath of Richard's death is not a glimpse into eternity but a fall into time—into the wholly historical world of Bolingbroke and his heir Henry V.

In short, Shakespeare uses the long dramatic tradition surrounding the king figure to underline a radical change in context. The king is still a representative of human mortality; but his mortality is no longer synonymous with the solution to it. It is not that the play world excludes the possibility of a transcendent dimension—indeed, Richard dies asserting a sacramental order ("Exton, thy fierce hand/Hath with the king's blood stained the King's own land" V.v.109-10). It is simply that nothing in the play confirms the existence of that dimension. Richard's death amounts to the death of all transcendental certainties, and death itself must henceforth be differently confronted.

Henry V illustrates the conditions within which the solution to death must now be sought. The king who presides over this play is a figure new to drama, a ruler who is associated with life and death at the same time.[40] Henry is, on one level, the saviour-king of English legend, a reformed scapegrace who unites his kingdom and leads his people to almost miraculous victory against the greater strength of the French. He is also a thoroughly calculating monarch who dispenses mercy (when he does dispense it) only because it is more effective ("when lenity and cruelty play for a kingdom, the gentler gamester is the soonest winner" III. vi. 112-13), and who is continually associated with the infliction of death—for example, the execution of the rebels (II,ii); the death of Falstaff, for which the king is indirectly responsible ("The King has kill'd his heart" II.i. 88); the declaration of war with France and consequent slaughter; the decision to kill the French prisoners; and the order to execute soldiers who loot, which results in the death of Hal's old companion.

Henry's speech at Harfleur exemplifies the ambiguity with which he is presented. The speech is a horrifying description of the torture and slaughter which will be visited on all the citizens of Harfleur, down to infants in arm, if the city does not yield. In this speech Henry places himself directly in the medieval wicked-ruler tradition.[41] Like Herod, he proposes to loose his soldiers to conduct a slaughter of the innocents— "fresh fair virgins" and "flow'ring infants" (III.iii.14). And Henry even invokes a direct comparison with Herod: the women of Harfleur will howl to see their children dead, as did the mothers of the babies Herod slaughtered (39-41). However, Henry's bloody speech convinces the citizens of Harfleur to yield, thus saving actual bloodshed as well as achieving English objectives. Here as elsewhere, the king is an undeniably effective head of the body politic; and he is, moreover, a "just" ruler, who subjects himself to the same discipline he imposes. Like the kingdom he heads, his virtues are inseparable from his defects, his nurturing and preserving aspects from his destructive aspects.

At the first mention of Henry in *Henry V*, he is associated with war (the Prologue); and the action of the play centers about his French campaign. But throughout the play attention is called to the enormous suffering and destruction which war will visit upon soldiers and civilians alike: in the king's address to Canterbury warning of the horrors of war; in his speech to the citizens of Harfleur, where he details the dreadful torments war entails; and perhaps most strikingly, in the scene the night before Agincourt, when the king and his soldiers debate the morality of war. Williams speaks graphically of "legs and arms and heads, chopped off in a battle," and reminds the king of the way soldiers actually die: "some swearing, some crying for a surgeon, some upon their wives left poor behind them, some upon the debts they owe, some upon their children rawly left. I am afeard there are few die well that die in a battle; for how can they charitably dispose of anything when blood is their argument?" (IV.ii.140-146). Williams' imagery of bodily dismemberment graphically evokes the impotence of the political body to restore the physical body; and the speech as a whole stresses both the irremediable suffering and the questionable morality of wars, especially *vis-à-vis* a Christian ethic. But the king's answer is responsive to none of these points, a fact made more troubling by our remembrance of the shaky basis on which the war was undertaken (the Salic Law speech).

The king's frequent infliction of the death penalty for crime is also stressed in the play, as in the execution of the three traitors; the king's orders to punish looting by death; and his "pious" order to punish by death anyone who boasts of the Agincourt victory, thus robbing God of the credit. The implicit irony of this is underlined by his instructions to bury the war dead "with charity" (IV.viii.126). But most significant, and most disturbing to our sensibilities, is the king's response to the news of his old companion's cruel death, his nose slit and his fire "out". Hal responds only, "We would have all such offenders so cut off" (II.vi.112). The unspoken irony of this is underlined because Bardolph was hanged for stealing a "pax" (*i.e*, a tablet used in the mass), whereas the king has just stolen a far greater *pax*, the peace between England and France.[42]

In fact, Henry's acquisition of France is simply the last, and most spectacular, of a long line of land-grabs beginning with Richard's attempt to seize Bolingbroke's inheritance, and Bolingbroke's subsequent acquisition of the English throne.

When a subject steals, whether petty thievery or aristocratic robbery on a grand scale, a power exists to define the actions respectively as theft and treason. But when the king himself indulges in the armed robbery of war there is no one to call it so, for no power higher than that of the state exists, either in the world of the play, or in the world of Tudor absolutism the play reflects.

Before each act of *Henry V* the Chorus sets the scene, ostensibly to rectify the inevitable lacks of a stage production attempting to present such vast armies and actions, but also to retail for us the official view of the forthcoming action, whether to present Harry to us as "the mirror of all Christian kings," or to promise us the treat of beholding "A little touch of Harry in the night." As the play progresses, the inadequacies of the Chorus' viewpoint become increasingly obvious. For our assent to the king's actions and sovereignty, constantly called for and, on one level, granted, is on another level undercut by our instinctive recoil from suffering and death.

Conflicts between communal and individual good remain a problem for us, as for any society; but for a complex of reasons, cultural and historical, the Elizabethans gave more weight to the communal factor than we would. In addition to the pervasive authoritarianism of the times, the bloody realities of civil turmoil were fresh in English memory, and kept sharply alive by fear of what would happen when the childless Elizabeth died. Consequently, no contemporary of Shakespeare's was likely to undervalue social order, even when obtained at the cost of individual suffering and death. Yet no individual gladly pays such a price himself. To acquiesce in the state-inflicted suffering and death so prevalent in *Henry V*, the onlooker must identify himself wholly with the nation, as many of the characters in fact do:[43] Henry himself; and the "good" characters, soldiers all, such as Henry's caricature-like echo and fellow Welshman Fluellen, a bully in love with official violence. Our ambivalence toward Fluellen is perhaps most sharply aroused by his ugly, supposedly comic beating of Pistol, which the "good" characters applaud. Pistol is a liar, a coward, a braggart, a self-confessed parasite on the body politic, who forthrightly declares his intention of going to

France "To suck, to suck, the very blood to suck!" (II.iii.56). Yet in this he is on a par with his betters who are doing precisely the same, and who reward Fluellen for aiding them in that endeavor.

If we compare Fluellen to that other Welshman Glendower, we see how diminished is the later figure: Glendower's lush poetry and invocation of love and magic replaced by Fluellen's Welsh provincialisms and reduction of all value to "the discipline of war." Yet the world of the play demands and rewards the Fluellen qualities—the military virtues of valor, competence and reliability in battle, even if accompanied by bullying and crudity.

At the start of the Prologue to the Fifth Act, the Chorus offers to "prompt" those who have not read the story. "Prompt" was used then, as now, for actors who forgot their roles. The Elizabethan audience, which constituted a cross-section of society, is being invited to assume its proper role, as Englishmen, thus as uncritical admirers of Hal and his splendid victories, and, by implication, an admirer of Tudor realities as well. Some among the audience doubtlessly did accept this role, including, probably, the censor who had to have passed on the play before its public presentation; but Hal's victories present the same dilemma as did the actual Elizabethan world. Critical assessment of each is necessary; but our response will vary according to whether we react as individuals recoiling from pain and destruction, or as Englishmen whose interests are completely identified with those of the collective body.[44] The point is that it is not possible wholly to accept or wholly to reject either of those alternatives.

In the prologue to the fifth act, the Chorus invites us to picture the welcome the victorious Harry received on his return to London by comparing it in our imaginations to the welcome Essex, then in Ireland, might receive if he were to return home victorious. In this contemporary reference Shakespeare closes the distance between "history," the past as safely done with, and the Elizabethan here-and-now. And even more significantly, he moves outward from the play to "reality," from the stage to the audience.[45]

The times in which these four plays were written were times of enormous change—psychological, social, political, economic, military, philosophical/religious. The tetralogy encapsulates the very process of this change, whether described concretely—transition from a feudal society to a capitalistic, centralized nation-state—or philosophically—the shift from a mythical and divine order which contains an inherent promise of immortality, to a secular and pragmatic one which does not. The end result is the exposure to view of what is in many essentials the modern world. The metaphysical certainties of Richard's world have vanished forever, and with them, the certainty of absolute and literal death-transcendence. Individualists and dreamers—Richard, Falstaff, Hotspur, Glendower, the tavern mates—are defeated or dead; and individual desire and identity are subordinated to the collective identity the Chorus wishes us to assume— patriotic Englishmen, members of a secular body politic for which sacred status is claimed. But the negative aspects of this social body force us back to an even sharper awareness of our irreducible separateness. Although the voice of individual desire is silenced within the beehive world of the play, we find it alive within ourselves, in the disparity between the role the chorus wishes us to assume—ratifiers of the official view—and our actual responses to what the play dramatizes. To the extent that we are unhappy with the world as is, even as we acknowledge our inescapable participation in it, the groundwork is laid for Shakespearean tragedy and comedy.

Conclusion

In the medieval understanding, history is the record of human union with the Corpus Christi—an endless repetition of death and resurrection centered around the source of the pattern, Christ's death and resurrection.[46] The collective history of mankind has always a comic shape, in that mankind as a whole is saved; but individual histories may assume comic or tragic shape according to whether the individual is assimilated to or cut off from the immortality-granting communal Body.

If we define a history play as a drama which recounts the story of a communal group, then the history play, drama recounting the collective fate and containing within it and subordinate to it the comedies and tragedies of individual fate, is the only form of medieval drama, for all medieval drama recounts the history of the Corpus Christi (see Chapter One). Moreover, individuals in the modern sense of the word do not exist in this drama, for there are only the saved and the damned, those incorporate with the Mystical Body and those cut off from it; and particulars of characterization serve chiefly to indicate where a character stands in relation to that revivifying Body. It follows that no true conflict is possible between the individual and the group, for their interests are actually identical. "Men come to recognize the body of Christ, the Corpus Christi, if they do not disregard their *being* the body of Christ"; and a character will have the perception of conflict between the two only to the extent that he fails to recognize his true interest. The communal Body is life, separation from it is death, and individual immortality is to be gained through acknowledgement of oneness with it.

Shakespeare's second history tetralogy retains the comic shape of medieval history, in that it records the death and resurrection of a communal body. However, the communal body is no longer a divine, immortality-granting entity, but a human polity, the Tudor nation state in its concrete actuality. And given the nature of this new communal body, individual and group interest are no longer necessarily identical. Although the new society claims status as the political embodiment of the divine community, it can offer at best only collective immortality—continuance of the race through successive generations within time, rather than individual immortality for eternity. Moreover, either separation from or incorporation with this life/death social body entails a form of death.[47]

Looked at as a strategy for confronting and mastering death, Shakespearean history is only partially successful. As in medieval drama, the comedies and tragedies of individual fate are subordinated to the story of the group—the fall and problematic redemption of the English nation; and our attention is thus deflected from the fate of the perishable individuals who compose the group to the fate of the immortal group itself (the group never dies).[48] But as individuals we find this only partially satisfactory, for the extent of our identification with the group is necessarily limited; and the extent to which we experience our separateness is the extent to which the communal solution to death fails.

Shakespearean comedy and tragedy address themselves to the unresolved problem of individual mortality. They do so, however, within the conditions set up by the histories. Whether depicted as a family, a city-state, a court or a nation, the community the comedies and tragedies begin with and return to is always some version of the law-bound, money-based, life-sustaining and death-inflicting world of the second history tetralogy, where "miracles are ceased." In comedy and tragedy alike, resurrection must be enacted within the constraints of this fully historical world.

Notes

1 Although written later, this sequence of course deals with an earlier period than that of the first tetralogy.

2 E.M.W. Tillyard, *Shakespeare's History Plays* (N.Y.: The Macmillan Co., 1946), established the importance to Shakespeare's English histories of contemporary ideas on kingship, and of the Tudor reading of history (England's punishment for the sin of deposing and murdering Richard II, followed by her redemption under the Tudor monarchs). Much subsequent criticism consists, wholly or in part, of elaboration, qualification or revision of Tillyard's views; and even critics who reject the notion that the plays are, preeminently, illustrative of Tudor political/ religious/moral orthodoxy recognize that such orthodoxy forms a constituitive element of the plays, and one of central importance.

In the tradition of Tillyard, Lily B. Campbell, *Shakespeare's "Histories": Mirrors of Elizabethan Policy* (San Marino, Calif.: Huntington Library, 1947; rpt. 1968), identifies contemporary political texts she believes are important to the English histories; and she views the histories as reflections of Tudor orthodoxy, didactic in purpose and nature. N.M. Reese, *The Cease of Majesty: A Study of Shakespeare's History Plays* [London: Edward Arnold (Publishers) Ltd., 1961], accepts the Tillyard-Campbell view that the histories reflect a Tudor reading of history and an orthodox conception of the nature of monarchy, but points out that such orthodoxy forms a starting point only, and that Shakespeare "never divorced 'politics' (a word he did not use) from the larger context of society and human relationships" (p. 91). Irving Ribner, *The English History Play in the Age of Shakespeare* (Princeton, N.J., 1957; rev. & rpt., London: Methuen & Co. Ltd., 1965), follows the Tillyard-Campbell emphasis: "The four plays taken together comprise a consistent and meaningful unit, but their unity is that of historical purpose rather than of artistic form or dramatic technique" (p. 193). Wilbur Sanders, *The Dramatist and the Received Idea: Studies in the Plays of Marlowe and Shakespeare* (Cambridge U. Press, 1968), reacts against simplistic historicism in general, and specifically, against the idea that Shakespeare's history plays straightforwardly present Tudor doctrine: "Shakespeare . . . voices the dialogue of sixteenth-century political controversy much more clearly than he adjudicates between the two sides" (p. 151). Robert Ornstein, *A Kingdom for a Stage: The Achievement of Shakespeare's History plays (Cambridge, Mass.:* Harvard U. Press, 1972), also reacts against the view that the histories simply embody conventional Tudor moral and political attitudes: "His [Shakespeare's] progress in the History Plays was a journey of artistic exploration and discovery that led almost unerringly beyond politics and history to the

universal themes and concerns of his maturest art" (p. 31); and
Ornstein's analysis stresses "what is original and individual" in the plays
(p.2). James Winny, *The Player King: A Theme of Shakespeare's Histories*
(London: Chatto & Windus, 1968), also objects to critical emphasis on
the English histories as embodying orthodox political conceptions, an
emphasis which "exalts the political and moral elements of a work
whose first characteristic is imaginative" (p. 9). Winny focuses on the
attempts of the three kings in the tetralogy "to assume the royal
identity" (p. 46), but feels that the historical material is used to express
psychological and imaginative concerns. Winny wants to separate
English history—"actual life"—and "the world which the poet brings
into existence" (p. 47). But in my view, not only is it not necessary, it is
in fact impossible to separate the political and the imaginative, public
and private, for each is in part constituitive of the other. For a fasci-
nating and suggestive discussion of the ways in which the self is constituted through an interplay with the culture, see Stephen Greenblatt,
Renaissance Self-Fashioning: From More to Shakespeare (Chicago & London:
The U. of Chicago Press, 1980).

3 The view of the tetralogy as a connected series of plays depicting a
transition from an older to a newer order is succintly yet comprehen-
sively set forth in Alvin B. Kernan, "The Henriad: Shakespeare's Major
History Plays," in *Modern Shakespearean Criticism: Essays on Style,
Dramaturgy and the Major Plays*, ed. Alvin B. Kernan (N.Y./Chicago/San
Francisco/Atlanta: Harcourt Brace Jovanovich, Inc., 1970), an essay to
which my discussion is wholly indebted. I am concerned to trace in
detail the highly specific ways in which the tetralogy reflects contemporary cultural changes and to relate those changes to the problem of
death.

For a recent discussion of the tetralogy in accordance with the view
expressed by Kernan, see H.R. Coursen, *The Leasing Out of England:
Shakespeare's Second Henriad* (Wash. D.C.: University Press of America,
Inc., 1982). Most critics accept Kernan's views. For an exception to the
critical consensus see Donna B. Hamilton, "The State of Law in
Richard II," *Shak. Q.*, 34 (1983), 5-17. Hamilton reviews contemporary
conceptions of the king's and the commonwealth's relation to the law,
demonstrating that the well-established idea that the king was not above
the law is functioning in *Richard II*; and from this Hamilton concludes,
"The presence of such concepts in *Richard II* would seem . . . to be
incompatible with interpretations that consider the play to be about the
passing of a period with a less modern kingship than that of the Renaissance, or interpretations that consider the play to be about the destruction of an era characterized by a kind and degree of order that could
never be recreated" (p. 16)—a view she identifies as Kernan's.
However, the fact that a long tradition held the king to be subject to law
(though also above it) does not contradict Kernan's view, because the
issue the tetralogy depicts is not that of whether a divinely-appointed
monarch had the right to flout the law, but rather the issue of what the
law itself is—a reflection of divine will and order, or simply relative,
secular, man-made (see above, the section of this chapter entitled *Law*,

Justice, Warfare). Moreover, emergent social configurations co-existed with older ones; and consequently, although the plays may be described as moving from one order to another, from the world of *Richard II* to the world of *Henry V*, on another level the two plays amount simply to two ways of looking at the same social/psychic/ metaphysical actuality.

4 Lawrence Stone summarizes the change as follows.

> Granted that change is a continuous process, that every shift has both earlier antecedents and later developments, it is nevertheless between 1560 and more precisely between 1580 and 1620, that the real watershed between medieval and modern England must be placed. It was then that the State fully established its authority, that dozens of armed retainers were replaced by a coach, two footmen and a page-boy, that private castles gave way to private houses, and that aristocratic rebellion finally petered out; then that the north and west were brought within the national orbit and abandoned their age-old habits of personal violence; then that the British Isles, England, Wales, Scotland, and Ireland were first effectively united; then that political objectives began to be stated in terms of abstract liberty and the public interest, rather than particular liberties and ancient customs; . . . then that the Lord Treasurer developed as the leading minister of the Crown, and the Exchequer as the most important administrative department; . . . then that London and the Court first began to sing their siren songs to the rural landlords; then that the ideal of stately, public living in the country was challenged by that of opulent, private pleasures in the City; then that foreign trade developed sufficiently to begin to preoccupy the minds of statesmen, and to make a London alderman the financial equal of a baron; then that usury was first openly legislated for, that interest rates fell to modern levels . . . then that capitalist ethics, population growth, and monetary inflation undermined old landlord-tenant relationships and old methods of estate management. . . .

Crisis of the Aristocracy 1558-1641, abridged edition (London/Oxford/ N.Y.: Oxford Univ. Press, 1967), pp. 12-13. (Although this and all subsequent references are to the abridged edition, the information has been checked against the unabridged version.) Every aspect of Stone's description is reflected within the four plays.

5 Cf. Graham Holderness, Shakespeare's History (Dublin: Gill and Macmillan, N.Y.: St. Martin's Press, 1985): "... in any society there are connected but separable and conflicting ideologies, dominant, residual and emergent; antagonistic and competing bodies of thought and systems of value, which in their perpetual struggle for power constitute the complex and contradictory structure of a given historical conjuncture" (p.20).

6   Cf. Stephen Greenblatt, *Renaissance Self-Fashioning*, who, in discussing the charges and counter-charges More and Tyndale, Catholic and Protestant, level at one another, comments, "It is as if the great crisis in the Church had forced into the consciousness of Catholics and Protestants alike the wrenching possibility that their theological system was a fictional construction; that the whole, vast edifice of church and state rested on certain imaginary postulates; that social hierarchy, the distribution of property, sexual and political order bore no guaranteed correspondence to the actual structure of the cosmos" (p. 113).

7   Cf. Greenblatt, who, in discussing the deep splits in the age's way of viewing actuality, notes that it is not a question of two world-views which can be held side by side for comparison and contrast, but rather of two worlds occupying the same space at the same time—a point compellingly illustrated in (among other places) his discussion of Holbein's *The Ambassadors*: the skull in the Holbein painting can be seen as such only when the viewer literally shifts his stance; and from the new position, the rest of the painting cannot be clearly seen.

8   Here, as elsewhere, the play-world reflects contemporary reality, for in Elizabethan England "all change had to be interpreted as the maintenance of tradition. In religion, the Reformation was defended as a return to the early church; in politics, parliamentary sovereignty was defended as the enforcement of fourteenth-century customs; in society the rise of new men was disguised by forged genealogies and the grant of titles of honor." Stone, p. 16.

9   Cf. W. H. Auden's statement: "In grasping the character of a society, as in judging the character of an individual, no documents, statistics, 'objective' measurements can ever compete with the single intuitive glance." "The American Scene," in *The Dyer's Hand* (1948; rpt. London: Faber and Faber, 1962), p. 313.

10 These and all subsequent quotations from the four plays which comprise the tetralogy are taken from the following Signet paperback editions, under the general editorship of Sylvan Barnet: *Richard II*, ed. Kenneth Muir (N.Y.: New American Library, 1963; *Henry IV, Part One*, ed. Maynard Mack (N.Y.: New American Library, 1965); *Henry IV, Part Two*, ed. Norman N. Holland (N.Y.: New American Library, 1965); *Henry V*, ed. John Russell Brown (N.Y.: New American Library, 1965).

11 Christopher Hill, *Reformation to Industrial Revolution: The Making of Modern English Society, Vol. I 1530-1780* (N.Y.: Pantheon Books, Random House, Inc., 1967), p. 38.

12 Stone, p. 22. By collecting data relating to the turnover of land, Stone has constructed a graph which vividly illustrates a "mountainous rise" in the 1590's in the transfer of land—a rise which represents "a tremendous upheaval in the mobility of land . . . which is without parallel in either the later Middle Ages or the late seventeenth and eighteenth centuries." Stone, p. 22.

13 Hill, p. 49.

14 Stone, p. 155.

15 Stone p. 27.

16 See Stone p. 237.

17 See Helge Kokeritz, *Shakespeare's Pronunciation* (New Haven & London: Yale U. Press, 1953; rpt. 1966), pp. 73, 320.

18 James L. Calderwood also notes the prevalence in *Henry IV, Part One* of "such concepts as debt, redemption, counterfeiting, and robbing," commenting, "monetary imagery of this sort is the measure of the play" (*Shakespeare and the Denial of Death*, p.27). But he sees it not as expressive of two irreconcilably opposed kinds of value, but rather as "a kind of mid-level metaphor between high honor and low appetite" (p. 27).

19 This view is of course central to the so-called new historicism.
    See also Stone, who, in discussing the financial crisis of the aristocracy (at a peak in the years in which these plays were written), emphasizes that the "crisis was not purely economic, it was moral and social as well, and the methods adopted to solve the one merely exacerbated the other." Stone, p. 75.

20 Stone, p. 29.

21 Stone, p. 31.

22 Stone, p. 76.

23 Hotspur was no anachronism. Lawrence Stone discusses at length the propensity of the sixteenth-century upper classes to resort to personal violence, and describes the disastrous effects this had on civil order and centralized government (see especially Chapter V, "Power," pp. 96-134). Ultimately, through a combination of social and natural forces, as well as through the persistent efforts of the Tudors, the great semifeudal families were eliminated or defanged. But the process was very gradual, and aristocratic rebellion remained a threat throughout Elizabeth's reign. The great northern families, including the Earls of Northumberland, were in fact among the last to succumb to royal power.

24 For example Hal, pretending to be Henry IV, describes Falstaff as "a devil . . . in the likeness of an old fat man" (*1 Henry IV*, II.iv.447-48). Falstaff himself comments, "Thou seest I have more flesh than another man, and therefore more frailty" (*1 Henry IV*, III.iii.166-68); and he earlier exclaims, "banish plump Jack, and banish all the world" (*1 Henry IV*, II.iv.479-80).

25 These definitions are drawn from the *OED*.

26 From Karl Marx and Frederick Engels, *The Manifesto of the Communist Party (1848;* rpt. Moscow: *Progress,* 1971), quoted in Paul Delaney, "*King Lear* and the Decline of Feudalism," *PMLA,* 82 (May 1977), p. 430.

27 Cf. David Scott Kastan, *Shakespeare and the Shapes of Time* (Hanover, New Hampshire: University Press of New England, 1982): "The histories ... reveal time to be intractable stuff. It cannot be recalled, and it cannot be rejected; at best it can be understood. The histories would help us to that understanding, as their open-ended structures make us confront our fragile existence as 'time's subjects' (*2 Henry IV,* I.iii.120) released in a world of contingency and flux" (p. 55).

28 Stone, p. 97.

29 Stone, p. 121. "By any standards the growth of litigation between 1550 and 1625 was something rather exceptional," as "All the pride, obstinacy, and passion that hitherto had found expression in direct physical action was now transferred to the dusty processes of the law." Stone, p. 117.

30 Stone p. 131.

31 Stone, p. 132.

32 Stone, p. 132. Stone continues as follows:

> These public expressions of devotion to the Moloch of the State—confessions curiously reminiscent of those pronounced in the Stalinist treason trials—were not the result of torture, for a nobleman's rank effectively protected him from racks and pincers. It is certainly possible that promises and threats about the disposal of the property and the treatment of the heirs may have played their part, but it is difficult to avoid the conclusion that the main explanation of these abject confessions was a profound belief in the inviolable sanctity of the state . . . .

Kantorowicz also notes the similarity between the Tudor concept of the king's two bodies and modern totalitarian versions of state deification.

33 Trial by combat was the ritualized and idealized form of aristocratic violence. In fact the actual expression of aristocratic power ranged from uprisings against the king, to feuds which drew in the surrounding countryside, to acts of malice and brigandage such as Stone reports of Lord Chandos, who, in the 1570's, "used armed retainers with guns at the ready to frighten off the under-sheriff, protected servants of his who robbed men on the highway near Sudeley Castle, so that the inhabitants dared not arrest the thieves nor the victims prosecute their assailants, rigged juries, and put in a high constable of the shire who used his office to levy blackmail on the peasantry." Stone, p. 111.

34 Stone, for example, comments on the increase after 1580 of lay power in the Upper House, in proportion to the decline in the "prestige and

social standing of the bishops," as they assumed "their now-familiar role of obsequious yes-men for the current ruling clique." Stone, p. 30.

35 Hill, p. 20.

36 Hill, p. 20.

37 Stone, p. 101.

38 In fact, the Elizabethan age was characterized by harsh and frequent punishments, including the infliction of the death penalty for petty theft and other minor crimes. Stone notes that "Physical punishment was used, as it had never been used before, as the prime means of enforcing obedience" (Stone, p. 20), and Hill points out that if "dirt and disease" took their toll of the lower orders, the law also "did its bit" toward killing them off (Hill, p. 30).

39 Critical views on Henry V vary: Henry as ideal Christian prince, or as cold Machiavel (extremes now largely out of critical fashion); Henry as a mixture of both (a mixture enforced, to greater or lesser degree, by the demands of the kingly role); or—my view—Henry as expressive of an irresolvably dualistic reality. Obviously, a critic's views of Henry are not separable from his overall views of the play and of the tetralogy.

Tillyard, *Shakespeare's History Plays*, and Ribner, *The English History Play*, both believe Shakespeare intends Henry to be taken, unqualifiedly, as the ideal Christian king the whole tetralogy has been searching for (although Tillyard feels Shakespeare's heart is not really in this project). Exponents of the view of Henry as a mixture of virtues and defects—as neither ideal king nor cold Machiavel—include Reese, *Cease of Majesty*; Ornstein, *A Kingdom for a Stage*; Michael Manheim, *The Weak King in the Shakespearean History Play* (Syracuse, N.Y.: Syracuse U. Press, 1973); and Derek Traversi, *Shakespeare from Richard II to Henry V* (Stanford, Calif.: Stanford U. Press, 1957), whose perceptive and detailed reading of the tetralogy culminates in his portrait of Henry as an inseparable blend of strengths and weaknesses, a blend produced in part by Henry's situation, in which political strength may be synonymous with personal limitation. Traversi's stress on the final dissatisfaction we feel with the play accords with mine, and is, significantly, associated with death.

> The inspiration of *Henry V* is, in its deeper moments (which do not represent the whole play), critical, analytic, exploratory. As we follow it, and in spite of our admiration for its hero's dedication to his chosen ends, a certain coldness takes possession of us as it took possession, step by step of the limbs of the dying Falstaff; and we too, as we come to the end of this balanced, sober study of political virtue rewarded by the success it deserves, find ourselves in our own way "babbling of green fields" (pp. 197-8).

The above critics stress balance, positives and negatives adding up to a complex but harmonious whole. In contrast, the following critics emphasize, as I do, radically irresolvable ambivalences in the histories. A.P. Rossiter, *Angel with Horn and other Shakespearean Lectures*, ed. Graham Storey (N.Y.: Theatre Arts Books; Longmans, Green & Co. Ltd., 1961), stresses the crucial and irreducible ambivalence at the heart of the histories (and elsewhere in Shakespeare), the existence of "meanings which point to opposite and irreconcilable systems of value" (p. 50). Sigurd Burckhardt, *Shakespearean Meanings* (Princeton, N. J.: Princeton U. Press, 1968), discusses the fact that in the tetralogy we get different answers, different interpretations, according to which model we apply; and that this truth is also what is being dramatized in the course of the tetralogy: "Some three centuries before Niels Bohr, Shakespeare discovered the need of complementarity—i.e., of operating with two mutually inconsistent and severally inadequate models because, and as long as, a single, consistent, and adequate model has not been found. Complementarity differs from and is superior to mixing because it remains aware of its "illegitimacy" and *pays the price* of choosing one model or the other" (pp. 183-4). Norman Rabkin, *Shakespeare and the Problem of Meaning* Chicago & London: The U. of Chicago Press, 1981) follows out the implications of Burckhardt's idea of complementarity, finding it to be central to Shakespeare's purposes in *Henry V*: "In *Henry V* the world is presented as equally reducible to opposite paradigms, each equally compelling, only one of which can be chosen" (p. 140). Although Rabkin does not specifically relate this to the problem of the oneness of life and death, his sense of the play's irresolvable doubleness is, like Rossiter's and Burckhardt's, close to mine: "*Henry V* is most valuable to us . . . because it shows us something about ourselves: the simultaneity of our deepest hopes and fears about the world of political action" (p. 62). Rabkin provides a good review of the play's critical history.

Other critics relate the doubleness of *Henry V*, and of the tetralogy generally, to their particular concerns. For example James R. Siemon, *Shakespearean Iconoclasm* (Berkeley/Los Angeles/Calif.: U. of Calif. Press, 1985), sees the conflicting elements of the histories, and especially of *Henry V*, as related to a profound conflict, in Shakespeare's work and in the culture at large, between iconic, or emblematic, representation, and naturalistic representation (the depiction of concrete particulars which subvert attempts to read iconographically, or allegorically). The conflicting forms of representation within the same work express deeper conflicts over the nature of reality. John W. Blanpied, *Time and the Artist in Shakespeare's English Histories* (Newark: University of Delaware Press; London and Toronto: Associated University Presses, 1983), traces the development of two forces in Shakespeare's English histories, forces he dubs the "antic" and the "Machiavel," the latter devoted to plotting and imposing order for the sake of achieving a future, the former devoted to the cracking and rupturing of all structure for the sake of the pleasure and energy of the moment. Blanpied's suggestive study is focused on the way in which a developing approach to history evident in Shakespeare's English histories enacts both the playwright's struggle with the seemingly fixed materials of actual history, and the attempts of all human beings to possess and shape their own lives, to give order and direction to the continual flux and chaos which characterizes all experience, private or public. From this perspective the distinction between drama and the material of actual history blurs, for the same forces are at work in drama and in our individual and collective histories.

For two recent psychoanalytically-oriented discussions of the Henriad, see Richard P. Wheeler, *Shakespeare's Development and the Problem Comedies: Turn and Counter-Turn* (Berkeley/Los Angeles/London: U. of Calif. Press, 1981), who discusses the tetralogy as part of Shakespeare's ongoing exploration and representation of the conflict between trust and autonomy, a conflict rooted in the primal mother-infant bond; and David Sundelson, *Shakespeare's Restorations of the Father* (New Brunswick, N.J.: Rutgers U. Press, 1983), who explores the Henriad in the context of a pattern he traces throughout Shakespeare's work: a concern with the absence, weakness, and/or destruction of a father figure, and a driving wish to restore a powerful and authoritative paternal presence.

As I do, Kirby Farrell, *Play, Death, and Heroism in Shakespeare*, considers Hal and the Henriad in relation to the effort to create a form of symbolic immortality. Farrell emphasizes the way in which in the presentation of Hal's fate prophecy and heroism conjoin to create a peculiar form of death transcendence—a form in which "the messianic provenance of the English crown" (p. 171) is at once demystified and reinforced. See Chapter 9, "Prophecy and Heroic Destiny in the Histories," especially pp. 148-50 and 159-71.

40 Cf. Anne Righter, *Shakespeare and the Idea of the Play* (N.Y.: Barnes & Noble, Inc., 1962), who comments, "The king is an abstraction, the representative of an eternal ideal, but he is also mortal. . . . The traditional formula concentrates upon the deathless passage of the ideal from one individual to another; yet the imagination persists in following the dead king to his grave . . ." (p. 115).

41 That Shakespeare knew the tradition is evidenced by Hamlet's request to the players not to out-Herod Herod (*Hamlet* III.ii.14).

42 Cf. Burckhardt: "What were crimes inside the border become acts of higher justice beyond . . ." (p. 181).

43 Cf. C.L. Barber and Richard P. Wheeler, *The Whole Journey: Shakespeare's Power of Development* (Berkeley/Los Angeles/London: U. of California Press, 1986): "There is something intrinsic to Henry V and his enterprise that *requires* the inhibition of conscious awareness of moral cruelty, and sexual cruelty, as elements of his character, unless we, shifting the gestalt, stand outside. We are either with him or against him, depending on whether or not *we* supply the dissenting or qualifying perspective" (p. 221).

44 Cf. Blanpied: "The 'audience' addressed by the Chorus is a part in the play that we are urged to fill. No other Shakespearean play has so

openly asked us to relinquish the myth of our individual solitudes" (p. 204).

A number of critics see the Chorus as in some sense epitomizing the play. For example, Michael Goldman, *Shakespeare and the Energies of Drama* (Princeton, N.J.: Princeton U. Press, 1972), remarks, "Once it is recognized that the Chorus sounds very much like the King, much of the play's method becomes clear. Like Henry, the Chorus is a man whose job is to rouse his hearers to unusual effort" (p. 59). Goldman's chief concern is to explore the subtle but profound effects deriving from Shakespeare's exploitation of the bodily nature of the theatrical experience. Ralph Berry, *The Shakespearean Metaphor* (Totowa, N.J.: Rowman & Littlefield, 1978), takes as central the play's stress on arguments, but arguments which do not prove what they purport to prove; and he sees the Chorus as embodying this tendency: "Just as the Chorus's reason for his own presence is not quite adequate, so his account of the action does not quite square with that amplified in the ensuing play. It is in that sense that I prefer to see the Chorus as the image of the play" (p. 49). Lawrence Danson, "*Henry V*: King, Chorus, and Critics," *Shak. Q.*, 34 (Spring 1983), 27-43, sees an analogy between Henry's relation to his on-stage audiences and the Chorus's relation to us, the off-stage audience—an analogy which should shape our interpretation of Henry's character. "In the historical world where Henry must lead, no choice can be absolutely right. . . . Yet the theatrical circumstances force us to choose, as the historical circumstances force Harry to choose. If we reject the Chorus' positive estimation of Harry we indulge, I believe, an impossibly romantic notion of heroism" (p. 37).

45 Cf. Marjorie Garber, *Coming of Age in Shakespeare* (London & N.Y.: Methuen & Co. Ltd., 1981), who focuses on the movement from stage to audience, and does so in the context of a discussion of the Shakespearean confrontation with mortality. In the relation of audience to play in *Henry V*, Garber sees the precursor of a way of dealing with death which is central to the tragedies: " . . . in the tragedies, the final act of transition and incorporation is performed, not by the players, but by the audience. To solve the dilemma of finitude and mortality, the silence of the grave, Shakespeare has created for his audience a crucial role that transcends the limitations imposed by the death of the hero—as well as the limitations implicit in 'the two hours traffic of our stage'" (p. 233). The whole of Chapter 7, "Death and Dying," is of special relevance to my general thesis.

46 David Jeffrey offers a concise description of the medieval view of history.

> The old view of history as an artificial frame for the recurrence of divine pattern had been common to several centuries of European culture, and had been codified in interpretations of Scripture as diverse as Augustine's *City of God*, the *Meditations of the Life of Christ*, the *Biblia Pauperum*, the programme of sculpture at

> Chartres, and all traditions of Christian haigiography. This view saw men of every generation participating in one great *historia* — in the *speculum humanae salvationis*. In this view nothing happened for the first time. What "happened" in the Old Testament recurs to fulfillment again in the New and again in the lives of the saints. The theme is recurrence. Christ lives and dies and is born again daily in the sacrament and in the hearts of men.

David L. Jeffrey, "English Saints' Plays," in *Medieval Drama*, Stratford-upon-Avon Studies 16, ed. Neville Denny [London: Edward Arnold (Publishers) Ltd., 1973], p.72.

47 This is precisely what is dramatized in *Romeo and Juliet*. See below, Chapter Four.

48 Cf. John Wilders, *The Lost Garden: A View of Shakespeare's English and Roman History Plays* (Totowa, N.J.: Rowman & Littlefield, 1970): " . . . the impression created by a history play is that the life of a nation has neither beginning nor ending" (p. 6).

Chapter Three

Love's Labor's Lost: Setting the Shakespearean Dramatic Task

Shakespeare's second history tetralogy portrays the limits of the communal solution to death, but leaves unresolved the problem of individual mortality. *Love's Labor's Lost* confronts that problem, and in so doing sets the task for Shakespearean comedy and tragedy. In the opening speech of *Love's Labor's Lost* Navarre poses the central problem of the play, and of Shakespearean drama in general—how to defeat death, imaged here as "cormorant devouring time" into whose gravelike maw all things will vanish (I.i.4).[1] The king's solution is immortal fame, to be achieved through the acquisition of extraordinary learning; and to accomplish this he plans to establish, with his companions, a "little academe/ Still and contemplative in living art" (I.i.13-14). But Navarre's description of the academy suggests, though unwittingly, the inherent contradictions which will render his scheme impossible to execute. "Still" had both an older meaning of "forever," and the modern sense of absence of noise, motion; of a stasis, a fixing in time and place. But as the word is spoken it suggests its own negation, for the young man speaking it is a living, embodied creature who cannot step out of time; and even as he endeavors to halt time, to make it stand "still," time is passing.[2] This same contradiction is suggested by the concluding phrase of Navarre's description, "living art." The gerund "living," with its sense of an ongoing action, echoes the ongoingness of all human life embedded in the flow of time which is carrying us toward death but which can be halted only by death. "Contemplative" extends the senses of "still," calling to mind the debate, going back to the Middle Ages and still current in Tudor times, over the merits of the active versus the contemplative life.[3] But a king cannot chose the contemplative life, for his position demands that he act on the iron stage of history;[4] and in fact the French princess, with her demand for negotiation, is waiting in the wings. The king is inescapably enclosed in his physical and in his social body, each of which has a death aspect which must be met and mastered. The emphasis in this comedy, however, is on the need to deal with the physical body, the root source of death. The whole of *Love's Labor's Lost* simply elaborates (with growing explicitness) on what we are shown at the start of the play in Navarre's opening speech. As Navarre speaks, his words are contradicted by the inescapable reality of his own physical being; and this subversion of language by the physical is the play's basic action — is, at one level of abstraction, its only action.

Certainly (as countless critics have noted), the most striking feature of *Love's Labor's Lost* is the frenetic, ubiquitous verbal play indulged in by virtually every character in the comedy.[5] The verbal play ranges from the merest quibble to the most structurally complex form of wordplay, literary art, and includes efforts as varied in style as the schoolmaster's barren pedanticisms, Armado's memorably eccentric verbosity, Moth's light-hearted quibbles, Berowne's polished elegancies. But these verbal efforts are on one level more alike than different; for like Navarre's opening speech all, whether deliberately or inadvertently, point to the ultimate inescapability of the body and its constraints, thus bringing us back, implicitly or explicitly, to the problem of death. Over and over the characters use language to deny, conceal, evade or transform the constraints of the body; but just as consistently sexuality and death break through the wall of words designed to bar them, opening language up to the reality of the physical.[6]

This characteristic action commences at the very start of the play, in Navarre's opening speech. In that speech Navarre attempts to use language — oaths and fiats — to establish an enclosure, the court turned academe, in which he and his companions will scant their bodily needs (food, sleep, women) while pursuing, through study, the fame intended to defeat mortality. The enclosure is designed to hold at bay time, history and the body, three related conditions of existence which are inseparable from death; the problem is that they are also inseparable from life. The basic action of the play consists of repeated assaults against Navarre's word-based enclosure by the very realities it was designed to protect against. Each time the would-be academe is breached it is forced to include more of what it would exclude, until the final assault, the entry of Marcade, a messenger of death. Marcade's news—the news of death—breaks apart the assembled court world and, by cutting off the action short of its expected comic conclusion, breaks apart the final verbal enclosure as well, the play world itself: the wall of words designed to close us off from actual life and the death which is an inseparable part of life. The verbal defenses mirror human resistance to dealing with death. But death is not an assault from without, it is inherent in our bodily nature; and until this fact is recognized and accepted, no attempt to meet and master death will succeed. But although *Love's Labor's Lost* exposes the death side of life, it does not enact a solution to the problem it exposes. Rather, it sets the task for other Shakespearean comedies and tragedies, which begin where this play leaves off: with acknowledgement of death's reality, and the generation of a dramatic strategy designed to deal with that fact.

In spite of the variety and brilliance of the play's kaleidoscopic surface, then, its verbal and structural elements are all referable to a single, central "action"—the erection of verbal defenses against mortality which are undermined even as they are erected, for the enemy is already within. Ralph Berry, in "The Words of Mercury," distinguishes between what "happens" in the play, and what the play is "about": "the movement toward reality is . . . the best way of describing what *happens* in *Love's Labor's Lost*," but "the play is *about words*."[7] In my view no such distinction can be made, since the thematic and structural elements are variations on the same symbolic action (the "literal" actions which compose the plot are of course also symbolic, being part of the dramatic fiction). Berry believes that there are three distinct attitudes toward words, each embodied by a different group of characters, and that each of these attitudes is finally tested by "Marcade-Mercury . . . the messenger of the gods, bringing the tidings of mortality" (p. 76). I agree with Berry that the characters' words are tested against a reality ultimately identified with mortality, but this testing is not reserved for the conclusion. It occurs throughout the play, it is what happens, and it is also what the play is about. To illustrate this I will discuss some of the many examples of wordplay in this comedy. Next I will look at some specifically literary uses of language in the comedy. Finally I will briefly trace the action of the play. I examine these elements separately for the sake of convenience, but literary and non-literary wordplay within the comedy are often indistinguishable, one shading into the other (all the language is of course literary in the sense that it is part of Shakespeare's own literary artifact); and wordplay and action are not ultimately distinguishable, since both are manifestations of the same symbolic action.

Wordplay

In terms of their typical way of using language, and also of their usual stage groupings, the characters may be divided into the following groups: (1) Moth and Costard, who mock the pedants and the courtier's impartially, and who are distinguished from the objects of their mockery by a lively awareness of the limits of language; (2) the pedants, who appear with their opposite number, the unlettered and laconic Dull; (3) the courtiers; (4) Armado, who moves between the courtiers and the pedants; (5) the ladies. I will consider examples of wordplay from each of these groups,to show how in each case the play of language actually points to the inescapability of bodily life, thus, to death.

(1) Moth and Costard
The wordplay of both Moth and Costard often depends on the pretense that physical fact can be altered through words. However, both characters are fully aware that such is not the case; and the effect of their wordplay is usually to emphasize

the intractability of the physical. A characteristic example is Moth's pretense that wordplay can alter the inexorable flow of time. In a dialogue with Armado, Moth asserts that he can convert three years (the time Armado has promised to study with Navarre) to an hour, and proceeds to prove it with a string of wordplay ending as follows: "Now here is three studied ere ye'll thrice wink; and how easy it is to put 'years' to the word 'three,' and study three years in two words . . ." (I.ii.50-53). But Moth's joke of course only emphasizes the impotence of words to alter time's progress—therefore, to fend off death; for time, as Navarre points out in his opening speech, is what is bringing us to oblivion.

Costard is a spokesman for another physical fact, sexuality; and like Moth, he pretends he can alter this fact through language. Confronted by Navarre with the details of his "crime" (consorting with Jaquenetta), Costard attempts to escape punishment by varying the word for the forbidden thing: for "wench" he substitutes "damsel," "virgin," "maid," (I.i.282 ff.). But Costard's attempts are unavailing. All his verbal variants cannot change Jaquenetta's womanhood and consequently Costard's trepass; and his very excuses are replete with bawdy puns (*e.g.*, "this maid will serve my turn," I.i.294) which only reinforce his implication in sexuality.

A close link between sexuality and death, both potentials of the body, is insisted upon throughout Shakespeare's work; but the degree to which the connection is allowed to surface varies greatly, and in this early comedy it is made chiefly through implication and innuendo. However, Costard delivered into Dull's hand and awaiting punishment for consorting with Jaquenetta is simply a lighter version of Claudio in the hands of the jailer anticipating death in *Measure for Measure* (I.ii). The men's trespass is essentially the same, as, in the long run, their penalty will be. Both men, caught in the trap of their bodies, are delivered to the law—to foolishly rigid human law (Navarre's proclamation and the Viennese edict), which must be bent to accommodate our bodily selves; and, on a deeper level, to the lethal law of nature which cannot be bent and which decrees death for all flesh. The difference in tone between the two plays is of course very great, as great as the difference between Costard's gently comic "Such is the simplicity of man to hearken after the flesh" (I.i.216-7), and Claudio's savage speech on the body and sexuality: "Our natures do pursue,/ Like rats that ravin down their proper bane,/ A thirsty evil, and when we drink, we die" (I.i.131-3). But the death taint associated with sexuality, insisted upon openly and intensely in the blacker *Measure for Measure*, is also central to the earlier and lighter *Love's Labor's Lost*. In part the association between sexuality and death is religiously based, for according to the traditional Christian view it is Eve, or woman, who fell and brought Adam with her, thus introducing suffering and death into the world (significantly, just before Costard attempts to escape punishment for his "crime" of consorting with Jaquenetta, Armado invokes this tradition by describing Jaquenetta as "a child of our grandmother Eve, a female; or, for thy more sweet understanding, a woman," I.i.259-60). But the religious tradition expresses (while coloring) a fact of experience, in that death does enter the world through women, through the flesh which is the inheritance of every new-born baby. Thus, the sexual act, which both springs from and perpetuates the death-bound flesh, is in fact associated with death as well as with new life.[8] Moreover, to the extent that the sexual act is a merely physical act as opposed to an act expressing human love, it is wholly bound to the mortal body. Whether viewed religiously or existentially, a love purely of the body cannot transcend death. The sexuality which humans share with animal creation *can* be transfigured by a distinctively human love, love which acknowledges but also goes beyond its bodily basis; and in Shakespearean drama the achievement of such love always constitutes a Lazarus-like version of resurrection in which the bodily nature of love—its death aspect—is at once accepted and transcended. Many of Shakespeare's plays, both comedies and tragedies, turn upon the idea of just such a resurrection, failed or achieved, including *As You like It, The Merchant of Venice, Measure for Measure, Romeo and Juliet, Hamlet, Othello, Antony and Cleopatra*. But *Love's Labor's Lost* does not show such a love actually achieved; for the achievement of fully human love, which is a form of mastering death, depends upon first confronting death; and that does not occur until the play's conclusion.

(2) The Pedants

Like Moth and Costard, the pedants Nathaniel and Holofernes also try to alter physical reality through manipulating language. This is strikingly exemplified in Holofernes' "extemporal epitaph on the death of the deer" (IV.ii.50-51) in which a sore (four-year-old buck)[9] is changed to a sorel by the simple addition of the letter "1," or one sore multiplied into fifty or a hundred by the addition of one or two "L's" (*i.e.*, Roman numerals for "fifty"). But in contrast to Moth and Costard, whose jests reveal awareness of the impotence of words in relation to the physical, the pedants' characteristic type of wordplay springs from their conviction that language is superior to mere physical actuality. They are frequently seen in the company of their fellow fool Dull, who is convinced of precisely the opposite. The typical responses of all three are well exemplified in a conversation in which they argue about the age and kind of deer the princess has killed (IV.ii). Nathaniel asserts it was "a buck of the first head" (10); Holofernes, who, like Nathaniel, prefers Latin and Latinate English, replies *"haud credo* (11); and Dull insists that "Twas not a *"haud credo"* [old gray doe], 'twas a pricket" (12) [a "two-year-old red deer"].[10] During this scene the two pedants generate a barrage of language to describe basic physical realities; and it is clear that for them words take precedence over the realities the words describe. Holofernes speaks of *"coelo,* the sky, the welkin, the heaven" (5-6) and *"terra,* the soil, the land, the earth" (7); and Nathaniel, who himself calls the moon "Phoebe" and "Luna" (39), is highly appreciative of Holofernes' efforts. "Truly, Master Holofernes, the epithets are sweetly varied, like a scholar at the least" (8-9), he exclaims, and at one point actually pulls out a tablet for the purpose of recording the schoolmaster's "singular and choice epithets" (I.i.17). Nathaniel's praise of the schoolmaster's "scholar"-like efforts constitutes a further, although subtle, undermining of Navarre's original ideal of scholarship (one function of the pedants throughout the play); for although the curate and the schoolmaster represent learning at its pedantic and parodic worst, there is still a sense in which all merely verbal learning is an equally vain manipulation of substanceless words. In the meanwhile Dull, spokesman for the corporeal, continues stolidly to insist upon the physical facts: the deer was no old gray doe, but a pricket. Dull always insists upon cutting through words to the bodily reality beneath them, as in his first appearance in the play when he tells us that although he may "reprehend" (represent) the "duke's own person," nevertheless he "would see his own person in flesh and blood" (I.i.182-4). Symbols of reality are for Dull no substitute for the corporeal thing itself.

In the interplay between the pedants and Dull, the pedants repeatedly discuss intellectual matters in language which suggests bodily functions. For the pedants, intellect is clearly superior to the physical; but the very language they use to assert this keeps before us the question of the relative merits of mind and body, and makes us wonder whether, as embodied creatures, we are not at our most foolish when we scant the means of renewal the body itself offers, renewal through children. This suggestion is central to the play's meanings (as it is to the comic solution to death). In his epitaph Holofernes multiplies the deer through wordplay; but the only way to multiply actual deer is through sexual reproduction, just as the only way to create new human life is through the sexual act. We are reminded of this especially strongly by passages such as IV.ii.25 ff., and IV.ii.66 ff., in which the pedants use the language of physical fertility to describe intellectual prowess. Nathaniel, for example, refers to the unlearned Dull as a "barren" plant (IV.ii.29), and adds happy self-congratulations on the intellectual abilities which, in contrast to the mentally barren Dull, "fructify" in himself and his fellow scholar (IV.ii.30). In the same scene Holofernes describes his literary "gift" (IV.ii.66) through a series of allusions to conception and childbirth. His "forms, figures. shapes, objects, ideas, apprehensions, motions, revolutions" (IV.ii.67-69) are *begot* in the ventricle of memory, *nourished* in the *womb* of *pia mater* [literally, "holy mother"],[11] and *delivered* upon the mellowing of occasion" (IV.ii.69-71, emphasis added). Thus the pedants denigrate the life of the body and extol the life of the mind; but even as they do their language suggests the barrenness of intellectual life and the generative potential of bodily life; and it is the celibate pedants who are the literally barren fools.[12]

(3) The Courtiers
The same suggestion also inheres in the courtiers' language. The link is deliberate, for the pedants' assertions throughout the play are intended as parodic commentary on Navarre and his lords.

For example, the pedants' denigration (just discussed) of bodily life in favor of the life of the mind is a deliberate echo, in burlesque form, of the discussion among the courtiers which opens the play. Navarre's proposal at the start of the play, and the ensuing debate among the courtiers, is initiated by the wish to deal with death. The pedants' conversation also opens with and centers upon death, the death of a deer. In his proposal, Navarre wishes his courtiers to scant bodily appetites (food, sleep, women) in favor of the "higher" life of the mind. The pedants take a similar tack, as when Nathaniel comments disparagingly on Dull's persistent misunderstanding of "*haud credo*" by comparing animal with intellectual appetite: "Sir, he hath never fed of the dainties that are bred in a book. He hath not eat paper, as it were, he hath not drunk ink. His intellect is not replenished. He is only an animal, only sensible in the duller parts" (IV.i.25-8). And perhaps most significantly, the courtiers, like the pedants, couch their denigrations of the body in language which only underlines the primacy of bodily life, and which continually reminds us of another way of meeting death—not immortality through fame, to be gained by denial of the body, but immortality through children, to be gained by acceptance of the body. A good example of this occurs in the debate which follows Navarre's proposal, a debate between the king and his lords, and Berowne, the only lord to protest Navarre's ascetic conditions.

The king wishes to defeat "cormorant devouring time" (I.i.4), that is to say, death; for time, like the body, is both an inescapable dimension of human existence and that which brings us to the grave. However, if time inevitably brings death it also brings race renewal, the succession of the generations; and the king suggests this potential of time also in the phrase "heirs of all eternity" (I.i.7). The king uses this phrase to describe the results of fame, but the word "heirs" reminds us of heirs of the body, the children through whom we can perpetuate ourselves and the race. Berowne keeps this same possibility before us, for his objections to the king's proposal are also couched in language which reminds us of the body's generative potential, the very potential which the king's strictures would keep in check. Berowne objects not to the idea of study *per se*, but to the stringent asceticism which is to accompany it: fasting, scanting one's sleep, foregoing the company of women. These conditions have in common the fact that they attempt to deny rather than allow for the reality of the body and its drives, and Berowne comments on them as follows: "0, these are barren tasks, too hard too keep,/ Not to see ladies, study, fast, not sleep!" (I.i.47-8). Significantly, it is not merely that the tasks are "too hard" — that is, too difficult, and also too harsh; it is also that they are "barren," a reminder that these tasks may not only *not* help the courtiers to overcome death, but may actually hinder them, insofar as they prevent the young men from employing the natural solution to death, immortality through offspring.[13] That solution is of course only partially successful in that the men as individuals will still die; but in contrast to the king's proposal, it has the great merit of being practicable.

As the debate proceeds Berowne continues to suggest, in his language, the primacy and value of the body. For example, he points out that sacrificing the body in search of illumination will bring only darkness — blindness from overstudying.

> Light seeking light doth light of light beguile;
> So ere you find where light in darkness lies,
> Your light grows dark by losing of your eyes.
> (I.i.77-9)

The physical and spiritual senses of illumination are mingled in these lines; and the final effect of their intermingling is to remind us that intellectual insight is of little value put against the loss of precious bodily sight. "Your light grows dark" refers to blindness, but also suggests the eternal darkness of death which will fall just as surely whether the men abuse their bodies in pleasureless, profitless scholarship, or whether they use their daylight springtime hours as nature intended: to pursue pleasure, love, marriage, children. Finally, the potential of the flesh itself to master the death inherent in the flesh is strongly suggested in the sonnet-like lines which climax Berowne's persuasions.

> Small have continual plodders ever won
> Save base authority from others' books.
> These earthly godfathers of heaven's lights,
> That give a name to every fixed star
> Have no more profit of their shining nights
> Than those that walk and wot not what they are.
> Too much to know is to know naught but fame;
> And every godfather can give a name.
> (I.i.86-93)

Literally Berowne is saying that the astronomers ("earthly godfathers") who label the stars have spent their time to no better effect than those who experience, wordlessly and directly, the beauty of the stars. At the opening of the play Navarre stated his intent to sacrifice full physical existence in the pursuit of a death-defying fame. Now his wish for an immortalizing fame is echoed—and undercut—in Berowne's use of the word "fame," for Berowne uses the word in its older sense of "public report," the words of others (see OED); and the fame the king seeks is perhaps no more than this kind of empty report, a vain verbal counter to death. Astronomers give names to stars, and godfathers give names to babies—both can label what is already created—but only through procreation can one continue the stream of creation itself.

Berowne continues his allusions to physical fertility in a series of references to the seasons: summer and the growing of corn (I.i.96); spring, "when green geese are a-breeding" (I.i.97); and winter with its "envious sneaping frost" (I.i.100) which destroys "the first-born infants of the spring" (I.i.101). These lines summarize the natural seasonal cycle of birth, fertility and death (green geese, corn and frost); but the seasonal references occur out of sequence (summer, spring, winter), just as the King wants to violate the natural sequence of human life by demanding restraints from those in the springtime of youth. Berowne puts the seasons back into sequence in his often-quoted assertion of the rightness—and inevitability—of the progression of the seasons, each of which has the pleasures and effects natural to it.

> At Christmas I no more desire a rose
> Than wish for snow in May's new-fangled shows,
> But like of each thing that in season grows.
> (I.i.105-7)

Berowne's viewpoint, then, is more inclusive than that of his fellow courtiers; but it is, nevertheless, still radically inadequate. As Berowne's own arguments imply, bodily life is locked into the flow of time; and time moves cyclically, but also in a linear way, depending upon whether we focus on the rhythms of nature and the race or on the rhythms of a single life—that is, on the perpetually recurring rhythms of day and night and the larger seasonal rhythms, or on the linear progression of a single human life which moves through the recurrent alternations of night and day, winter and spring, until the final winter of age and the spring that will never return. Berowne argues, through his imagery, for acceptance of nature and man's place in it. But as that same imagery suggests, "great creating Nature"[14] dwells in and works through the same flesh which will destroy us; and accepting our bondage to nature therefore requires nothing less than acceptance of death itself. However, Berowne does not realize this implication.[15] Persistently, he (and other characters) employ imagery which evokes mortality. But it requires the whole play to make clear to the characters—and to the audience—the full dimensions of human mortality, including the inescapable link between sexuality and death.[16]

The failure fully to confront mortality is evident in Berowne's wordplay in general. Repeatedly, Berowne pushes toward verbal acknowledgment of the sexual basis of love (thus, by implication, of the link between love and death). For example, at the end of the third act, in the monologue in which Berowne confesses his subjection to "Dan Cupid"

Love's Labor's Lost: Setting the Dramatic Task 119

(III.i.175 ff.), he calls attention to the sexual basis of love and to the anarchic character of purely sexual desire (for example, his love is a "wanton" who "will do the deed,/Though Argus were her enunch and her guard," 200-01). Moreover, in his jesting Berowne often links sexuality and death. At the opening of the sonnet-reading scene, for example (IV.iii.), Berowne speaks a monologue which insists on the sexual basis of love, and which associates sexually-based love with death. In this monologue (IV.iii.1 ff.) Berowne compares love to hunting, an act of pursuit which ends in the death of the animal. Earlier the Princess pursued and killed a deer; thereafter the King "pitched a toil" (IV.iii.2); and now Berowne too is trapped, "toiling in a pitch" (2-3), a "pitch that defiles" (3). The trap is the trap of Berowne's own body, the source of sexually-based human love and also of death. "Pitch" brings together the senses of "trap" and of black tar, to which Berowne has previously compared his mistress's eyes (III.i.199). He is caught, stuck fast, in the trap of his own animal nature. Under the influence of love mad Ajax killed sheep, and Berowne, a sheep in love, will meet a similar fate. But although Berowne connects sexuality and death in his wordplay, he never faces the connection in earnest; for to do so would require a confrontation with the full weight of human mortality, and such a confrontation is not enacted within the playing space of this comedy (it is, however, what Rosaline bids Berowne undertake at the play's conclusion).

The animal self makes us vulnerable to both the sexual impulse and to death; and Berowne's reference to himself as a sheep is one of many references in the play to deer and sheep, animals destined for slaughter. These references, common to all the groups of characters, often include allusions to horns, almost always with the standard Shakespearean wordplay on horns and cuckoldry. The references form a web of allusions linked by association which together suggest the at once fruitful and lethal potentials of the flesh. Many of the references involve Moth. For example, in the fifth act Moth and Holofernes exchange repartee involving puns on letters of the alphabet, the hornbook (the horn-covered parchment from which children were taught their letters), sheep with horns and, inevitably, cuckoldry. This wordplay keeps before us one potential of sexual love, adultery, which is potential in two ways. It may never be actualized, because the restraints of love or law may restrict animal promptings to their exercise in marriage; and it is alluded to by a boy, one who is only potentially a sexually mature male. Because he is a boy Moth is, simply in his physical presence, a walking emblem of bodily life in time, and of the progression of the generations, and his wordplay emphasizes this. For example, in Act Three Moth offers to prove a jesting contention to his master. Armado asks, "What wilt thou prove?" and Moth replies, "A man, if I live" (III.i.40-41). As so often in the play, an unpalatable physical fact pushes against a screen of language (the jests). If Moth lives he will reach maturity but also, eventually, death; however, the only alternative to aging is untimely death. The question is not if, but when, death comes.

The implications of Moth's jesting are picked up in the next scene in an exchange between Longaville and Katharine. Katharine calls Longaville a calf and mocks him, and the following dialogue ensues:

Longaville. Look how you mock yourself in these sharp mocks.
Will you give horns, chaste lady? Do not so.
Katharine. Then die a calf before your horns do grow.
Longaville. One word in private with you ere I die.
Katharine. Bleat softly then. The butcher hears you cry.
(V.ii.252-56)

Sexual maturity may bring horns—that is, make a man a cuckold; but the only alternative to sexual maturity is early death ("Then die a calf before your horns do grow"). To die had a double meaning in Elizabethan English, the modern meaning, and also to reach sexual climax; and both senses operate in Longaville's rejoinder, "One word in private with you ere I die." Death and sex are further associated in Katharine's next remark, "Bleat softly then. The butcher hears you cry." A grown man may escape cuckoldry; but just as the animal reaching maturity is eventually butchered, so in time the little death of sexuality, and death itself, inevitably await the mature man. Again, however, the only alternative to sexual maturity, aging and eventual death is premature death. A connection between sexuality and lethal disease—another form of death—is also suggested in this comedy in the frequent wordplay picturing love as a mortal sickness. Berowne, for example, refers to love as a "plague" (III.i.203). Berowne and Rosaline trade quips picturing love as a mortal disease (II.i.184-88). Dumaine, in the sonnet-reading scene, refers to his love as a "fever" which "reigns in my blood" (IV.iii.94,95), and Berowne repeats the phrase and recommends blood-letting as the cure. Later Berowne comments, "Light wenches may prove plagues . . ." (IV.iii.384). Love, a potentially fatal illness, has actually killed Katharine's sister, who died of a broken heart (V.i.13-15). Katharine reports her lover's description of her as a "Qualm" ["sudden sickness"],[17] and the Princess responds, "sickness as thou art" (V.ii.281). And Berowne, after the Russian masque, employs a series of dense and witty puns to describe love as a plague and the ladies as plague carriers who have infected the lords (V.ii.418-24).[18] The insistent wordplay linking love and disease keeps before us the death side of sexuality, reminding us that the sexual drive is inseparable from the mortal body.

(4) Armado
Armado, the link between the courtiers and the pedants, also buries physical fact in a barrage of words; for his fantastic verbal elaborations are often built around an acknowledgment of the bodily basis of human life. For example, we first hear from Armado through a letter which he sends to Navarre describing the circumstances in which he caught Costard with Jaquenetta (I.i.229 ff.). As always with Armado's use of language, ornament threatens to overwhelm content. Nevertheless, what Armado describes are the conditions of creaturely existence, including place—exactly where in the park he met Costard—and time, a description of time which stresses the link between animals and men: "the sixth hour; when beasts most graze, birds most peck, and men sit down to that nourishment which is called supper" (I.i.233-36). Thus his

screen of words conceals, but also reveals, our bondage to space, time and animal necessity. And in the end it is he, alone among both courtiers and pedants, who most profoundly acknowledges the ultimate bodily reality, death, in his eccentric but powerful rebuke to the shallow courtiers who are mocking the pageant: "The sweet war-man is dead and rotten. Sweet chucks, beat not the bones of the buried. When he breathed, he was a man" (V.ii.661-63).

(5) The Ladies
In contrast to the pedants and courtiers, the noblewomen deliberately use language to point to bodily reality, especially the related realities of sexuality and death. This tendency is well illustrated in the hunting scene (IV.i), with its plethora of sexual allusions and its insistence on the death of the deer at the hands of the Princess. In this scene it is the Princess herself who insists, although jokingly, on her part in inflicting death, asking "where is the bush/ That we must stand and play the murderer in?" (IV.i.34-35), and chiding herself for her lethal intentions ("I for praise alone now seek to spill/ The poor deer's blood that my heart means no ill," IV.8.7-8). The jesting takes on added significance because of the recurrent wordplay, discussed above, linking men in love with animals destined for slaughter.

The Princess is allowed to remind us of death; but in keeping with royal dignity it is her ladies, and not she, who engage in sexual badinage. After the hunting discussion the Princess exits, and Boyet, Rosaline, Maria and Costard are left on stage to indulge in a passage of obscene punning which in length and explicitness is remarkable even for Shakespeare.[19] In this passage, the banter exchanged between the four links shooting and hunting (thus aggression and death) with sexuality and adultery; and the net effect of the repartee is to reduce sex to an animal, even mechanical, activity in which one organ fits another in mechanical and loveless fashion (see the series of puns culminating in IV.i.134, "Let the mark have a prick in 't, to mete at if it may be"). Some readers are puzzled by the fact that the noblewomen joke so grossly. However, it is totally appropriate that they joke in this manner, for it is their function in this play to cut through language to the physical facts beneath. The ladies' insistence on calling a spade a spade is not limited to romantic matters, but extends to all areas of life, as when the Princess responds to Navarre's words of welcome by pointing out that in fact they are not welcome in the King's court, since they are only in his park: " . . . 'welcome' I have not yet. The roof of this court is too high to be yours, and welcome to the wide fields too base to be mine" (II.i.91-94). However, the ladies are above all objects of love, and as such their most important function in the play is their refusal to let their suitors divorce love from its bodily component. It is not that either Shakespeare or the ladies consider merely physical love to suffice for humans. But if human love cannot be reduced to its sexual component, neither can it be divorced from that component; and true love must acknowledge before it can go beyond its bodily basis, an acknowledgment synonymous with the acknowledgment of mortality. The ladies push this unwelcome truth on their lovers not only through the kind of wordplay described above, but also through their actions. For example, because of the ladies' plotting, in the masquing scene the men make love not to their chosen mistresses but to signs and tokens which they mistake for their flesh-and-blood lovers. This scene and its aftermath constitute a dramatic parallel to the ladies' characteristic wordplay. Both are devices, one dramatic, one verbal, to force exposure of the flesh-and-blood reality beneath the protective concealments of clothing as of language.

Literature

Whether the characters use language to fend off, or to point to, bodily reality, the ultimate effect of all the wordplay is the same: to refer us, whether deliberately or inadvertently on the character's part, back to the problem of the body, thus back to the problem of death. The language which calls attention to mortality often suggests a solution to it, immortality through children. But as is also often suggested through the same language, this solution is flawed. Individuals still die, and they can give birth only to equally mortal offspring. Another possible way of countering death is through the creation of literature, and one form the verbal activity in *Love's Labor's Lost* repeatedly takes is the creation of literature. If literature is held to consist of formally structured verbal artifacts which can immortalize their subjects and survive their flesh-and-blood makers, then the idea of literature as a strategy against death is as old as literature itself; but for Shakespeare the nature and function of literature includes but goes beyond that of a potentially enduring aesthetic object. The art he seeks, an art capable of confronting and mastering death, is kinetic and transformational. Since what is to be transformed is the death taint in our bodily-based existence, the transformation actions are versions of resurrection. This concept of art finds expression in (among many other places) Ariel's song from *The Tempest*, "Full Fathom Five," and in *The Tempest* as a whole.[20] The song tells of the "sea-change" by which bones are transformed into coral and pearls into eyes—the perishable body transformed into something precious and undying, although also unliving—a Yeatsian "artifice of eternity."[21] Moreover, *The Tempest* repeatedly enacts resurrection. Human beings and destinies rise from the grave of the past ("the dark backward and abysm of time," I.II.50),[22] and the seemingly dead spring up from the oozy mud in which we are repeatedly told they lie buried.[23] Unlike *The Tempest*, however, *Love's Labor's Lost* presents the search for rather than the demonstration of an efficacious art.

Early in *Love's Labor's Lost* Berowne suggests, by implication, what kind of art is needed. In his rebuttal to Navarre's initial proposal Berowne refers to the plodding astronomers, those "earthly godfathers of heaven's lights/ That give a name to every fixed star" (I.i.88-89). In this reference Berowne implicitly contrasts the creative energy of nature, manifest in its effects ("heaven's lights," Creation itself), to the astronomer's sterile verbal efforts which are confined to naming that which already exists.[24] But simply naming what exists is the definition not only of pointless learning but also of a kind of art, the kind which consists merely in the rearranging of words—Holofernes' "sweetly varied" epithets, for example, or the lords' graceful arrangements of shopworn poetic cliches. Although this kind of art is opposed rather than allied to nature, "there is an art which . . . shares/ With great creating nature" (*Winter's Tale*, IV.iv.87-8), if by nature we understand not only the visible, material phenomena of the natural world, but also the invisible, immaterial animating forces which give rise to and transform those phenomena. This kind of art is suggested by certain Elizabethan meanings of the word "art." The word had, among other meanings, the meanings of "Human skill as an agent, human workmanship. Opposed to nature"; of "An artifice, contrivance, stratagem, wile, trick, cunning device"; and, in a sense which includes the other meanings and is especially relevant to Shakespeare, of "magic art,"[25] the phrase Prospero repeatedly employs in *The Tempest*.[26] Starting with materials drawn from nature — therefore materials which, like Friar Lawrence's herbs, have both a life and a death aspect—art (both magic and literary art) attempts to transform that very nature which is its basis. "This is an art/ Which does mend Nature, change it rather; but/ The art itself is Nature" (*Winter's Tale*, IV.iv.95-7). In the end art may be judged as unable to transform mortal reality, but we will know this only by including in a work of art that which we hope to transform.[27] *Love's Labor's Lost* pushes towards an art based on recognition, inclusion and transformation of the death aspect of our bodily-based existence. Drama is inherently more inclusive of the body than other forms of literature, for it is composed of a meld of words and of the living bodies of actors who move through actual space and time. Accordingly, the push towards a more inclusive and transformational art is mirrored within *Love's Labor's Lost* in the shift from the examples of non-dramatic literature which dominate the first four acts (Armado's Euphuistic prose, the pedants' verse, the courtiers' sonnets), to the dramatic literature of the last act (the masque, the pageant, the songs of the Owl and the Cuckoo), to the confrontation with the actual with which Shakespeare's play concludes. All these examples of literature, non-dramatic and dramatic, are centered around attempts to deal with the body, therefore, with death. However, none succeeds; for although at the end of the play we face the reality of death directly, the art which might transform that reality remains to be achieved. To illustrate this I will briefly examine some examples of literature within the play, including Holofernes' epitaph on the death of the deer; the noblemen's sonneteering; Armado's Euphuistic prose; the masque; the pageant; the lyrics which conclude the play (the songs of the Owl and the Cuckoo); and finally Shakespeare's own play *in toto*, embracing and commenting upon all its constituent forms. The authors of these pieces are all men, for the way of dealing with death proper to Shakespearean women is not literature but marriage and children; and as we have seen, the ladies' verbal wit is characteristically employed in directing the men away from verbal solutions and back to the body.

Holofernes, in his "extemporal epitaph on the death of the deer," uses poetry to confront our mortal vulnerability, the potential for experiencing pain and death which we as embodied creatures share with the deer. Suffering is acknowledged in the wordplay on "sore": "Some say a sore [four-year-old buck],[28] but not a sore till now made sore with shooting" (IV.ii.58). However, pain and death are dealt with simply by adding the letter "l" to "sore": a wounded, dying sore beset by dogs is transformed into an untouched "sorel" [young buck][29] who "jumps from thicket" (59) as good as new. This is indeed a resurrection, but this revivification through art is a ludicrously literal one in the root sense of "literal" (the letter). The transformations of art must involve the spirit, not merely the letter. And successful art must begin with the acknowledgment that the reality of the flesh is not, finally, transformable and that the ills the flesh makes us heir to are not, ultimately, escapable.

As authors, the King and his courtiers specialize in love sonnets. All three lords and the King are shown at the height of their sonneteering in IV.iii, in which we watch Berowne watching the King watching Longaville watching Dumaine, each entering with a poetic confession of love. The poetry is the polished conventional stuff of countless sixteenth-century sonnet sequences, full of fashionable conceits, paradoxes and oxymorons, praising the lady in quasi-divine terms and vowing devotion to her as to a deity. Longaville's love is a "goddess" (64), Dumaine's love is fairer than Juno herself (116-7), and no "tongue of mortal" can tell the excellence of the King's beloved (39-40). Mistress-deification is of course a standard feature of sixteenth-century love sonnets, but within the context of *Loves Labor's Lost* it reveals the lords' failure to come to grips with the body. Here, as elsewhere in the play, it is the iconoclastic Berowne who insists on the bodily nature of the deified ladies. At the opening of the sonnet-reading scene Berowne speaks a monologue which pictures love as both defiling and potentially lethal, and so sets up a satirical conditioning context for the extravagantly romantic sonnets which follow. Moreover, as the sonnets are read the hidden Berowne engages in a series of mocking comments designed to emphasize the fleshly nature of the beloved women. For example, at the conclusion of Longaville's sonnet Berowne calls attention to the folly which makes a man idolize a flesh-and-blood girl as if she were a goddess: "This is the liver-vein, which makes flesh a deity,/ A green goose a goddess. Pure, pure idolatry" (IV.i.73-4). To Dumaine's epithets for his mistress, "divine" and "heaven," Berowne counters with "profane" and "earth." And when Berowne finally reveals himself to his companions, he calls attention to the female body which prompts the love poetry:

> When shall you hear that I
> Will praise a hand, a foot, a face, an eye,
> A gait, a state, a brow, a breast, a waist,
> A leg, a limb . . .
> (IV.iii.182-5)

What inspires the men's poetic effusions to their "goddesses" is the mortal body — "a brow, a breast, a waist,/ A leg, a limb." Earlier in the play Berowne calls "Dan Cupid" (III.i.182) "Regent of love-rhymes" (183) and "Dread prince of plackets, king of codpieces" (186). The sexual nature of the force underlying the rash of courtly sonneteering could not be stated more plainly. Now, as Longaville wonders if he should recast his sonnet into prose the better to move Maria, Berowne comments, "O, rhymes are guards [trimmings, ornaments, as well as the modern sense] on wanton Cupid's hose;/ Disfigure not his shop [codpiece or phallus]," IV.iii.57-58). That is, the formal, ordering device of rhyme "guards" (both ornaments and restrains) the naked sexual impulse which is its generating force.

After Dumaine, the last lord to read his sonnet, finishes, Longaville steps forward and reveals himself to Dumaine; the King reveals himself to both lords; and finally Berowne reveals himself to all three, openly mocking them. But Berowne himself, in spite of his mocking disclaimers, has already groaned and rhymed for his Joan; and no sooner does he begin to mock his fellow lords then Jaquenetta and Costard appear bearing his love sonnet to Rosaline, and he is exposed as a fellow fool: "I confess, I confess" that "you three fools lacked me fool to make up the mess" (IV.iii.204,206). Berowne follows this confession with a rueful acknowledgment of their shared creatureliness.

> We are as true as flesh and blood can be.
> The sea will ebb and flow, heaven show his face;
> Young blood cannot obey an old decree.
> We cannot cross the cause why we were born.
> (IV.iii.214-17)

Man through his body is part of nature, and sexuality, inherent in that nature, is no more resistible than the movement of the tides and the sun. Moreover, we cannot detach ourselves from "the cause why we were born," the sexual imperative which has produced us and all of that living creation of which we are a part. But although Berowne insists upon the sexual basis of both love and love poetry, his own sonnet to Rosaline (IV.ii.107 ff.) is as conventionally idealizing, as full of mistress-deification, as those of his fellow lords: "Celestial as thou art, O pardon love this wrong,/ That sings heaven's praise with such an earthly tongue" (119-20). Moreover, he follows his forceful reminder of human rootedness in the body ("We are as true as flesh and blood can be") with a lapse into extravagant poetic praise of his mistress, full of the same flowery and deifying language for which he has just castigated his fellow fools (see IV.iii.220-27, 231-45, 247-52, 256-64). Thus none of the love poetry in the play, Berowne's included, succeeds in coming to terms with the body. In his jests and wordplay Berowne may acknowledge, even insist upon, the bodily (therefore death-tainted) basis of love; but he does not succeed in creating love-poetry which reflects that acknowledgment. Rather, he vacillates between jokes based on a harshly satirical reduction of love to mere sex (the point of view of the intellect), and what may be called the sonnet-view of love which does not acknowledge that the mistress is a sexual being at all. The failure of Berowne's art points to a deeper failure of vision. If love poetry, like love itself, cannot be divorced from the body and its drives, neither can it be reduced merely to those drives. A fully human love acknowledges but also goes beyond its bodily basis, just as a fully human art acknowledges in order to transcend our shared corporeality. The underlying reason for the inadequacy of both Berowne's vision and his art is suggested in passages such as the following, in which Berowne praises Rosaline.

> A withered hermit, five-score winters worn,
> Might shake off fifty looking in her eye.
> Beauty doth varnish age as if new-born,
> And gives the crutch the cradle's infancy.
> (IV.iii.241-4)

Love may create renewal on a psychological level; but except for the limited form of physical rebirth possible through children, love cannot give "the crutch the cradle's infancy." To really love one must accept mortality, both one's own and that of one's beloved, who is no goddess but a human being who will age and die.[30]

At the end of the sonnet-reading section, after all the lords have acknowledged their complicity in love, Berowne supplies a rationale to release the courtiers from their vain oath, and they plan an assault on their respective mistresses. The men have taken a step toward accepting the imperatives of the body, and this acceptance is reflected in their shift from poetry, which employs words alone, to the masque which, as drama, makes use of the living bodies of actors.[31] Both sonnets and masque share a common aim—to win the ladies' affections, thus to master death through generational immortality. But the masque is no better than the sonnets at coming the grips with the body, and in the masque the men make love not to their actual flesh-and-blood mistresses but to tokens of their beloveds. Moreover, Berowne is scolded roundly for his affected love-making. Thus, whether considered as wooing devices or as forms of art, both sonnets and masque fail to master death. Berowne forswears courtly elaboration in favor of plain speech, but he still does not see the deeper problem. No words, whether "Taffeta phrases, silken terms precise" *or* "russet yeas and honest kersey noes," will suffice until the underlying wordless bodily reality is fully acknowledged and accepted.

Armado, the last of our litterateurs, is the link between the two chief groups of authors, the courtiers and the pedants. Much of Armado's speech is a kind of literary creation— Euphuistic prose gone mad. But Armado's chief "literary" effort is perhaps his love letter to Jaquenetta, which parallels Berowne's sonnet to Rosaline. The letter, couched in Armado's eccentric, bombastic, Lyly-like prose, has more to do with Armado's vanity than with his mistress' charms; but it does acknowledge the ultimate source of his interest in her when he declares, "I profane my lips on thy foot, my eyes on thy picture, and [suggestively] my heart on thy every part" (IV.i.86-7). Further, Armado has a deeper understanding of love than do his fellow courtiers. We see this clearly in the monologue he speaks at the end of the first act, in which he acknowledges love's power (I.ii.165 ff.). Armado alludes to great heroes—Samson, Solomon, Hercules, the strongest and the wisest, a company in which Armado clearly places himself. All were overcome by love, which is to say, by their own bodies; and Armado has been similarly overcome. Armado concludes his acknowledgment of love's irresistible power with a declaration that he will turn author. "Assist me some extemporal god of rhyme, for I am sure I shall turn sonnet. Devise, wit; write, pen; for I am whole volumes in folio" (I.ii.181-3). For Armado, the sonneteering of the lords (his own included) is a little like the singing of birds: birds mating chirp, lords in love "turn sonnet." In each case nature works through the individual, producing sounds which may seem to the creature

Love's Labor's Lost: Setting the Dramatic Task 131

to be individual expressions of passion, but which are really simply musical expressions of the generative impulse. To turn sexual passion to fully human love, and the twitterings of lovers to fully human art, requires simultaneous acknowledgment and transcendence of the natural reality which underlies love.[32] At the end of the play the songs of those other birds, the Owl and the Cuckoo, will suggest what is missing from the springtime twitterings of the courtly lovers in Navarre's park (see below, p. 133 ff.).

The vanished heroes Armado alludes to in his monologue were overcome by the body in two senses: sexuality and, ultimately, death. But the motif of heroes conquered by death is held in abeyance until the performance of the pageant; and therefore it is not until the pageant scene that we see why Armado as a literary artist is comparable to Bottom in *A Midsummer Night's Dream*. Both these fools are not altogether fool, but are on one level wiser than the nobles who mock them; for both understand the fundamental realities underlying art—love and death, those twin potentials of bodily life.

The pageant, which consists of bringing dead heroes to momentary dramatic life, amounts to an attempt at resurrection. To this extent the pageant attempts to perform the proper function of art, but only Armado realizes the deeper significance of what they are doing. Costard as Pompey, Nathaniel as Alexander, Holofernes as Judas Maccabaeus and Moth as the infant Hercules all appear in turn, and each is jeered off the stage by the noblemen, whose rude mocks thus frustrate the enactment of resurrection. As the nobles jeer, references to death ring through their taunts: Judas (Iscariot) and his suicide, "A death's face in a ring" (V.ii.621). Shadows, literal and figurative, are gathering: the day is turning to darkness as spring will to winter, youth to age and death; and Boyet calls for light—"A light for Monsieur Judas! It grows dark, he may stumble" (632). The black notes are strongly though unexpectedly reinforced by Armado's reproof to the jeering nobles, as he asks for respect not for himself but for Hector, the dead hero he represents. "The sweet war-man is dead and rotten. Sweet chucks, beat not the bones of the buried. When he breathed, he was a man" (V.ii.661-3).

Armado's eccentric but powerful lines reveal a respect for mortality which the seemingly wittier lords lack. Armado alone sees that Hector was once a man as fully alive as any now present, and that all present will one day be as dead as Hector;[33] and through his language he forces on us awareness of the corruptible body which will bring us to Hector's fate: the bones that will lie in the earth, the flesh that will rot.

Through the imagination, we can lend ourselves to Hector's momentary resurrection; and the Princess graciously requests Armado to continue. But before Armado can proceed very far, the attempted dramatic resurrection is again broken off, this time by the intrusion of literal physical reality: first, of sexuality—the announcement of Jaquenetta's pregnancy; and finally, of death—Marcade's announcement of the death of the King of France. The connection between sexuality and death, those allied yet opposed potentials of the body, is caught perfectly in the wordplay on "gone." Armado declares of Hector, "The party is gone" [*i.e.*, "dead"], and Costard responds, "Fellow Hector, she is gone [*i.e.*, pregnant]. She is two months on her way" (V.ii.671-2). In a burlesque of chivalry Hector/Armado, stung by the accusation that he is the father of Jaquenetta's child, challenges Pompey/Costard to a duel, and is urged on to combat by the mocking courtiers. But in the course of the quarrel it emerges that Armado is naked under his coat. With this revelation of the naked body beneath the trappings of courtly clothing and (mock-)chivalric ritual, Marcade appears bearing the news of death, news which breaks off not only the pageant but, some lines later, Shakespeare's play as well. The ladies postpone the expected conclusion to the action, marriage, by sending the lords into the world outside the playing space to receive instruction in their own mortality. Thus, the "wooing doth not end like an old play; Jack hath not Jill" (875-6); and Shakespeare's comedy does not enact any of the possible solutions to death—renewal through love, through children, through art. Both the plays-within-the-play and the enclosing wider play must come to terms with mortality before effecting such transformation of it as is possible.

The presentation of the "dialogue . . . in praise of the owl and the cuckoo" (V.ii.888) is the third and last presentation of a play-within-a-play. The songs of the Owl and the Cuckoo bring together the audience on stage and the audience in the playhouse, as all listen to their recapitulation of the very realities the art within the play, and the play itself, keep trying, unsuccessfully, to master.[34] At first glance it seems as if the traditional opposition of pleasing springtime and harsh winter is the point of the songs. But actually, the emphasis in both songs is on man's subjection to the simultaneously pleasing and "unpleasing" natural realities bodily being entails: in the Cuckoo's song, anarchic sexuality; and in the Owl's song, the still less pleasing realities of bodily suffering (cold, labor, illness) and, ultimately, death.

The springtime world of the Cuckoo's song is painted in terms of flowers, colors, delight, fertility. In this world humans are as much a part of the natural landscape as the daisies, violets and larks. Turtledoves, rooks, daws mate, and maidens bleach their summer smocks—both activities are presented in the same sentence and in parallel grammatical order, which conveys a sense that the maidens' and the birds' activities are essentially alike. "Turtles tread," and maidens prepare their garments to entice young men in the human version of the mating game. For this is above all a world of sexual fertility in which every element of creation—plants, birds, maidens—renews itself in accordance with nature's promptings. But in this world, pleasurable as it is, what is distinctively human is overwhelmed by the nature we share with animal creation; and from every tree the cuckoo reminds us of the power of the sexual drive to destroy human love.

In the Owl's song nature has dropped her pleasing springtime aspect. Men have retreated inwards to the man-made comforts of hearth and hall as protection against, and solace for, the assaults of winter. But although human beings do have culture to mitigate the rigors of winter, they are still, as in the Cuckoo's song, bound to the rest of creation: for inanimate things, animals and humans all suffer from nature in her winter aspect—the milk "frozen," the blood "chilled," the birds "brooding in the snow," Marian's nose "red and raw."

Although both songs stress our implication in animal existence, both also allude to the means whereby anarchic sexuality and mortality—the penalties of creaturely existence—might be at least partially mastered. The Cuckoo's song reminds us that indiscriminate sexuality might be overcome through marriage, whether marriage is considered in religious terms or humanistically. Seen in its religious aspect, marriage is a ritual which literally sacramentalizes bodily love. But humans must choose to enact this ritual to make it effective; and marriage as an act of choice represents the commitment two unique individuals undertake to love one another exclusively and unselfishly, thus transfiguring the purely animal imperatives of sex into something distinctively human. In like fashion, the Owl's song reminds us that the ills of mortality—vulnerability to discomfort (winter cold and blasts), to labor (Tom bearing logs, Joan keeling the pot), to illness and death (coughing)—could be revalued by human culture. Culture includes the domestic, social and religious ordering of life, all epitomized in the Owl's song (the indoor scenes; the social ordering according to which shepherd, plowman and maid have their parts to play; the parson's words). Above all, culture includes not only the specific social forms of a given society, but the value systems which shape and are shaped by those forms, and which help us to revalue and mitigate, if not dissipate, the ills of mortality.[35] But although the two songs allude to these transfiguring possibilities—human love, communal value systems (especially religious systems)—they do not show them operating effectively. Rather, the Cuckoo mocks the married man—that is, the power of the sexual drive mocks human attempts to transfigure sex through love; and "coughing drowns the parson's saw"—the power and reality of suffering and death drown out the religious/social orthodoxies which purport to explain them.

At the conclusion of the songs the enigmatic final words of the play return us to the real world of bodily existence—of desire, pain and death—with the solution still to be found: "The words of Mercury are harsh after the songs of Apollo" (V.ii.931-2).[36] That is, after escape into the Golden World of art (the songs), the real world (the stage world surrounding the presentation of the Owl and the Cuckoo songs and, by analogy, the actual world surrounding Shakespeare's stage world) will seem harsh. But the songs contain, indeed are built upon, the materials of harsh reality: confinement to the body, therefore vulnerability to indiscriminate sexuality, labor, winter, cold winds, illness, pain, and the inexorable passage of time carrying us from springtime youth and pleasure to winter age and death. The seeming opposition of Apollo and Mercury, art and life, is therefore false, belied by the songs themselves which incorporate the worst of bodily reality and transform it through lyric loveliness into something pleasurable. They point the way for what art in general, and Shakespearean art in particular, might accomplish, although the actual accomplishment is still to seek. And they tell us that the transformations art seek have an analogue in reality, in that we must acknowledge before we can master the harsh facts of mortality, exactly as the characters within the play are enjoined to do.

Action

Clearly, the assorted literary efforts in this comedy vary widely in type and in degree of finish. But all the literary efforts aim to master those twin potentials of bodily existence, sexuality and death; and none, Shakespeare's own play included, succeed. For when we examine Shakespeare's play as a whole, we see that it does not enact a solution to the problem it poses. Instead, the action of the play within scenes, from scene to scene, and overall, simply repeats what we see in little in the various instances of wordplay, literary and non-literary. Again and again a verbal defense against mortality is erected; and again and again the defense is shattered even as it is erected, for the enemy is already within.

At the start of the play Navarre declares his intention of defeating death by converting his courtiers into a community of ascetic scholars. Navarre's "schedule" (I.i.18), his collection of articles establishing the ascetic conditions of the academy, is therefore the first of the play's verbal defenses against death—the first effort to control, through language, the importunities of the body. By swearing to obey the terms of Navarre's schedule the lords will fight their own bodily urges—for food, for sleep, for women—and in so doing will win the ultimate victory over the body, victory over death in the form of the undying fame their efforts will bring them. But no sooner is this defense erected than it is breached; for even before Berowne, the last of the lords to capitulate, agrees to the articles, the French princess is at the gates forcing Navarre to violate his own prohibition against speaking with women. Moreover, the Princess's mere entry into the park is a breaching of Navarre's enclosure at another level, for she brings with her reminders of the body and of history, the very realities Navarre's enclosure is designed to exclude.[37]

The Princess, a "maid of grace and complete majesty" (I.i.135), suggests both the life and death sides of the body. On the one hand she carries with her the potential for renewal of life, for physical renewal through children and for spiritual renewal through love. On the other hand, she also bears with her reminders of sickness, aging and death—the problem of individual mortality which continuance through children cannot solve—since she is come on behalf of her "decrepit, sick and bed-rid father" (I.i.137). Moreover, she also reminds us of the death aspect of the social body, the iron world of the history plays characterized by conflicts over money, territory, power; for she is come to negotiate about the "surrender up of Aquitaine" (I.i.136). The passage in which Navarre responds to the French requests (II.i.128 ff.) sounds unlike any other passage in *Love's Labor's Lost*. As Navarre speaks he seems to invoke the world of *Henry V*, a world of man-made legal obligation backed by military might in which all value is reducible to cash value—here, a hundred thousand pounds, which can be equated precisely to the value of a part of the French kingdom, and which represents debt incurred through past military proceedings and enforceable by human legal documents backed by implicit threat of present military action. Moreover, the language Navarre uses is not the formal, figurative rhetoric we might expect from a king negotiating with a fellow sovereign, but rather an accountant's rendering of the situation, a straightforward insistence on debt and contractual obligation in which attention is drawn over and over to the exact sum owing, "a hundred thousand crowns." Because there is nothing like this passage elsewhere in *Love's Labor's Lost*, its effect is similar, in inverse fashion, to the effect of the scene in *1 Henry IV*, in which love-making between Mortimer and Glendower's daughter is accompanied by the sweet sounds of Welsh, music, song, poetry (III.i.191 ff.). In both instances we are reminded of what is excluded elsewhere in the play: in *1 Henry IV*, the related forces of love/pleasure/magic/art/ imagination, which might partially transform the lethal world of law, money and state-imposed slaughter; and in *Love's Labor's Lost*, precisely the opposite—the death aspect of the social body, the subject of the English histories, which, except for this passage, remains outside the playing space of *Love's Labor's Lost* while a still more urgent aspect of death is confronted, the death inherent in our individual physical being.

Although the French princess and her ladies appear as intruders at the gates, the threat they represent is not extrinsic, but is inherent in the men's own nature. Just as Navarre's initial challenge to death contains its own contradiction, because the speaker is a living creature who cannot escape his own mortality, so his oath-based academy, his would-be defense against death, is doomed from its inception, because those who man the defenses exemplify the very creatureliness they wish to defy. The rest of the play simply repeats and expands upon the initial action, as one after another the men fall victim to the urges of their own bodies.

Just after Navarre realizes he must speak with the French princess, Costard enters, having been caught in the company of a woman, the same fault Navarre is about to commit in speaking to the princess. The sexual innuendos which Costard cheerfully insists on even while attempting to deny his fault suggest the deeper meaning of what Navarre is trying to avoid—implication in sexuality, and therefore in death.

In the scene which follows Costard's entrance, Armado, the man who turned Costard over to punishment, confesses that he is about to commit the same fault as Costard, for he is in love, and with the very woman Costard was taken with. In the ensuing scenes the men's defeat continues as, one after another, Navarre, Berowne, Dumaine and Longaville, following Costard and Armado, succumb to their conquerors — on one level the women, but on a deeper level, their own bodies.

Throughout the comedy, Shakespeare deliberately parallels Armado and Berowne. Armado's rueful confession of subjection to love which concludes the first act (I.ii.165 ff.) is exactly paralleled by Berowne's better-known confession at the end of the third act (II.i.175 ff.). At the end of his confession of love Armado declares his intention to "turn sonnet" (I.i.182); and at the end of *his* confession, Berowne announces his intention of embarking on a similar course of love-prompted authorship ("I will love, write, sigh, pray, sue, groan," III.i.206). The paralleling of the two men continues in the fourth act in the mix-up of the letters intended for their respective mistresses. This paralleling is entertaining, but it also makes a point. Berowne is as superior to Armado in easy intelligence, polish, elegance, as his gently-born mistress is to Jaquenetta, Armado's beloved. But on another level the differences are meaningless. The sexual drive, a great leveler (the other great leveler is death), works through individuals causing them to select one person rather than another as the object of their affections. But just as the passion driving the fantastic Armado, the elegant Berowne, and the clownish Costard is precisely the same, so for the purposes of nature there is no essential difference between Jaquenetta the country wench, the various noble mistresses, and royalty herself in the person of the French princess. At this level the various lovers and their mistresses are all indistinguishable, and all subject to the common enemy, not the women, but the body to which men and women, royalty, nobles and commoners, alike are bound, and which dooms Navarre's oath-based academy and all merely verbal defenses to defeat. But Shakespeare is concerned to indicate not merely the likeness, but also a crucial difference, between the two men; for Armado points the way toward a solution to the problem of our common animal nature (thus, toward a solution to death). Through the power of his imagination (inseparable from his language)

Armado, in Don Quixote-like fashion, creates his beloved—transforms a dairymaid into a Dulcinea-like mistress worthy of a soldier's and courtier's admiration. The point is that love is a creative achievement on the part of the lover; and to achieve love, one must go beyond the satiric reductionism of a Berowne, which can expose, but cannot transfigure, mortal reality.[38] Here, as elsewhere, *Love's Labor's Lost* asks to be read in conjunction with *Midsummer Night's Dream*; and to do so casts light on Theseus' association of the lover and the poet. The lords' rude mockery of the Pageant (which contrasts sharply to Theseus' courteous reception of the mechanicals' equally inept performance) is the equivalent of Berowne's satirical posture *vis-à-vis* love. It is true that all women, whether Jaquenetta or the princess, are merely flawed mortal beings, and also true that no play, whether the Pageant of the Nine Worthies or a Shakespearean masterpiece, is more than a play—unless, that is, "imagination amend them" (*Midsummer Night's Dream*, V.i.213). For imagination, as Armado understands, is an animating force capable of transforming death-tainted animal passion into human love, and also capable of transforming a construct of words, subject to all the limitations of actual actors and theaters, into a dramatic vision faithful to, yet also transcendent of, the confines of the naturalistic world represented. Imagination, then, is a resurrection force which can bring to life both love and "living art." But to exercise this force, that which requires reanimation—death in its various guises—must first be admitted to the mind's eye, and to the dramatic equivalent of that eye, the playing space; and in *Love's Labor's Lost* this does not happen until the play's conclusion.

Act Four is the turning point of the play's action.[39] The first scene of this act, the hunting scene, with its abundance of sexually explicit puns and of jests connecting sexuality and death, reminds us of what remains to be mastered. In the second scene we see the pedants, fools in love with language, insisting on the superiority of words. These fools are still more foolish than the foolish lovers, for by refusing to acknowledge the claims of the body they lose the opportunity for even the partial immortality conferred through love and children. These scenes prepare us for the third, climactic scene, the sonnet-reading scene, in which the king and his lords acknowledge that they are caught—by one another, but more importantly, by the trap of their own bodies, the sexuality which decrees that they must fall to their fair conquerors. Caught in this trap, the hunted become the hunters, as all vow to mount an assault upon their respective mistresses in language which combines military metaphor with sexual innuendo: "Advance your standards and upon them lords" (IV.i.366). As the lords vow to win their ladies, they are turning from evasion to embracing of the body. This assent to the power of the body is matched by a change in their wooing technique, as they turn from sonnets, composed of words alone, to drama (the masque).

The first scene of Act Five is a kind of a verbal interlude which recapitulates the play's action. Dull stands silently and stolidly by as Nathaniel, Holofernes, Armado, Moth and Costard, each of whom exhibits his characteristic way of using language, trade flights of linguistic fancy, jests and puns, many based on treating words and even letters as if they were actual things. Thanks especially to Moth and Costard, this extravaganza of language is shot through with references to sexuality, especially illicit sexuality, the bodily reality which here as throughout the comedy pushes hard against the pedants' screen of language.

If the first scene of Act Five consists almost wholly of wordplay, the second scene shifts back to the dramatic mode; for in addition to advancing the play's love action it is centered on two internal plays, the masque and the pageant, each of which attempts to enact rather than merely to assert mastery over the body. At the end of Act Four, the lords acknowledged defeat by their own sexuality, one aspect of bodily being; but that other aspect of bodily being, death, was still not admitted openly into the playing space. In this scene, the final scene of the play, death bursts openly and shockingly onto the stage, shattering the last of the verbal enclosures—first the pageant, the play within the play; and finally Shakespeare's own play which, like the pageant, is broken off by, and left open to, the reality of death.

Love's Labor's Lost: *Setting the Dramatic Task* 141

The scene opens with death pressing hard for admittance, as the ladies discuss the lords' love offerings in banter filled with sexual allusions. The ladies also present love as actually lethal, for Katharine's sister has died of it. After this reference more banter follows in which love is linked to disease, thus reinforcing our sense of love as potentially lethal. The lords then present their masque, and later re-enter to trade repartee with their mistresses, repartee which stresses both the deeply sexual basis of love, and death. At the height of the verbal duel between the lords and the ladies Costard enters, asking to present the pageant. During the presentation of the pageant the atmosphere of festivity shifts to a mood of feverish, even frantic, revelry, as the lords interrupt the pageant with ever-harsher mocks, forcing the actors one after another off the stage. References to death gather thick and fast in this section, and the total effect is of a death's head at a feast, an effect reinforced by Berowne's reference to "a death's face in a ring" (V.i.612). Berowne's reference not only introduces an image of an actual death's head, but also links sexuality and death especially strongly, for a death's-head ring was worn by Elizabethan prostitutes. This especially strong linking of death and tainted sexuality, and the introduction of explicit death imagery, reflects the fact that at this point the characters have openly embraced women and the sexual life; but to do so is also to embrace death, and this fact, not yet acknowledged, is pressing hard for admittance. The men's wild and whirling words, their harshly discourteous jests, their almost feverish "merriment," reflect a heightened verbal resistance to death's ever-more insistent presence. And in fact the pageant, a little verbal enclosure within the greater verbal enclosure of Shakespeare's play, is not only repeatedly disrupted by the lords' ever-ruder mocks, but is finally broken off altogether—first, by sexuality (the announcement of Jaquenetta's pregnancy); and then by the intrusion of death itself in the person of Marcade, who "interrupt'st our merriment" with the announcement of the death of the king of France. The entrance of Marcade marks the final breaching of Navarre's verbal enclosure, this time by death itself, the ultimate thing we are "forbid to know" (I.i.60). For the first time in the play death is confronted directly rather than through a barrage of language which partly conceals, partly reveals the unpalatable fact.[40] The pageant, a play within a play, is an analogue of the surrounding play, Shakespeare's own comedy; and the court assembled to watch the play is an analogue of the audience watching Shakespeare's play. Marcade's announcement breaks off both the little play and Shakespeare's play world as first the lords and ladies, then we, the audience, are sent out into the world outside the playing space to encounter the darker potentials of mortal existence: "frosts and fasts, hard lodging and thin weeds" (V.ii.802), "mourning" (V.ii.811), illness, "agony" (V.ii.858), and finally death itself, inherent in the time-bound world which the lords will be forced to experience as they wait for the "annual reckoning" to come round (V.ii.799). This reckoning could, in the short run, replace hardship and suffering with pleasure and joy, when the postponed marriages finally take place; but it will also, in the long run, force the lords to the ultimate reckoning, the death which is the debt we owe to nature. The songs of the Owl and the Cuckoo recapitulate these realities for the audiences on-stage and off-stage. But here, the play concludes. The movement of the play therefore is not, contrary to virtually all critical opinion, from problem to resolution.[41] We begin as we end, with death and the need to master it. But at the end we understand what is only implicit at the start: that to master mortality, we must first confront it fully; and that, paradoxically, any "solution" to death must begin with the acknowledgment that death cannot in fact be escaped. The comedy is set in Navarre's Arcadian park, a postlapsarian garden; but unlike the Adamic story, what is enacted is the fall into knowledge of death, not the fall into death itself, for we are already there.

Conclusion

The conclusion of this early comedy[42] articulates a task central to Shakespeare's work and to our own lives as well: the need fully to confront our own mortality and still affirm. In one sense virtually all Shakespearean drama takes place in the gap

Love's Labor's Lost: *Setting the Dramatic Task*   143

between the actual ending of *Love's Labor's Lost* and the promised ending, the happy ending we—and the characters— desire. This ending—love and marriage, the victory of pleasure and new life over suffering and death (the resurrection pattern)—is postponed. It will take place, if at all, only outside the play world: in the year that is to come round, or perhaps, in the real world outside the play, the "hospital" where human beings suffer and die. Berowne is enjoined to go out into this world and to "move wild laughter in the throat of death"—to jest with those who are suffering and dying (potentially, and ultimately, all of us), and see if he can force them to rejoice. This is precisely the task Shakespearean drama as a whole undertakes: to confront suffering and death ever more directly, assimilating them into a whole the characters—and we —can in some sense acknowledge as positive. Berowne raises the question of whether the task can in fact be carried out: "It cannot be, it is impossible./ Mirth cannot move a soul in agony" (V.ii.857-8). It remains for us to decide to what extent, and in what way, Shakespearean drama succeeds in this most difficult yet most emotionally central of human tasks.

Notes

1 This and all subsequent quotations from the play are taken from the Signet paperback edition of *Love's Labor's Lost*, ed. John Arthos, The Signet Classic Shakespeare, ed. Sylvan Barnet (N.Y. and Toronto: The New American Library, 1965).

2 For human beings, time stands still only in death; and Shakespeare uses the word in this sense elsewhere, as in "still as the grave" (*Othello*, V.ii.94); "this counselor [the dead Polonius]/ Is now most still, most secret, and most grave" (*Hamlet*, III. v.214-125); "Dost thou lie still?" (referring to the dead Iras, *Anthony and Cleopatra*, V.ii.296).

3 Sidney, for example, refers to this debate in his allusion to "the philosophers . . . wrangling . . . whether the contemplative or the active life do excel" (Sir Philip Sidney, "The Defense of Poesy," in *Sir Philip Sidney: Selected Prose and Poetry*, ed. Robert Kimbrough (N.Y.: Holt, Rinehart & Winston, Inc., 1969), p. 125.

The Elizabethan ideal was of course to sacrifice neither, as shown in Sidney's own life which would fit Ophelia's description of Hamlet—courtier, soldier, scholar (*Hamlet*, III.i.154).

4 Cf. Prospero in *The Tempest*, who neglects his princely duties in favor of his studies, with disastrous results.

5 However differently they may interpret the play, virtually all readers agree that words are somehow central to this comedy. Anne Barton, for example, in "Shakespeare and the Limits of Language," *Shak. Survey*, 24 (1971), 19-30, believes (as her title suggests) that the play is concerned to show the limits of language, and that it "ends with the defeat of the word" (p. 23). Nevertheless, she remarks that "*Love's Labour's Lost* stands out among the comedies as a play overtly about language, filled with verbal games, with parody and word patterns, firing off its linguistic rockets in all directions" (p. 23). William Carroll believes that the play does not illustrate the defeat of language, but rather creates a larger, synthesizing viewpoint composed of the play's many seeming oppositions. But he, too, remarks that "The life of *Love's Labour's Lost* centers, beyond all else, in its language, in crackling exchanges of wit and in mind-stretching wordplay that must be heard to be believed" [*The Great Feast of Language in* Love's Labor's Lost, (Princeton, N.J.: Princeton U. Press, 1976), p.8]. And even Frances Yates, who is concerned chiefly with identifying possible topical allusions, comments on the linguistic extravagances in the play: "the brags and high-flown hyperbole of Armado, the proverbs, synonyms, strange words, Latin and foreign tags

which fall from the lips of Holofernes" [*A Study of Love's Labor's Lost* (1936); rpt. Folcraft, Pa.: Folcraft Library Editions, 1973), p. 18].

6 Louis Adrian Montrose notes the often frantic quality of the characters' verbal play, and even links this quality with the threat of sexuality and death: "The spell of the playwright's magic circle is weakened from within before it succumbs to the pressure of an inexorable outer reality. It is threatened from the play's beginning, and is only maintained by an anxious and at times frantic group effort. The play's texture is filled with ominous prolepses and disturbing images, knit together by an undercurrent of lust and obscenity and the symbolism of the hunt. Berowne and his comrades playfully draw their imagery of love and courtship from disease . . . . The obsessive series of these images hints continually at the world of pain and death from which the courtiers try to insulate themselves in living art," *"Curious-Knotted Garden": the Form, Themes, and Contexts of Shakespeare's* Love's Labour's Lost, Salzburg Studies in English Literature, Elizabethan & Renaissance Studies, 56, ed. James Hogg (Salzburg, Austria: Institut für Englische Sprache und Literatur, Universitat Salzburg, 1977), p. 154.

7 *Shak. Survey*, 22 (1969), p. 69.

8 Cf. Calderwood, *Shakespeare and the Denial of Death*, who comments on "the death-threatening aspect not merely of wantonness but of all sexuality..." (p. 46), and also notes the association of women with death in Shakespeare's work: "...the mere presence of a woman reminds a man that despite his symbolic self-aggrandizement he is corporeally no different from other dying animals" (p. 54). See Chapter IV (pp. 46-57), "Death, Sex and the Body."

9 The meaning of "sore" is given in a note in the Signet edition of *Love's Labor's Lost*, ed. John Arthos. See also OED.

10 The meaning of "pricket" is given in a note in the Signet edition of *Love's Labor's Lost*, ed. John Arthos.

11 The meaning of *"pia mater,"* a "membrane enclosing the brain," is given in a note in the Signet edition, ed. John Arthos.

12 Holofernes' "fertility" begets poetry—the absurd epitaph; and bodily fertility begets flesh-and-blood children. But children will die, and a better epitaph might survive to immortalize both its subject and its maker. The question of the limits and powers of art remains to be explored.

13 In the sonnets, Shakespeare repeatedly advocates having children as a solution to death. See, for example, Sonnets 1-13 (among others), which all, in one way or another, reflect agreement with the message expressed in Sonnet 12: "And nothing 'gainst Time's scythe can make defense,/ Save breed, to brave him when he takes thee hence."

14 *Winter's Tale*, IV.iv.88. Many of the issues dealt with in this early play are dealt with more fully and explicitly in *Winter's Tale*.

15 For this reason (among others) it would be a mistake to identify Shakespeare's viewpoint with Berowne's, as certain critics do. Here as elsewhere, it is no one character, but rather the whole action of the play, which carries the playwright's meanings (that action being understood in the inclusive sense described above).

16 At the end of the play what Berowne and the audience must learn is summarized in the songs of the Owl and the Cuckoo; and at the end of Shakespeare's career the same understanding is recapitulated, with greater depth and fullness, in *The Winter's Tale*.

17 This meaning of "qualm" is given in a note in the Signet edition, ed. John Arthos.

18 As Montrose points out, "references to plague . . . . presumably had a more visceral effect on Elizabethan audiences than they do on us" (*"Curious-Knotted Garden,"* Ch. 7, n. 1, p. 216).

19 Eric Partridge, *Shakespeare's Bawdy* (1948; rev. N.Y.: E.P. Dalton & Co., Inc., 1969), calls this "one of the most greasy passages in the whole of Shakespeare" (p. 45).

20 The best guide to Shakespeare's conception of art is of course the plays themselves. As Montrose points out, "Shakespeare's conception of the nature and function of his art is embodied in that art—not merely in some explicit and generalized way but through the manipulation of particular techniques and devices: internalization of poets and other artists, and of specific artifacts (books, paintings, statues) within the fictions; implanting of plays-within-plays to generate complex mirrorings of action and themes; presentation, in the context of dramatic speech, of explicit discussions about art and nature, fantasy and reason; inclusion of masques, lyrics, sonnets to create generic contrasts; pervasive and critical treatment of language—the medium of both playwright and characters—as thematic in itself" (*"Curious-Knotted Garden,"* p. 6.).

21 W.B. Yeats, "Sailing to Byzantium," in the *Collected Poems of W.B. Yeats* (N.Y.: Macmillan Company, 1956).

22 Compare "cormorant devouring time" (I.i.4), Navarre's conflation of time and death. The association of the grave with the jaws of death, swallowing up its prey, is also traditional.

23 See, for example, *Tempest*, I.ii.399; III.iii.100; V.i.151-2.

24 M.M. Mahood, *Shakespeare's Wordplay* (1957; rpt. London: Metheun & Co., 1965), refers to "The argument of sixteenth-century astronomers that no new star could be discovered because there would be no name to call it by . . ." (p. 170). Whether or not Shakespeare was familiar with

this argument, he is certainly aware of—and anxious to reject—the conception of language which underlies such an argument.

25 These definitions are taken from entries under "art" in the *OED*.

26 Prospero himself connects magic art with resurrection when he declares, "graves at my command/ Have waked their sleepers, oped, and let 'em forth/ By my so potent art" (V.i.48-50).

Alvin B. Kernan, *The Playwright as Magician: Shakespeare's Image of the Poet in the English Public Theater* (New Haven & London: Yale U. Press, 1979), discusses *The Tempest* as Shakespeare's fullest exploration of the limits and powers of the playwright's art (see specially chapter 7). Kernan's primary concern is with the relationship between an ideal theater, "some pure theater of the imagination, free of the limitations of real actors, stages, and audiences" (p. 135), and conditions in the actual Elizabethan public theater.

27 For a discussion of *Love's Labor's Lost* which treats the limits and powers of Shakespeare's art in relation to death, see Calderwood, *Shakespeare and the Denial of Death*, especially Chapter XV, "Immortalizing Art," pp. 169-181.

28 The meaning of "sore" is given in a note in the Signet edition, ed. John Arthos.

29 The meaning of "sorel" is given in a note in the Signet edition, ed. John Arthos.

30 This idea, still only implicit in this early comedy, is given full expression in (among other places) Shakespeare's late work *The Winter's Tale*, in the statue of Hermione sixteen years more wrinkled than when Leontes last saw her. This moving statue is both literal example and ultimate emblem of "living art." Compare also the many sonnets in which the feeling of love is inseparable from grief at the beloved's mortality, an emotion caught in the following lines from sonnet 64: "This thought [that the beloved will die] is as a death, which cannot choose/ But weep to have that which it fears to lose."

31 Cf. Calderwood, *Shakespeare and the Denial of Death*, who links the embodied nature of drama with death: "Theater is implicit with death because it is full of life, because it features not merely voices chattering, intoning, and screeching but also bodies dancing, drooping, embracing, battling, and of course dying. Indeed dying in fact as well as fiction, Olivier proceeding at life's slower pace while Hamlet makes pace toward his stage grave" (p 180).

32 Cf. Rosalind's view of love in *As You Like It*. Touchstone stresses the sexual quality of love, Orlando espouses the familiar sonnet view, and Rosalind integrates the two.

33 Cf. Lysander's remark on Pyramus' "death" in the play-within-a-play in *Midsummer Night's Dream*: "he is dead, he is nothing" (V.i.307-8).

34 However differently they interpret the songs and the play as a whole, most readers are in agreement that the songs are integrally related to the play's meanings. See, for example, Cyrus Hoy, "*Love's Labour's Lost* and the Nature of Comedy," *Shak. Q.*, 13 (1962), 31-40; Catherine M. McLay, "The Dialogues of Spring and Winter: A Key to the Unity of *Love's Labour's Lost*," *Shak. Q.*, 18 (1967), 119-127; S.K. Heninger, Jr., "The Pattern of *Love's Labour's Lost*," *Shak. Studies*, 7 (1974), 25-53; Robert G. Hunter, "The Function of the Songs at the End of *Love's Labour's Lost*," *Shak. Studies*, 7 (1974), 55-64; William C. Carroll, the *Great Feast of Language* in Love's Labor's Lost (Princeton, N.J.: Princeton U. Press, 1976); Louis Adrian Montrose, "*Curious-Knotted Garden": The Forms, Themes and Contexts of Shakespeare's* Love's Labour's Lost (Salzburg, Austria: Institut für Englische Sprache und Literatur, Universität Salzburg, 1977). These authors offer detailed readings of the two songs.

35 "Believing, with Max Weber, that man is an animal suspended in webs of significance he himself has spun, I take culture to be those webs, and the analysis of it to be therefore not an experimental science in search of law but an interpretive one in search of meaning," Clifford Geertz, *The Interpretation of Cultures* (N.Y.: Basic Books, Inc., 1973), p. 4. Geertz's understanding of culture as a network of symbolic actions in which meaning and action are inseparable seems especially applicable to Shakespearean drama as well as to the social world that drama reflects; and it offers a theoretical basis for understanding the senses in which, and way in which, a Shakespearean play reflects the actual world. For a fuller description of Geertz's theory of culture see chapter one of *Interpretation*.

36 The speaker of these lines is not given in the 1598 quarto of *Love's Labor's Lost*, but the Folio gives him as "Brag" (i.e., "Armado," who appears sometimes as "Armado," sometimes as "Brag").

There is considerable critical disagreement on how to interpret these lines, and many critics attempt to identify the "words of Mercury" and the "words of Apollo" with one or the other of the songs.

37 Cf. Bobbyann Roesen [Anne Barton], "Love's Labour's Lost," *Shak. Q.*, 4 (1953), 411-26, who comments, "The Princess and her little retinue represent the first penetration of the park by the normal world beyond, a world composed of different and colder elements than the fairy-tale environment within. Through them, in some sense, the voice of Reality speaks . . ." (p. 415).

38 Cf. Jacques in *As You Like It*, who embodies the satirical point of view.

39 Montrose, "*Curious-Knotted Garden*," points out that "by line count, the numerical center of the play is the sonnet scene in the early part of IV.iii". (p. 167).

Love's Labor's Lost: Setting the Dramatic Task   149

40 Bobbyann Roesen [Anne Barton], whose "Love's Labour's Lost" *Shak. Q.*, 4 (1953), 411-426, offers the best overall description of the comedy's feeling-tone and effect, points out that the play begins with death and that death shatters Navarre's world at the close; but she does not see that the question of avoiding death is the play's central question from start to finish, in part because she thinks of death in contrast to, rather than as an inseparable part of, "the gentler forces of life" (p. 420).

41 Although critics vary as to what problem *Love's Labor's Lost* addresses — therefore, as to what resolution is achieved — virtually all see the play as concluding with some kind of resolution. One exception to this view is James L. Calderwood, *Shakespearean Metadrama: the Argument of the Play in* Titus Andronicus, Love's Labour's Lost, Romeo and Juliet, A Midsummer's Night Dream, *and* Richard II (Minneapolis, Minn.: U. of Minnesota Press, 1971), who sees the ending as pointing toward a resolution achieved only elsewhere: "through the raising and purging of linguistic delight, he [the playwright] has perhaps come to realize how language in the service of the comic vision can create an image of social communion shared not only by the characters within but by the audience without as well. That achievement is not to be found here, but it, like the marriages, stands in the offing" (p. 332).

42 There is scholarly disagreement on the dating of *Love's Labor's Lost*, which in any case seems to have been reworked at different periods, to greater or lesser degree; and proposed dates vary from the late 1580's to as late as 1595. Nevertheless, scholars agree that the play belongs with Shakespeare's earlier, if not with his very earliest, work.

Chapter Four

Romeo and Juliet: Death Confronted

In medieval drama, death is overcome through union with the immortality-granting Corpus Christi and its institutional embodiment, the Catholic Church. Shakespearean history approaches death through a modification of the earlier strategy. In Shakespeare's second history tetralogy, which traces the death and resurrection of the English nation state, death is overcome to the extent that the individual is able to identify with the communal body England, for England's continuance is then his own continuance. In *Henry V* identification between the individual and the state is pushed as far as it can go; and the extremity of the identification reveals its limits as a means of mastering death. For by its very insistence on the assumption of corporate identity the play arouses in the audience a sense (greater or lesser according to the individual) of the irreducible difference between any communal body and his own individual being, mental and physical. And as the play repeatedly makes clear, the body politic, unlike its model and predecessor the Corpus Christi, can inflict individual death but cannot confer individual life. As a literary/psychological strategy for overcoming individual death, then, the strategy of Shakespearean history—identification with the body politic—is radically flawed.

Love's Labor's Lost insists upon the reality of individual mortality, and tells us that we must confront this reality before we can master it; and Shakespearean comedy and tragedy both take, as their starting point, the fact of individual death. The strategy of Shakespearean comedy, however, is more akin to that of Shakespearean history, for it depends, at the conclusion, on reintegration with a communal body. In the course of a Shakespearean comedy death in some form threatens the protagonists.[1] As the action unfolds, the lovers move apart from the communal body; but the threat of death is successfully overcome, and the protagonists are incorporated back into the communal body, united with one another and with their society.[2] The result is always a completion of the resurrection pattern, a victory for individual pleasure and life over suffering and death, with a promise of race renewal in the offspring to come. But as the comedies themselves repeatedly remind us, the victory is both temporary and partial. For the comic solution is brought about only by stopping the dramatic action, as, in time, the lovers will age and die. To individuals, therefore, the comic solution—marriage and children—is only partially satisfactory; and as with the history plays, the success of the strategy depends upon the necessarily limited extent to which individuals can identify with the community, finding immortality through children and through the continuance of the group: the family, the nation, the human race.

Comedy acknowledges individual death; but tragedy focuses on that fact and takes us to the moment of death, the moment comedy always deflects and delays. The enactment of death necessitates a new dramatic strategy, one built on full inclusion (rather than deflection) of the death it seeks to master. Any given tragic strategy therefore constitutes, implicitly, a rejection of the comic strategy. But in *Romeo and Juliet*, an early tragedy (only *Titus Andronicus* is earlier), that rejection is actually dramatized within the play.

Many commentators (although differing in their interpretation of the fact) have noticed the links between this play and Shakespearean comedy, and have discussed the way in which *Romeo and Juliet* is in some sense an aborted comedy.[3] Repeatedly the play evokes the possibility that a comic resolution will be enacted—the delay of the protagonists' deaths to a time and space beyond the play's action; and the union of the lovers with one another and with the community, a union which can offer communal, and partial individual, renewal through children. Moreover, the other major characters in the play all urge some version of this solution on the protagonists, and the enactment of such a solution in fact remains possible until the play's penultimate moments. But the play evokes the comic solution only to expose its limits *vis-à-vis* individual life. The exposure of those limits prepares us to accept another solution, one built on the embrace, rather than the deflection, of the inescapable death taint in mortal life. In this respect (as in others), *Romeo and Juliet* exposes and epitomizes an essential of Shakespearean tragedy generally.[4]

Death happens to individuals, and the fact of death is not separable from the fact of individuality. We all begin life in the womb, as part of the mother's body. But the necessary precondition of life is separation from that body, birth and weaning. We also begin life as part of a social body—on the smaller scale, as members of a family; on the larger scale, as members of a city-state, a dukedom, a nation. And the differentiation of one's self from that social body—the development of an individual personality and value system—repeats, on a psychological level, the physical individuation of birth and weaning. The analogy between physical birth and the birth of personality is especially close in Shakespeare's work because for him the social body headed by a male governor—a father, a duke, a king—is an abstract male version of the maternal body (Shakespeare's imagining of the community as such a body is evident throughout his work, for example, in *Hamlet*, in the reference to "those many many bodies . . . / That live and feed upon your majesty," III.iii.9-10). But these acts of separation—birth and the birth of personality—while necessary precursors of life, are also the source of death. We are born into a physical body which makes us always vulnerable to death, and ensures eventual death ("Well, we were born to die," *Romeo and Juliet*, III.iv.4).[5] Thus birth is the first step of the journey to the grave, and every moment of living only brings us that much closer to aging and dying (when the Nurse asks where to find the young Romeo, Romeo replies, "the young Romeo will be older when you have found him than he was when you sought him," II.iv.125, 126-128). And the birth of personality is also associated with death. A sense of identity with the community allows us to find immortality in the ongoing life of the community (the solution propounded by both history and comedy). But the sharper our sense of individual separateness, the more we experience our own mortality; and in fact it is the unique self which dies. That which we share with our fellow mortals lives on in them, reborn with each new life; but the degree to which we are unique, irreplaceable individuals is the degree to which we finally, irremediably, die. The Nurse—an embodiment of the comic viewpoint—gives focus to the problem of individuation and its relation to death. To the Nurse, individuals are replaceable because they are interchangeable according to their stages and positions in life. Thus Juliet, whom she has nursed, has taken the place of her dead daughter Susan—two girl children, each of the same age (I.iii.16 ff.)—and she advises Juliet to adopt the same course of action. Romeo banished is as good as Romeo dead, and Juliet should substitute Paris for Romeo, one handsome, eligible young man for another (III.v.214 ff.). But Romeo and Juliet not only accept, they insist upon, one another's irreplaceability—which is to say, they accept and embrace the reality of death; and that acceptance is both validated and made literal in the play's closing moments by the lovers' enacted willingness to die.[6] Their death is therefore synonymous, literally and figuratively, with ultimate separation from the communal body. But the community itself has a death aspect, which the play stresses from start to finish; and therefore the lovers' separation from the communal body is death, but also, a form of death-transcendence. For in choosing physical death, they overcome the death aspect at the heart of the community itself, the very thing comedy, which depends for mastery over death on group continuance, cannot fully confront.[7]

The basic communal body in *Romeo and Juliet*—the social body which is both life-sustaining and death-dealing—is not a kingdom, nor a court, nor a city-state (although the play is set in Verona), but rather the family, the basic unit of which those other, more abstract communal bodies are composed. The family has a biological and also a social existence, each of which is a source of both life and of death: the maternal and paternal bodies ("From forth the fatal loins of those two foes / A pair of star-crossed lovers take their lives," Prologue, 5-6); and a socially constructed existence—Italian, Veronese, rich or poor, upper or lower class—everything symbolized by the name "Montague" or "Capulet," as opposed to the corporeal reality the name designates ("What's Montague? It is nor hand, nor foot,/ Nor arm, nor face," II.ii.40-41). The central action of the play is the emergence, from the parental/ communal body, of the two lovers who find, in that emergence, both death and death-transcendence.

As is appropriate to a play where the family is the basic social unit, *Romeo and Juliet* is the most domestic of the tragedies. It is true (as has often been remarked) that all Shakespearean tragedy is involved to greater or lesser degree with family bonds. However, in other tragedies we are made aware of the public standing of the protagonists (Hamlet is a son and a prince; Lear a father and a king; Macbeth a husband and a king; Julius Caesar a ruler of Rome; Antony and Cleopatra rulers of half the world; and Othello is a great general, linked with the defense of the Venetian commonwealth, as Titus Andronicus and Coriolanus are with that of Rome.)[8] But in *Romeo and Juliet* we feel that we are looking into the interior of a bourgeois Stratford household.[9] This effect is created by a number of vignettes depicting domestic life in the Capulet household. These include the Nurse's maternal recalling of an anecdote from Juliet's childhood (I.iii.16 ff.); the Capulet's interchanges, which reflect their longstanding marriage, whether Lady Capulet is deflating her husband by suggesting he call for a crutch rather than a sword (I.i.79), or supporting his self-image as a gay dog ("Ay, you have been a mousehunt in your time;/ But I will watch you from such watching now," IV.iv.11-12); the servants exchanging commands, requests, complaints as they bustle about the household business ("Save me a piece of marchpane," I.v.9); "Where's Potpan, that he helps not to take away? He shift a trencher! He scrape a trencher!" I.v.1-3); the exchanges between Juliet and the Nurse, which reflect an affectionate intimacy rooted in childhood bonds; the preparation for the festivities (the masque and the wedding) which Capulet, the "cot-quean," personally supervises, drawing up guest lists, shopping lists, menus; and other brief looks into kitchen and hall where servants and masters scurry about cooking, moving furniture, bantering, bickering and getting in one another's way.[10] Together, these glimpses into a domestic interior depict the quotidian reality which forms the background of all existence: the stream of domestic life, spilling over through a network of friendship and kinship to form the fabric of society. For in this play, public life is clearly an extension of private life. Indoors and out, from highest to lowest, friends, servants and blood relations all identify themselves with one or another of the households, their alliances and feuds reflecting the family alliances and feuds. Romeo and Juliet represent the only exception to this assumption of familial identity, for though they are inextricably involved with their respective families, they also insist upon a being that transcends that familial identity. But to understand the meaning of their deviance, we must examine that which they deviate from—the society (the family) as portrayed in this play. The key point in Shakespeare's presentation of the family is that the family, the source of life, is also a source of death; and that the protagonists are inextricably involved in this life-giving and death-dealing social unit.

The life/death nature of the family is made clear from the start. The play opens with the words "Two households" (Prologue, 1), naming first not the lovers, but the parental/communal bodies from which the lovers emerge; and those bodies are immediately described as a source of the lovers' lives, but also, of their deaths. "From forth the fatal loins of those two foes / A pair of star-crossed lovers take their life" (Prologue, 4-5). The loins are of course fatal in the special sense of the feud, for the feud threatens the lovers with physical death, and also with psychological death, the death of individuality entailed in forced capitulation to a group vision or will. But they are also fatal simply in the sense that all parents, themselves mortal, bequeath to their children mortal bodies, and so bequeath death as well as life (as the Friar points out, IV.v.69, the Capulets' "part" in Juliet is the perishable flesh, which they cannot "keep from death"). Thus the play's opening lines describe its central situation: the family, origin and ground of individual physical and social being, is a source of life, but also, of death. Because this is so, either incorporation with, or separation from, this life/death communal body involves a form of death, but also, as the play demonstrates, of death-transcendence. The inescapable death taint in mortal life is fully confronted in this as in other Shakespearean tragedies; and that very reality becomes the basis for such transcendence of death as the play affords. To illustrate this I will first discuss the characters who compose the parental/communal body. I will then discuss the lovers, for their actions take on significance only in relation to the communal body they arise from and leave behind.[11]

The Communal Body

A central group of characters in the play are parents, including biological parents—the Capulets and Montagues—and also those who play a parental role—the Friar, Romeo and Juliet's "ghostly father", and the Nurse, Juliet's foster mother (the biological parents in the play are actually of lesser importance than the Friar and the Nurse). Like the familial body they help compose, all of these characters are presented as both life-giving and death-dealing.

Of the two sets of biological parents, the Capulets have the larger part. The Friar describes the three components of a human being—"birth," "heaven," and "earth" (III.iii.120), by which he means family origin, soul, and body; and the Capulets have bestowed on their child Juliet two of these three components, "birth" and "earth." But as the Friar also points out, when the Capulets discover the supposedly dead Juliet, "Your part in her you could not keep from death" (IV.v.69). For the parental "part" in Juliet proves to be precisely the elements which cannot avert but which actually lead to, her death: her family identity ("birth") which prevents open acknowledgement of her marriage; and her fleshly self ("earth"), the part which decrees that sooner or later, she must die. Moreover, Capulet and Lady Capulet's actions contribute directly to Juliet's death. By insisting that she marry Paris, and that she do so almost immediately, they push the desperate Juliet into her ultimately fatal course of action. And when insisting that she marry Paris, they treat her with callousness, even cruelty. Capulet rails at her with shocking violence: "An you be mine, I'll give you to my friend./ An you be not, hang, beg, starve, die in the streets" (III.v.193-4).[12] Lady Capulet is little better, for after Capulet storms out, and Juliet pleads with her mother to delay the wedding, her mother coldly repulses Juliet: "Talk not to me, for I'll not speak a word./ Do as thou wilt, for I have done with thee" (III.v.204-5). And carried away by anger, both parents, in scolding and pressuring Juliet, wish her dead. Capulet declares that even this one surviving child is too much, not a blessing, but "a curse" (III.v.165-68); and Lady Capulet exclaims, "I would the fool were married to her grave" (III.v.141). The parental wishes seem horribly and ironically to come true at the end of the play when, partly due to the parents' behavior, Capulet does lose his only remaining child, and Juliet is "married to her grave." Thus the progenitors of Juliet's life are associated with, and also actual causes of, her death, a fact which perfectly expresses the simultaneously life-giving and death-dealing nature of the family.

The Montagues have smaller parts than do the Capulets, but they play the same role. They appear only three times in the play, in each case at a moment of potential or actual death associated with the feud. They initially appear in I.i., during the first feud-related brawl, a brawl which Montague attempts to join (78 ff.). They appear next after the play's first deaths, the duelling deaths of Tybalt and Mercutio. And finally, Montague appears in V.iii (his wife has died of grief) after the discovery of the final deaths, the deaths of Paris, Romeo and Juliet. At each of the Montagues' appearances, what is stressed is their implication in both life and death. As parents they have given their offspring life, but as perpetuators of the feud they are contributors to their offsprings' deaths. Thus, both the Montagues and the Capulets play the same role, each helping to define the nature of the familial body: parents, who confer on their children physical and social existence (bodily life and familial identity), each of which is a source of life, but also, of death.

The Nurse is a foster mother to Juliet. Although not Juliet's biological mother, she represents the natural mother-child bond, whereas Lady Capulet represents parental authority as construed by society. The Nurse offers affection and bodily nourishment; Lady Capulet commands respect and obedience. Juliet's first words to her mother reflect the formal, respectful tone which characterizes their interchanges throughout: "Madam, I am here. What is your will?" (I.iii.5-6). The Nurse, in contrast, uses endearments—"lamb," "ladybird," (I.iii.3)— and in her first long speech she recounts anecdotes from Juliet's childhood, of the sort only fond parents find amusing.

Lady Capulet is concerned to promote a good match for Juliet, ensuring her an advantageous social position; and this is certainly an important part of parental care as the society Juliet lives in construes it. But the ease, affection, emotional intimacy of a natural (as opposed to a culturally construed) parent-child relationship exists only between Juliet and the Nurse. The fact that Shakespeare assigns different qualities to the Nurse and the mother is not merely a reflection of their differing social positions, for in other plays Shakespeare assigns natural maternal tenderness to women of high as well as low degree. In *Hamlet*, for example, Gertrude is conceived of as both Queen and mother, as when, in the midst of the duel, she wants Hamlet to mop his forehead: "Here, Hamlet, take my napkin, rub thy brows./ The queen carouses to thy fortune, Hamlet" (V.ii.290-291). And in this play Lady Montague, even in the brief glimpses we have of her, is depicted in terms of strong natural feeling, as when, after the opening brawl, she exclaims in relief that Romeo was not present to be endangered. "O, where is Romeo? Saw you him today?/ Right glad I am he was not at this fray," I.i.119-120). Thus the social and physical aspects of motherhood, which might have been combined in a single character, are split between two characters in this play, showing the more clearly what each represents, and also, the death-side of each. As discussed above, Lady Capulet, who gave Juliet physical life and also social identity, is associated with her death (by her insistence on the socially desirable marriage to Paris, and her cold response to Juliet's pleas, she drives Juliet toward an ultimately fatal course of action). And the Nurse, who has suckled Juliet, and who is even more strongly representative of the physically nurturing aspect of parenthood, is even more strongly associated with death; for she represents both the powers and the limits of the physical solution to death (that is, the comic solution: marriage, children, and the continuance of the race).

The Nurse has suckled Juliet—nourished Juliet's body with her own body—a fact stressed at the Nurse's first appearance when she recalls Juliet as an infant, and embarks on a long-winded anecdote involving Juliet's weaning (I.iii.16 ff.). And throughout the play the Nurse is strongly associated with other natural bodily functions as well, especially, with sexuality. For the Nurse is the spokesman for life at the level of its lowest common denominator: an endlessly repeated cycle of birth; nursing and weaning; growth into adulthood and sexual maturity; marriage and reproduction; and death. This is reflected in her opening speech, in which she recounts an anecdote about Juliet, as a toddler, falling. The Nurse's now-dead husband remarked, " '. . .dost thou fall upon thy face?/ Thou wilt fall backward when thou hast more wit,'" and Juliet, unconscious of the husband's sexual innuendo, stopped crying and answered "'Ay'" (I.iii.16 ff.). On a naturalistic level the tone is at once individual, and expressive of a class and type: the garrulous stream of association; the delighted repetitions of the husband's crude witticism; the choice of the kind of babyhood anecdote only doting parents find amusing. But the Nurse's anecdote is also symbolically expressive of the point of view she represents.[13] She thinks backward to Juliet's babyhood and ahead to her future (a future conceived of wholly in sexual terms) because for the Nurse the sequence of childhood—sexual maturity and parenthood—death summarizes the whole of human life. Individuals arise out of the common matrix of humanity only to repeat the race experience, reproduce, and die.

Bearing and raising children, then, is the key to sustaining and continuing life; and the Nurse's devotion to this project is reflected in her continual stream of bawdy allusions, many deliberate, equally many inadvertent. Her view of marriage, for example, is gleefully sexual. In contrast to Lady Capulet's formal, highly rhetorical description of the marital rewards—

physical, social and material—which await Juliet (I.iii.79 ff.), the Nurse gets right down to what for her is the heart of the matter, sex and children. Lady Capulet sums up her speech as follows—"So shall you share all that he doth possess,/ By having him making yourself no less"; and the Nurse responds, "No less? Nay, bigger! Women grow by men" (I.iii.95). And again and again in the play, she returns to the theme of sexual activity in marriage. For example, she announces Romeo's nuptial visit to Juliet by declaring, "I am the drudge, and toil in your delight;/ But you shall bear the burden soon at night" (II.v.76-77); and trying to wake Juliet on the morning of her marriage to Paris, she exclaims, "Sleep for a week; for the next night, I warrant,/ the County Paris hath set up his rest/ That you shall rest but little" (IV.v.5-7). And the Nurse's inadvertent references to sexuality are if anything even more frequent, as when, in Friar Lawrence's cell, she declares that Romeo is "even in my mistress' case" (III.iii.84), and follows that up with a series of probably unintended phallic puns, adjuring Romeo to "Stand up, stand up! Stand, and you be a man./ For Juliet's sake, for her sake, rise and stand!" (III.iii.88-89). Significantly, it is also the Nurse who declares "Death's the end of all" (III.iii.92), by which she means that all woes will end when we die; that nothing is hopeless until one is dead; and also that all—everyone and everything—will die. For the Nurse's view, based as it is on—indeed, revelling in— the body, includes and accepts the reality of death, countering death only with the continuance of the stream of mortal life. Thus the Nurse is on the side of life, but of physical life, and of life for the race rather than for the individual; and to individual death she counterposes a denial of individuality— in fact, the essentials of the comic solution to death. Juliet replaces the dead Susan, and Paris should replace Romeo, because for the purposes of continuing the race, one young woman or man is as good as another; and for the Nurse, grief can be assuaged by such a substitution. Thus, the Nurse offers her own formula for turning suffering and death into pleasure and new life.

The Nurse represents not only our common bodily life, but also human values at their lowest common denominator—

acknowledgement of the importance of those things which conduce directly to pleasure and survival, including sex; money (whoever has Juliet will also "have the chinks," as she tells Romeo, I.v.119); and a flexible pragmatism, the willingness to compromise and carry on with life, making whatever adjustments are necessary to survive. She is, in short, the epitome of the nourishing body, which nourishes everything but what is individual and, potentially, transcendent of the perishable body. In this the Nurse epitomizes the comic view of life. The point is that the Nurse-view is, on one level, correct; for without a dose of Nurse-values, men would not (as Romeo and Juliet do not) survive. But the Nurse's point of view leaves out that which is specifically and uniquely human; and therefore the Nurse, like comedy itself, works to avert immediate death, but can offer nothing to counteract ultimate death.

The Nurse's insufficiency—and the insufficiency of the Nurse point of view—is made clearest in III.v, where, as countless critics have noticed, the Nurse's values are most sharply tested and defined. In this scene Capulet and Lady Capulet behave toward their daughter with callousness, even cruelty—he violent, she cold. Effectually abandoned by both parents, Juliet turns to the Nurse for comfort and advice. "Comfort me, counsel me"; "What say'st thou? Hast thou not a word of joy?/ Some comfort, Nurse" (III.v.210; 212-214). And thus appealed to, the Nurse does proceed to offer comfort, but a comfort which drives Juliet to near despair, and prepares her to undertake her desperate mock-death. The Nurse is not capable of Lady Capulet's cruelty, for she is the epitome of "kindness," in both the modern sense, and in the older sense of "naturalness," that which is appropriate to us as creatures of nature. But for this very reason the Nurse is incapable of offering Juliet the comfort Juliet craves. Instead, she offers Juliet some quintessential Nurse advice—forget Romeo, and marry Paris. True, Juliet is already married to Romeo. But Romeo is banished—as good as dead—so Juliet may as well make the best of things and marry Paris. This advice, the essence of practicality, ignores the claims of love or of religion (of anything which is potentially transcendent of our merely physical being), because for the Nurse, those claims do not really exist. To carry her point she begins to praise Paris and disparage Romeo: Paris is "a lovely gentleman," compared with whom Romeo is a mere "dishclout" (III.v.220,221). A "dishclout" is a perfect Nurse object, invoking the homely world of everyday domestic life, and suggesting also a limp penis—thus, that Romeo compares unfavorably with Paris in the department which, to the Nurse, is most to the point. To this "comfort" Juliet responds, ironically, "Well, thou hast comforted me marvellous much" (III.v.232).

The Nurse's response to Juliet's plea for comfort and counsel reflects the strengths, and the limits, of the natural. Nature decrees that as "Cat will after kind" (*As You Like It*, II.ii.103), and as "the man shall have his mare" (*A Midsummer Night's Dream*, III.ii.463), so young men and women fall in love, marry and reproduce. But for this purpose any young man would suffice, and Juliet wants only Romeo, the man she has elected to love above all others. Juliet's love is both sexually based, and transcendent of the sexual drive; both a part of, and outside of, physical nature. Accordingly, Juliet seeks a remedy which recognizes the uniquely human quality of her love—love which includes but transcends the merely physical; and this the Nurse, the epitome of the natural, cannot provide.

The transcendent is, traditionally, the province of religion, and within *Romeo and Juliet*, the spokesman for traditional religious values is the Friar. The values of the natural and of the community (embodied both in the Nurse and in the two sets of biological parents) have failed Juliet—have, indeed, helped to place her in her present predicament; and now she turns in desperation to the Friar, her "ghostly father," who is both her last "parent," and a spokesman for the transcendent.

Like the Nurse, the Friar plays a parental role, more so than either the Montagues, whom we never see together with Romeo, or the Capulets, whose coldness, impatience, even cruelty towards Juliet contrast to the Friar's patience and concern. In part, the parental effect is created simply through the use of parent/child terms. Romeo and Juliet address the

Friar repeatedly as "Father" (for example, III.iii.4; IV.i.37), and he addresses Juliet repeatedly as "daughter" (for example, II.vi.22; IV.i.39; IV.i.68), and Romeo as "son" (for example "That's my good son," II.iii.47; "Be plain, good son," II.iii.55; and "my dear son," III.iii.7). Those terms are of course traditional between a priest and members of his flock, but they are so because the relationship is that of spiritual father and children; and Shakespeare deliberately emphasizes use of parental terms in the dialogue. In addition, the content of the Friar's addresses to Romeo and Juliet is parental, whether he is admonishing his "children" to control themselves, offering them advice, or devising "comfort" and "remedy" for the ills which befall them. And the tone of his interchanges with them, especially with Romeo, is often the universally recognizable tone of a parent towards an adolescent offspring. For example, at their first meeting in the play the Friar gently teases Romeo, pointing out that only yesterday the Romeo who now wishes to marry Juliet was madly in love with Rosaline.

> Holy Saint Francis! What a change is here!
> Is Rosaline, that thou didst love so dear,
> So soon forsaken?
> . . .
> Jesu Maria! What a deal of brine
> Hath washed thy sallow cheeks for Rosaline!
> How much salt water, thrown away in waste
> To season love, that of it doth not taste!
> The sun not yet thy sighs from heaven clears,
> Thy old groans ring yet in mine ancient ears.
> Lo, here upon thy cheek the stain doth sit
> Of an old tear that is not washed off yet.
> . . .
> Thou and those woes were all for Rosaline.
> And art thou changed?
>   II.iii.65-67; 69-76; 78-79

The tone is that of a parent regarding youthful excesses with fond amusement. But if the Friar, like the Nurse, functions as a parent, like the Nurse he is also something more. The Nurse speaks for the body, the Friar, for the soul (provided soul is conceived of in orthodox religious terms). The Nurse has nourished Juliet with bodily milk, the Friar offers Romeo the "milk" of philosophy ("adversity's sweet milk, philosophy/ To comfort thee, though thou art banished," III.iii.55-6). Each parent attempts to nourish the child, but each proves inadequate; for human beings are composed of both body and spirit, and while in the hereafter we may be spirit only (nothing in the play contradicts this possibility), on earth we are both at once, and both must be acknowledged and dealt with. Contrary to the Nurse's view, Juliet needs the man she loves, not merely any young man; and contrary to the Friar's view, the milk of philosophy cannot sustain a part bodily creature, who yearns for the body as well as the soul of his beloved.

The Friar, then, is a parental figure, ready to advise and aid in earthly matters such as Romeo's marriage, and also a "ghostly," or spiritual, father, a spokesman for the counsels and consolations of orthodox religion, to be applied when earthly comforts fail. And when those comforts begin to fail, the adequacy of the Friar as a spiritual father is increasingly tested, until the final testing at the conclusion, the testing against death itself.

The testing of the Friar begins in III.iii, the scene in which he tells Romeo that he is banished. Romeo responds to the news with extravagant, almost hysterical, grief; and the more the Friar tells Romeo he is lucky the sentence is exile, not death, the more strongly Romeo insists that exile—separation from Juliet—*is* death, and hell besides. The Friar offers to "comfort" Romeo for the loss with "philosophy" (55,56), to which Romeo responds, "Hang up philosophy! / Unless philosophy can make a Juliet,/ Displant a town, reverse a prince's doom" (57-59)—that is, alter actuality. The Friar then, in one of the play's funnier moments, offers to "dispute" with Romeo (63). Disputation, a form of debate calling for formal logic and reasoning, and tied to systematic philosophy and theology, is hardly appropriate to the distraught adolescent we see on stage; and Romeo promptly responds to the Friar's offer to "dispute" with him by flinging himself on the floor and refusing to get up even when a knock is heard which both think may be an officer coming to take Romeo. In the Friar's reaction to Romeo's extravagant gesture, Shakespeare captures the response of an exasperated and anxious parent to a maddeningly foolish and obstinate child.

> Hark how they knock! Who's there? Romeo, arise;
> Thou wilt be taken. — Stay awhile! — Stand up;
>   [*Knock*]
> Run to my study. — By and by! — God's will,
> What simpleness is this, — I come, I come!
>   [*Knock*]
>   III.iii.74-77

How are we meant to view Romeo and the Friar in this scene? If Romeo's loss is only temporary (as it may be at this point in the action), the extravagance of his emotion seems like adolescent excess, and the Friar appears correspondingly sensible. But when the separation is forever — loss in death — the Friar's comforts are put to the ultimate test; and they are found, in the end, inadequate.[14]

The inadequacy of the Friar is made clear only as the play proceeds. The Friar initially appears as a benign figure, allied with the Nurse. Together, they contrive to effect a marriage between Romeo and Juliet, thus attempting to bring about the comic solution to death: individual fulfillment and pleasure in married love; physical renewal through children; and social renewal, the union of the lovers with a reformed society, a society whose death aspect is controlled and bent to the service of life (this is symbolized by the potential of the marriage to resolve the feud, for, as the Friar points out, the "alliance may so happy prove/ To turn your households' rancor to pure love," II.iv.91-92). But after actual death enters the play — the deaths of Mercutio and Tybalt — and the Friar is forced to confront and deal with the consequences of those deaths, he is shown as increasingly unable to do so, and increasingly implicated in death itself. After Tybalt and Mercutio's deaths and Romeo's consequent banishment, the Friar does succeed in calming and comforting Romeo, promising him future joy and life. Romeo will go to Mantua,

> Where thou shalt live till we can find a time
> To blaze your marriage, reconcile your friends,
> Beg pardon of the Prince, and call thee back

> With twenty hundred thousand times more joy
> Than thou went'st forth in lamentation.
> (III.iii.150-154)

And Romeo responds, "How well my comfort is revived by this!" (III.iii.165). Thus, the Friar promises Romeo a form of resurrection: suffering and death (the death of exile) will be transformed to joy and life (return and reunion with his beloved and with the larger society). And here, since Romeo and Juliet are still alive, such a "resurrection" may indeed be enacted. But as actual, irreversible death looms larger and larger—first, Juliet's mock death, for which the Friar has planned a mock-resurrection; and finally Romeo and Juliet's actual deaths—the Friar becomes less and less able to deliver on his promise. Throughout the play he is depicted as being asked for, and offering, comfort and remedy against suffering and death; but his "comforts" end only in greater grief, and his final remedies in increasingly serious disaster, until the final, irreversible disaster, death.

The chief scenes in which the Friar's remedies against sorrow and death are tested are the scene of Juliet's mock-death, in which he administers comfort to those grieving for her; and the concluding scene, in which he again tries to administer comfort, this time in the face of real, irreversible death.

In the first of these scenes, the scene where Juliet's mock-death is discovered (IV.v), Capulet, Lady Capulet, the Nurse and Paris join in passages of formal lament for their lost daughter and bride (IV.v.14 ff.), and the Friar breaks in on their laments, scolding them for grieving. His consolations are the conventional consolations of philosophy and orthodox Christianity. Their "part" in Juliet, the flesh, was bound to perish, but her immortal part lives on ("heaven keeps his part in eternal life," 70); and they should be rejoicing at Juliet's "promotion" (71) to heaven, not grieving. Here, where the Friar and the Nurse—spirit and body—are no longer confederate (the Nurse does not know the death is a mock-death), we see most clearly what the Friar represents. The Nurse speaks for our physical nature (on which the comic solution to death depends), the Friar, for the spirit, but for the spirit as orthodox religion conceives of it—spirit divorced from body. Thus the Friar caps his consolations to the mourners with the declaration that while "fond nature bids us all lament,/ Yet nature's tears are reason's merriment" (IV.5.82-3). But the problem is that we *are* partly natural beings who feel natural grief, and therefore even if we accept the Friar's religious views as truth—even if we believe in his promise of immortality hereafter (something which *ipso facto* could not be demonstrated either on earth or in a theater limited to representing life on earth)—we still feel grief for the dead, and the Friar's words do not satisfactorily address the emotion as we feel it. In the discrepancy between any assent we might make to the Friar's words, and the power of actual grief, we feel the inadequacy of the Friar's consolations, and the need to seek another way of mastering death—a way created by and for the mortal humans, part soul, part body, who experience grief at the death of those they love, and fear and sadness at their own mortality. Our sense of the inadequacy of the Friar's comforts is reinforced because he himself has engineered Juliet's "death"; and while, presumably, he will undo that death, he is nevertheless the cause of the grief he is ministering to.

The death in this scene is only a mock death, and the mourner's laments are deliberately stylized (in the Nurse's case, ludicrous as well).[15] Accordingly, we do not, at this point, feel the full weight of death. That weight is fully felt in V.iii, and therefore, it is there that the Friar's consolations are ultimately tested—tested and found wanting.

The Friar arrives at the Capulet monument just too late to save Romeo. His first words on entering are "St. Francis be my speed! How oft tonight/ Have my old feet stumbled at graves" (V.iii.121-22). And the grave is a stumbling block for the Friar, literally and figuratively. His resurrection plot—his plot to "kill" and revive Juliet—has foundered, leading not to resurrection but to the grave (the grave which the play presents as ever waiting). The plot fails most immediately because the aged Friar, trying to hurry through the dark churchyard, stumbles and is delayed. But if the whole chain of events leading to the final deaths is examined, it is truer to say that the plot fails through accident (the good news failing to be delivered, the bad news arriving); illness (the plague which causes the letter to be returned; time (the Friar arriving just too late); old age (the Friar's age, which helps prevent him from arriving sooner); human law (which decrees Romeo's banishment); human limit in general (the Friar's inability to foresee all the accidents of time and chance which cause his plot to go astray); hatred/aggression/failure of love (the feud, parental anger and coldness); and passion itself, Romeo's love for Juliet which leads to his, and ultimately to her, death. In short, the Friar's efforts at "resurrection" are thwarted by mortality itself, the death aspect of nature, human nature and society which can be momentarily, but never permanently, fended off. Thus death itself—the implacable, ever-waiting grave—is the true stumbling block in the way of the Friar's efforts. But in the face of actual death, the Friar fares even more poorly than he did at the scene of Juliet's mock-death. Juliet greets him, as always, with the expectation of receiving comfort: "O comfortable Friar! Where is my lord?" (V.iii.148). Yet the Friar's only response is a conventional religious one: "A greater power than we can contradict/ Hath thwarted our intents" (V.iii.153-4). It's all the will of heaven—an answer which neither acknowledges the Friar's own part in the miscarriage of the plan, nor is responsive to Juliet's emotion. The Friar declares flatly that Romeo is dead and, frightened by the approach of the watch, urges Juliet to leave, telling her he will dispose of her to a nunnery—a kind of living death, a place devoid of natural pleasure, life, fertility (cf. *A Midsummer Night's Dream* and *Measure for Measure*; in both plays, although lip-service is paid to the idea of nunneries, they are presented as sterile, anti-life). And when Juliet refuses to leave the tomb, the Friar, who is not overanxious to gain his "promotion" to heaven, runs away in fear, thus paving the way for Juliet's death, which his presence would have prevented.[16] We see, then, that the Friar, the spokesman for conventional religion, is associated with the promise of immortality, a promise he often alludes to in the course of the play. But in the end, what we see him bring to his "children" is not immortal life, nor even earthly life, but rather, death. And when his faith is put to the test, it proves inadequate to counter his fear of death.

At the Friar's first appearance in the play he points out that earth yields herbs which heal and also poisons which slay, and that both "poison" and "medicine" may reside within the same plant: "Within the infant rind of this weak flower,/ Poison hath residence, and medicine power" (II.iii.23-24). Characteristically, the Friar turns his statement to orthodox religious moralizing, using it to point a conventional religious moral: "Two such opposed kings encamp them still/ In man as well as herbs—grace and rude will" (II.iii.27-28). But the entire play works to demonstrate the simple existential truth of the Friar's statement, a truth rooted in bodily being. For the death aspect of our life is not presented in the play as a consequence of, or punishment for, sin, but as a simple fact, affecting the good and the evil, the innocent and the guilty, alike. And the Friar's conventional religiosity fails increasingly to address what we experience in the play, or in our actual life, which the play symbolically represents.

We have seen that none of the parents in the play—the Capulets, the Montagues, the Nurse, the Friar—offer a viable way of dealing with immediate grief and death; and all are to some extent implicated in their offsprings' deaths. And throughout the play imagery occurs presenting earth, the mother of all creation, as being—like human parents—a source of life but also of death. The key statement of this is the speech the Friar makes at his first appearance in the play, as he gathers earth's produce, herbs which include both "baleful weeds and precious juiced flowers" (II.iii.8): "The earth that's nature's mother is her tomb./ What is her burying grave, that is her womb" (II.iii.9-10). The chiasmus—"mother"/"tomb"/"grave"/"womb"—perfectly expresses the life/death nature of nature itself, in which life-giving and lethal aspects are inextricably intertwined. Moreover, the Friar's depiction of the earth as both womb and tomb is echoed throughout the play in imagery depicting earth, the literal ground of our being, as a grave waiting to swallow us. For example, Capulet, in speaking of his sole remaining child, says, "Earth has swallowed all my hopes but she,/ She is the hopeful lady of my earth" (I.11.14-15); Juliet, wishing for death, cries, "Vile earth [her body], to earth resign" (III.ii.59); Romeo, throwing himself on the ground, declares that he is "taking the measure of an unmade grave" (III.iii.70) — that is, it is only a matter of time before the earth he lies alive on will receive him in death; and at Juliet's grave Romeo cries out to the "womb of death," the grave which is swallowing Juliet who is "earth": "Thou detestable maw, thou womb of death,/ Gorged with the dearest morsel of the earth" (V.iii.45-46). Thus earth, source of all natural life, is also an ever-waiting grave; the grave is also a womb. And the "earth" we are made of, our flesh, is also a source of our life, and an ever-ready grave ("a womb of death," which will give birth to our death). When the Friar exclaims of the still-living Juliet, interred in the monument, "Poor living corse, closed in a dead man's tomb!" (V.ii.29), he might be describing any human being born into the body which will become, in the course of time, a tomb. The point is that the birth of anything in nature is synonymous with death, the death that, in time, awaits all created beings. What is needed is the birth of something beyond the natural; and that is precisely what Romeo and Juliet create as together they give birth to a love which is tied to, yet transcendent of, their merely physical (therefore perishable) selves — a love which defies animal nature in the ultimate degree by defying and embracing death itself. But the form of death-transcendence Romeo and Juliet enact is not that offered by orthodox Christianity — the soul's immortality — but rather a form of death-transcendence which, like the death it seeks to overcome, is inseparable from actual bodily life in the here-and-now.[17]

A feature worth mentioning in Shakespeare's depiction of the parental figures is his emphasis on their age. The biological parents are presented not merely as older, but as old — older than we would expect the parents of children that age to be; and throughout the play, Shakespeare stresses the advanced age of all of the parent figures. In part this is done simply by references to their age. For example, at Montague and Capulet's first appearance, they are represented as old men past their fighting days, now dominated by their wives.

Capulet calls for his sword only to be told by Lady Capulet that he'd do better to call for a crutch; and Montague, entering and waving his sword about, is held back by Lady Montague. The Prince, on entering, refers to "old Capulet and Montague" (I.i.93), and speaks of "old partisans in hands as old" (I.i.97). The Nurse, depicted as almost toothless, complains of the aches of old age: "Fie, how my bones ache! What a jaunce have I" (II.v.26). The Friar refers to his "old feet" stumbling over the churchyard graves (V.iii.122), and refers to his "old life" (V.iii.267). And at their final appearance in the play, Lady Capulet laments, "O me, this sight of death is as a bell/ That warns my old age to a sepulcher" (V.iii.206-7), and Montague exclaims, "What further woe conspires against mine age?" (V.iii.212).

The stress on the parents' age is also created through the quality of their interchanges with their offspring, in which the age and youth of each are stressed in both their respective viewpoints and their way of speaking. Over and over they are presented almost as morality-play figures, *Senex* and *Juventus*, each speaking from, and representative of, two opposed stages of life—the impatience, romanticism, hot blood of youth; and the pragmatism, muted passion and relative slowness of age. For example Romeo, reacting to the Friar's attempts to calm him after the news of his banishment, responds with an impassioned outburst stressing the universe of difference between his outlook and the Friar's.

> Thou canst not speak of that thou dost not feel.
> Wert thou as young as I, Juliet thy love,
> An hour but married, Tybalt murdered,
> Doting like me, and like me banished,
> Then mightst thou speak, then mightst thou tear thy hair,
> And fall upon the ground, as I do now.
> (III.iii.64-69)

And Juliet, feverishly impatient to hear of Romeo's reply, and tormented by the Nurse's delay in bringing it, exclaims, "Had she affections and warm youthful blood,/ She would be swift in motion as a ball," "But old folks, many feign as they were dead—/ Unwieldy, slow, heavy and pale as lead" (II.v.12-13, 16-17). And when the Nurse finally enters, only to delay giving her news by complaining about her aching bones, Juliet exclaims, "I would thou had'st my bones, and I thy news" (II.v.27). But Juliet will, one day, have the Nurse's bones, old bones with their accompanying aches and pains. For if youth and age are opposed, as the play also repeatedly reminds us, youth will turn to age. Juliet will become her mother, who "was a mother much upon" Juliet's own age (I.iii.72), and Romeo will become not the extravagant adolescent he now is, dancing, brawling, moping, loving, but another old man sitting on the sidelines reminiscing about long-gone festivities.

This is dramatized for us in (among other places) the treatment of Capulet during the masque scene, the scene where Romeo and Juliet first meet. For Capulet, fighting and womanizing—young men's pursuits—are things of the past. Earlier in the play he declares of himself and Montague, " 'tis not hard, I think,/ For men so old as we to keep the peace" (I.ii.2-3); and now, he gives evidence of this by preventing Tybalt from drawing on Romeo, refusing to allow him to quarrel with one who is his guest. And he welcomes his guests with references to his own days of courtship and flirtations, as things long past.

> I have seen the day
> That I have worn a visor and could tell
> A whispering tale in a fair lady's ear,
> Such as would please. 'Tis gone, 'tis gone, 'tis gone.
> (I.v.23-26)

As his guests dance, Capulet reminisces with another aged kinsman about their vanished "dancing days" (I.v.33), which he swears were a mere 25 years past, not 30. For the two aged men sitting on the sidelines the years have slipped away imperceptibly; and the scene evokes, powerfully, a sense of the inevitable passing of youth into age, and of the whole cycle of birth, aging and individual death. The two old men last met at a wedding. But unlike comedy, in which a marriage concludes the action, life did not stop with that wedding, and the offspring of that marriage is now himself 30. Parents hope to renew themselves through children; but the children, being themselves mortal, are also vulnerable to aging and death.

Thus, Romeo and Juliet are each their parents' only children, on whom the parents' hopes are set ("Earth has swallowed all my hopes but she [Juliet],/ She is the hopeful lady of my earth," Capulet tells Paris, I.ii.14-15). But by the end of the play the children are dead, dashing also their parents' hopes for continuance through offspring. And even if offspring survive to continue the family line, individual parents and children still age and die. Had Romeo and Juliet escaped untimely death, choosing instead the comic solution of fulfilled love, marriage and children, they would have faced only future aging and death, declining from their youthful passion into the Capulets' affectionate bickering and bantering, and from the spring of youth to the aches and peevishness of wintry age. The stress on the parents' age, then, reinforces our sense of the limits of the comic solution, and drives us to search for a different way of meeting and mastering death, preparing us to understand how the denouement—the embrace of death—may represent both death and a partial solution to it.

The communal body in *Romeo and Juliet* is, most fundamentally, the family, but the community is also a political unit bound by law; and the head of, and representative of, the community in its political rather than its familial aspect is Prince Escalus. Although Escalus heads the body politic, as is appropriate to a play centered on the family, his kinship ties are stressed. He is related to Mercutio and to Paris, and he speaks of them as kinsmen rather than as subjects; and he expresses anger at the deaths occasioned by the feud as much in terms of personal, familial loss as in terms of disturbance to the state. For example, after Mercutio's death he exclaims, "My blood for your rude brawls doth lie a-bleeding" (III.i.191); and in commenting on the deaths at the conclusion he declares, "And I, for winking at your discords too,/ Have lost a brace of kinsmen" (V.iii.294-95).

The Prince is presented as powerful and authoritative, a just and rightful ruler. He makes his entrance with appropriate pomp, surrounded (as the stage directions tell us) with "his Train" (S.D. ff. I.i.83), and he is always spoken of with respect and awe; but throughout the play he is associated with death, especially death in the form of law. The Prince appears three times in the play, and each time he enters at a moment of threatened or actual death. At each appearance he attempts to prevent death through invoking the power of the law to inflict it; and in each case he is unsuccessful.

He first appears at a scene of potential death, the opening brawl. He does succeed in stopping that fight, but he fails to prevent the deaths which follow. He appears again at those deaths, the deaths of Mercutio and Tybalt, at which time he banishes Romeo, in part as a deterrent to further quarrels; but again the Prince is unsuccessful in preventing death, for his sentence sets in motion a chain of events leading to the deaths of Romeo, Juliet, and Paris, and also of Lady Montague, who dies of grief at her son's banishment. The Prince appears for the third and last time at the churchyard, the scene of the final deaths, where he attempts to take control of the situation by meting out just punishment. But in the face of these deaths (deaths to which his own actions have inadvertently contributed), his limitations are shown finally. There is no one to punish, for no one is deliberately responsible. The Prince is facing, not human wrongdoing, but human mortality; and against that fact, mortal rulers are powerless. The Prince can neither punish the culprit—death itself—nor undo the deaths he, and we, see before us at the play's conclusion. Moreover, as the action unfolds, it becomes increasingly clear that Escalus is not only powerless against death, but is strongly associated with it.

The play opens with the feud breaking out between the Montague and Capulet servants, and then spreading from lowest to highest as the young Capulet and Montague kinsmen Tybalt and Benvolio enter and take up the quarrel, followed by the Capulet and Montague parents, who also attempt to join the fray. Onto this scene of would-be carnage comes Prince Escalus, the head and representative of the body politic, and the law incarnate. Escalus does succeed in ending the fight before blood is shed; but he stops the quarrel not by appeals to love or to reason, but by threats of torture and death: "On pain of torture, from those bloody hands/ Throw your mistempered weapons to the ground" (I.i.89-90); "If ever you disturb our streets again,/ Your lives shall pay the forfeit of the peace" (I.i.99-100); "Once more, on pain of death, all men depart" (I.i.106). In rebuking the brawlers, the Prince stresses the animal nature of their aggression: "You men, you beasts,/ That quench the fire of your pernicious rage/ With purple fountains issuing from your veins!" (I.i.86-8); and his threats—of torture and death—are directed at that animal self. But although the Prince, wielding the power of the law, can hurt or kill that animal self, he cannot transform it—cannot transform the animal aggression that fuels the conflict. And consequently, although he can inflict death, he is only momentarily successful in averting it; for a day later Mercutio, the Prince's own kinsman, and Tybalt, will lie dead.

The Prince's limits reflect the limits of the law which he embodies. The social order, bound by law, differentiates men from beasts, and ideally it operates to control animal impulse and so sustain and enhance life; but in the Verona of the play, the social order aggravates rather than mitigates animal aggression, producing dissension and death (the feud, a cause of the deaths in the play, is of course tied to social identity). Thus society, which should help to sustain life, is a source of death. But law, which is the means used to check the death-aspect of society, is also a source of death. For in this play (as so often in Shakespeare's work) law is virtually a synonym for death. "Justice," in one meaning, was actually a synonym for death, according to the *OED*; and the equation of the two reflects contemporary actuality (see above, Chapter Two), and also suggests the theological scheme whereby law and justice demand man's death for Adam's sin, and love and mercy, made effective through Christ's sacrifice, save man from the consequences of that sin, suffering and death. And repeatedly the Prince, the embodiment of the law, is referred to in terms which invoke that theological scheme, and which suggest Doomsday, the day of ultimate judgement, when some will be granted eternal life, and others doomed to everlasting pain and death. We see this, for example, in the Prince's sentence of exile. Exile, a separation from the communal body, is a form of death, and is certainly so for Romeo, to whom Juliet is life. And Romeo specifically refers to exile as both death and damnation.

> There is no world without Verona walls,
> But purgatory, torture, hell itself.
> Hence banished is banished from the world
> And world's exile is death. Then "banished"
> Is death mistermed.
> (III.iii.17-21)

The Prince backs up his "doom," his sentence of banishment, with a threat of actual death: "Let Romeo hence in haste,/ Else, when he is found, that hour is his last" (III.ii.196-7); and his sentence is in fact a key link in the chain of events leading to Romeo's (and Juliet's, Paris's, and Lady Montague's) deaths. This is only one of many places in the play in which the Prince and the law are linked with death and/or Doomsday. Benvolio, warning Romeo to flee because he has killed Tybalt, cries, "The Prince will doom thee to death/ If thou art taken" (III.i.136-7). Lady Capulet, invoking an Old Dispensation morality—justice, not mercy—begs the Prince to kill Romeo ("For blood of ours shed blood of Montague," III.i.151), and demands "justice," by which she means death: "I beg for justice, which thou, Prince, must give./ Romeo slew Tybalt. Romeo must not live" (III.ii.182-2). Capulet, in interceding for Romeo, points out that the law would have demanded Tybalt's life: "His [Romeo's] fault concludes but what the law should end,/ The life of Tybalt" (III.ii.187-88). The Friar brings Romeo "tidings of the Prince's doom," (III.iii.8), and reminds Romeo that "Thy fault our law calls death" (III.iii.25); and the apothecary tells Romeo that "Mantua's law/ Is death" to anyone who dispenses poison (V.i.66-7). And climactically, the Prince appears in the concluding scene to dispense final judgement on the preceding chain of events. But here, as everywhere in the play, his judgement is associated not with happiness and life, but with punishment and death (his comment on the deaths is, typically, "All are punished" (V.iii.295). The scene in which the Friar told Romeo of the Prince's sentence of exile (III.iii.) was filled with images of Doomsday; and these images take on even greater significance at the play's conclusion, as the Prince, in a secular version of Doomsday, enters to sift guilt and innocence and pronounce final judgement. The Friar tells his tale, and submits himself to judgement.

> if aught in this
> Miscarried by my fault, let my old life
> Be sacrificed some hour before his time
> Unto the rigor of severest law.
> (V.iii.269)

And the Prince prepares to play his Christ-like role as arbiter of life and death ("Some shall be pardoned, and some punished," V.iii.308). But the play invites a comparison to Doomsday only to emphasize the crucial difference. Unlike Christ the Prince of Peace, who can save as well as destroy, and who can grant eternal life, this Prince is an inflictor of death only, and is powerless either to prevent or undo death. At the end, the witnesses (the Prince, the Friar, Montague, the Capulets, the onlookers), like the witnesses in the *Quem quaeritis* drama, are gathered at a tomb; but the bodies they are faced with do not, and will not, rise; and against that demonstrated reality, the Prince's doom is powerless.[18]

It is clear that Escalus is a typically ambiguous Shakespearean ruler figure, one in a long line of ambivalently presented authority figures who demonstrate the truth of John of Gaunt's remark to Richard.

> Shorten my days thou canst with sullen sorrow
> And pluck nights from me, but not lend a morrow;
> Thou canst help time to furrow me with age,
> But stop no wrinkle in his pilgrimage:
> Thy word is current with him for my death,
> But dead, thy kingdom cannot buy my breath.
> (*Richard II*, I.iii.231)

Like Henry the Fifth (see Chapter Two), Escalus is a good ruler who is, nevertheless, associated from start to finish in the play with the imposition of legally sanctioned death. Escalus is not a tyrant. He is treated always with awe based on awareness of his potentially lethal powers; but although he frequently backs up his exercise of power with threats of death, his actual judgements are not excessively harsh, but just, even moderate. For as with Henry the Fifth, Shakespeare's treatment of Escalus expresses not the limits of the individual ruler, but the limits of rulership itself. The point is not that Escalus is bad or weak, but rather, that even the best and most powerful of rulers is impotent against death and also, in part, an inflictor of it. For the state may control, but it cannot transform, animal nature, including both the aggression that leads to death, and the vulnerability of the animal self to death. Moreover, its means of controlling human animality are founded on that very animality, rather than on anything uniquely human — on the fear of punishment, of pain and death, which the physical self makes us vulnerable to.

Like the parental body, then, the body politic in this play is not only powerless to avert death, but is also a source of it. But Escalus is even more strongly associated with death than are the Montagues, the Capulets, and the Nurse; for in contrast to the power of the parents to produce new life, the state can produce no new life, but can only help to preserve or destroy that which is already created (neither Escalus nor of course the Friar, representatives respectively of the body politic and of the Church, are biological parents). Again we are pushed to seek a solution to death, a solution built on full acknowledgement of the inescapable death taint in every aspect of human life.

Of the remaining characters in the play other than the lovers, Mercutio is the most important. He is the wittiest and most elegant of the young aristocrats, and he presents the communal values in their most attractive and most compelling light;[19] but they are the same values seen in the Nurse[20] and the servants prattling of sex and money, and in Capulet and Lady Capulet trying to force a socially desirable match on their reluctant daughter. These values are associated with tremendous natural vitality, the energies of life itself, imaged in Mercutio's own vitality; but we also see the essentially reductive nature of Mercutio's viewpoint (the death side of these values) in his Queen Mab speech (I.iv.53 ff.), and in his "conjuring" speech (II.i.6 ff.).

In the description of Queen Mab and her chariot, Mercutio creates a delicate, enchanting fantasy. But if we look at the materials of which the fantasy is built, we see that they are all drawn from physical nature: "spinners' legs," grasshopper's wings, spider webs, moonbeams, cricket's bone, a hazelnut shell. Moreover, the dreams Queen Mab confers are also related to physical nature, being the dreams of natural man, desires pertaining to the physical self and to the passions associated with that self: ambition and greed (the courtier dreaming of "smelling out a suit," the parson of "another benefice"); lust (the ladies dreaming of kisses with "blister-plagued" lips—a suggestion of unclean desire, and of actual sexual disease); aggression, animal appetite, and fear (the soldier dreaming of "cutting foreign throats," of "healths five fathom deep," and of "Drums in his ear," at which he wakes in a fright). Thus, in the Queen Mab speech modes of human activity associated with ideals, with non-material realities—lover, courtier, parson, soldier—are in each case reduced to merely animal impulse: love to lust, courtliness and sanctity to greed and ambition, military glory to animal fear and aggression.[21]

Mercutio's conjuring speech (II.i.6 ff.) is similarly reductive. The speech, while not pitched at the same level of enchanting fantasy as the Queen Mab speech, exhibits wit and imagination, and is, in a more forthrightly satirical manner, equally amusing. But it displays the same reductive view of human activity, in this case, the activity of love, which for Mercutio is entirely reducible to the sexual impulse. In the first part of the conjuring speech, Mercutio makes fun of Romeo as the epitome of a mooning, versifying Petrarchan-style lover.

> Nay, I'll conjure too.
> Romeo! Humors! Madman! Passion! Lover!
> Appear thou in the likeness of a sigh;
> Speak but one rhyme and I am satisfied!
> Cry but "Ay me!" pronounce but "love" and "dove";
>   (II.i.6-10).

When Romeo fails to respond to this invocation, Mercutio declares he will have to "conjure him"; but the ensuing calling up of Romeo (who is the very spirit of romantic love) makes clear what for Mercutio is the essence of that love.

> I conjure thee by Rosaline's bright eyes,
> By her high forehead and her scarlet lip,
> By her fine foot, straight leg, and quivering thigh,
> And the desmesnes that there adjacent lie
> (II.i.17-20).

Thus the conjuration, which begins in typical Petrarchan style, by describing the mistress' charms, ends in very un-Petrarchan style, by specifying the exact and sexual nature of those charms (her "quivering thigh,/ And the desmesnes that there adjacent lie"). And Mercutio follows this description with a barrage of witty and very funny wordplay, all with sexual innuendoes (II.i.23-29; 33-39). The first passage of wordplay (II.i.23-29), which revolves around conjuring, uses "spirit," "raise," and "mistress' circle" to mean also semen, erection, and the female sexual organ. And the second passage of wordplay (II.i.33-39) centers on "medlars" and a "pop'rin pear," fruits which resemble the female and male sexual organs. Mercutio pictures Romeo sighing and wishing, in traditional lover's fashion, for his love to be requited; but he then makes clear, in most untraditional fashion, what that requital would consist of: "O, Romeo, that she were, O that she were/ An open *et cetera* [medlar, *i.e.*, an open female sexual organ], thou a pop'rin pear" (II.i.37-38). The point of all this wordplay is the same: to reduce love to the sexual impulse, mocking any pretensions that love is something more.

There is much to be said for the Mercutio view, since common sense tells us that we cannot escape the dictates of social and natural necessity. And Mercutio's style ensures that this view is presented in the most attractive and compelling light possible. But although the values Mercutio speaks for are necessary to sustain life, they are also values with death at their heart. For if love is merely lust (the conjuring speech), it is wholly associated with the perishable animal self, and so with death. And if dreams, which are uniquely human, are reducible merely to animal impulses—lust, greed, aggression (the Queen Mab speech)—then nothing exists which can transform or transcend our mortal selves. What Mercutio does, then, is precisely the opposite of what occurs in *Midsummer Night's Dream*. In that play, through the related forces of love and art, expressed as magic and dreams, animal nature is transformed into something including, but also transcendent of, the death-bound animal self. Here, magic (the conjuring speech) and dreams (the Queen Mab speech) are reduced back to animal impulse, therefore back to what is, ultimately, wholly perishable. In short, to Mercutio natural man—the physical self and the passions associated with that self—is the only man; and the art which Mercutio employs so well is employed to decorate, not to transform, that animal self.

Mercutio, then, for all his charm, wit, linguistic ebullience, is a doubter figure, one of the many Shakespearean descendants of the doubter figures in medieval drama. Medieval doubters may be Jews and wicked kings, who doubt the truth of the Resurrection, or simply skeptics, like the midwives in the Chester Nativity who doubt Mary's virginity. But what they doubt is always essentially the same: that nature can be transcended, therefore, that death can be overcome; and they are what a given play exists to confound.[22]

The remaining characters in the play fall mainly into two groups, the young aristocrats, and the servants; and like extras in opera, these characters serve to flesh out and extend the picture of the communal body. That body is, as said above, most fundamentally the family; and accordingly the minor characters (as well as those with larger parts) are shown in terms of their family connections. Benvolio is identified as a Montague, Tybalt as a Capulet, and Mercutio as a friend of Romeo's and also a kinsman to the Prince. The servants, too—Sampson, Gregory, Abram, Balthasar, Peter, and the unnamed servants (*e.g.*, the servant who is sent about with the guest list in I.ii, and the servants in I.v. and IV.iv)—are allied with one or another of the two households. Moreover, like the households they are connected with, these characters are associated with life, but also, with death.

The young aristocrats whom we see exchanging banter, gossip, and plans to meet, together compose a portrait of youth in a certain time and place (ostensibly Verona, actually

Elizabeth's England), but also, in all times and places. They are depicted in carefree fellowship, eating, drinking, dancing, bantering, fighting, falling in love. Above all, they epitomize the energies natural to youth—the hot-blooded passion ("mad blood," III.i.4) which can be turned to the service of love and life, or of aggression and death. Both potentials inhere in each young man, as we see in Mercutio, Paris, Romeo; but in Tybalt and Benvolio, Shakespeare also splits the life and death aspects of youth in two. Benvolio, as his name suggests, exemplifies good will, and he continually attempts to avoid bloodshed; and Tybalt, in contrast, is aggression incarnate, a death's head at the feast (literally so at the masque, where he is barely prevented by Capulet from turning the festivities into a scene of carnage). "Turn thee, Benvolio, look upon thy death," Tybalt cries at his first appearance in the play (I.i.69); and he is indeed a figure of death, the cause of Mercutio's death and, indirectly, of the ensuing deaths, since they in part follow from Romeo's revenging of the killing of Mercutio.

The servants in the play, another important group of minor characters, are also pictured in relation to the two main family groups, the Capulets and the Montagues. And they, too, are associated with both life and death, whether they are shown carrying the family feud (the death side of the family) to the streets, as in the opening scene where Sampson, Gregory, Abram and Balthasar meet and take their respective masters' parts; or whether we see them preparing for the masque and the wedding, occasions of fellowship, feasting, joy, associated with the life side of the family.

The servants and the young aristocrats, like all the characters in the play except for the lovers, share a common set of values—what we might call the Nurse values—although the servants express these values crudely, and the aristocrats with elegance and, in Mercutio's case especially, with wit. These values are given succinct expression in the curious little scene which follows the discovery of Juliet's mock death. The mourners exit, and the musicians, who have come to play at the wedding, remain on stage exchanging heavy-handed jokes and puns revolving around music and musical terms.[23] In doing so Peter, the Nurse's servant, quotes from a song which describes the "silver sound" of music as offering comfort against grief and death.[24]

> "When griping grief the heart doth wound,
> And doleful dumps the mind oppress,
> Then music with her silver sound"—
> (IV.v.128-30)

The description of music's "silver sound" recalls Romeo's exclamation, "How silver-sweet sound lovers' tongues by night,/ Like softest music to attending ears" (II.ii.165-66). For Romeo, this silver-sweet music is the music of love, which can offer comfort against, and partial transcendence of, sorrow and death. But the musicians, who, like the other servants, embody the values of the communal world (the importance of money, sex, social position), do not hear that music. Instead, they hear the "sweet sound" of silver in the sense of money, the payment they expect to receive for creating their music ("musicians sound for silver," IV.v.135-6); "musicians have no gold for sounding," IV.v.142).[25] Peter finishes the song he begun: "'Then music with her silver sound/ With speedy help doth lend redress'" (IV.v.143-44); and the scene leaves us suspended between the two forms of "silver" (money, and love), epitomizing two opposed realms of value, each offered as remedy for sorrow and death (and each associated also with a form of death).

The values the musicians express—the values shared by the Nurse, the servants, the Capulets, the young aristocrats, *et al.*—have their own validity, as the scene between Romeo and the apothecary reminds us. For although man may be more than a body, without the means of sustaining bodily life, he is nothing at all. And when the apothecary's physical survival conflicts with his life as a moral being, he is forced to bow to the dictates of bodily necessity, and sell the deadly poison. In the first four acts of the play, the supporting characters, minor as well as major, stress bodily-based needs. But the apothecary appears in the concluding act, where the values Romeo and Juliet stand for—values transcending (though also tied to) the body—are being finally asserted and confirmed. And accordingly, the scene with the apothecary expresses both sets of values. If the apothecary were only an animal being, he would not regret the action he is forced to take. But although he is a part bodily being, forced to traffic in death in order to sustain his bodily life, another part of him—his "will"—stands aside and regrets the action: "My poverty but not my will consents" (V.i.75). This scene helps prepare us for seeing Romeo and Juliet's self-murder as a means of avoiding a different kind of death, the death of the uniquely human self—the very self the apothecary, in the act of saving his physical self, did violence to.

We see, then, that Mercutio, the Nurse, the Capulets, the young aristocrats, the servants, the musicians all share, in their different ways, a common set of values based on awareness of the needs of the body and of the ways of the world. This set of values is hardly unique to this play. It finds expression in Shakespearean history and comedy as well as tragedy; and it is often epitomized in aphorisms scattered throughout the plays. "I like not such grinning honor as Sir Walter hath. Give me life" (*1 Henry IV*, V.iii.58-60). "Cat will after kind," and "the property of rain is to wet" (*As You Like It*, III.ii.103,26). Prostitution would be lawful "if the law would allow it" (*Measure for Measure*, II.i.227). "Court holy-water in a dry house is better than this rain water out o' door" (*King Lear*, III.ii.10-11). These truisms express realities of physical and social existence, to be ignored at one's peril. But although they express truths which, if heeded, tend to sustain and promulgate life, they are also, at another level, truths with a death aspect. However, only tragedy faces this fact directly.

In *Romeo and Juliet*, nothing exposes the limits of the communal values more powerfully than the death of Mercutio.[26] In terms of the action, the death of Mercutio is the point at which the play passes from potential comedy to actual tragedy,[27] and, concomitantly, the point at which the inadequacy of the comic solution to death becomes incontrovertibly clear.[28] It is the first actual death in the play; and it is death in precisely the form comedy can least successfully cope with—the untimely, senseless death of a highly individualized young man at the height of his vital powers (as opposed to death coming at the end of a fulfilled life cycle). To such a death, the values of the community offer no counter. What is needed is a way of mastering death which acknowledges, yet transcends, our subjection to the social and physical necessities the community speaks for. And of the characters in the play, only Romeo and Juliet point the way toward such a solution.

Romeo and Juliet

In looking at the characters who compose the social world from which Romeo and Juliet emerge, we see that our picture of this world is created in good measure through those characters' distinctive voices, which (along with action and imagery) compose the substance of this play: the voices of the servants, the musicians, the Nurse, the two sets of parents, the Prince, the Friar, the apothecary, Paris, Tybalt, Benvolio, Mercutio, each of whom has an individual voice, yet all of whom are in underlying agreement on a basic view—the reality of social and natural necessity, and the concomitant importance of sex, money, social position. Emerging from this aural composite are the voices of the lovers which are differentiated from, but also defined in relation to, the composite voice.[29] The total effect is a musical one, operatic in nature. The lovers' duets diverge from, but are also heard against, a chorus-like background, creating a musical figure clearly distinct from, yet also inseparable from, its ground. Together, the lovers create poetry—both actual poetry (for example, the sonnet of I.v.95-108), and, more generally, an intense, exquisite poetic lyricism different from anything we hear elsewhere in the play.[30] This distinctive lyricism is the linguistic expression of the lovers' values; and those values are not separable from the problem of death. Individuals die; but the subordination of individuality to group identity equals another form of death. When the lovers meet, they assert one another's uniqueness (thus, irreplaceability), and that assertion is both the cause of, and the counter to their deaths.

In the play the Friar describes the three components of a human being: "body" (the physical body), "birth" (family origin), and "soul." "Body" and "birth" thus equal the parental/communal body, which is strongly associated in this play with death (especially, the feud) as well as with life. But "soul," which, as the Friar often points out, should be our immortal part, is not defined in the play as a whole in the Friar's conventionally religious terms, terms which invoke a hereafter, but rather in terms of the here and now; for "soul" is what the lovers both express and create as they assert, and die for, their love. Thus "soul," as we see it in the play, may be consonant with, or correspond to, the orthodox religious idea of it; but it is defined in human terms, through the lovers' language, and through the actions which validate that language, as they transform the tired Petrarchan conceits of dying for love into actual death. "Soul," therefore, amounts to an enacted demonstration of the existence of something which may or may not perish with, but which cannot be reduced to, either "body" or "birth"; it is inseparable from the lovers' creation of a love springing from, and expressive of, their own and one another's unique individuality; and it offers a form of death-transcendence, but a limited form, and one different in kind from orthodox religious ideas of it.

We have seen that the family—the all-encompassing ground of physical and social life in this play—is strongly associated with death as well as with life. But exactly the same is true of Romeo and Juliet's "death-marked love" (Prologue, 9), the counter to the death inherent in the communal values; for that love, being partly of the body, cannot escape death.[31] This point is made over and over in the play's language, and in its action as well. The passages which associate love and death are too numerous (and too often noted) to list. They are, in fact, one of the most striking features of this play, a feature commented upon by virtually all critics. Significantly, many of the allusions linking love and death are introduced by the lovers themselves, especially by Juliet; for from the start it is she who has the most realistic apprehension of death, as when, at their first private meeting, she tries to warn Romeo that if he is found in the Capulet orchard he will be murdered, and he responds to this warning with Petrarchan conceits of the mistress as murderer.

> Juliet. If they do see thee, they will murder thee.
> Romeo. Alack, there lies more peril in thine eye
> Than twenty of their swords! Look thou but sweet,
> And I am proof against their enmity.
> (II.ii.70-73)

I will trace some of the play's allusions to love and death as linked, in order to show how we are reminded, with increasing power, of the death-taint inherent in even the most profound and idealized of mortal loves; for that death-taint must be fully confronted in order to be overcome, in a play in which mortal love is offered as a solution to mortality itself. To trace the links between love and death — especially, between married love and death — is also to trace the play's action.

The key point in the play's association of love and death is that the love is not sonnet-style unrequited love, in which the mistress is an unattainable goddess, but married love, love with an avowedly sexual component, in which the beloved is mortal and desire is fulfilled.[32] But if the passion between Romeo and Juliet is not asexual sonnet love, neither is it merely physical sexuality such as that suggested by the servants' jests in the opening scene. Rather, it is sexuality triumphantly transformed by a fully human love — love which includes but also transcends its physical (death- tainted) basis. The sexual basis of love, which the lords in *Love's Labor's Lost* deny, is in *Romeo and Juliet* fully acknowledged; but to acknowledge the sexual basis of love is to acknowledge the body, thus to acknowledge death. And accordingly, Romeo and Juliet's love is associated with death throughout the play. The connection is made at the level of language, and also of action, as the play provides us with a dramatic image of the link between love and death — an image which unfolds in time and space, as we move from a scene of sexual fulfillment intensely anticipated (III.ii.1 ff.), to a scene in which the fulfillment of desire in marriage is powerfully conveyed (III.v.1 ff.), to a scene in which sexual union in marriage and sexual union in death become wholly inseparable (V.iii.74 ff.). The love depicted is married love because for Shakespeare marriage is the ultimate expression of specifically human love, whether marriage is conceived of in religious terms — a sacrament which sanctifies and transforms the physical act of sexual union—or simply in human terms—the decision of two people to commit themselves exclusively and selflessly to one another. In either case, married love carries the same expressive weight in the play: a form of love in which the sexuality (and mortality) of oneself and one's beloved are simultaneously acknowledged and, partially, overcome.[33]

As is appropriate, the linking of *married* love and death does not occur until Romeo and Juliet's first meeting. Death and love are linked in the Prologue ("death-marked love," 9); and death is then linked to sexuality—one component of mortal love—but not to love itself, in the opening scene, in which the servants exchange crude banter filled with wordplay associating aggression and sexuality. Death next enters the play in the form of imagery as Montague, describing the melancholy and secretive Romeo, compares him to "the bud hit with an envious worm/ Ere he can spread his sweet leaves to the air/ Or dedicate his beauty to the sun" (I.i.154-56). This precisely forecasts the course of the action: Romeo and Juliet's untimely death. But the worm is the worm of death that waits in all created things, and is therefore latent also in mortal love. This idea is present in the next passages in which images linking love and death occur: the flood of conceits which Romeo, on entering, spouts. They are conceits familiar from countless sixteenth-century sonnets, based on the convention of the hard-hearted mistress whose heartlessness is killing her lover (I.i.174 ff.). Romeo's spate of sonnet-like lover's complaints includes a declaration that if Rosaline will not marry and have children, "when she dies, with beauty dies her store" (I.i.219). This thought (a common one in Shakespeare's own sonnets) reminds us of the double aspect of the flesh: death, and physical fertility, the bodily potential on which the comic solution to death is based.[34] But in *Romeo and Juliet*, the comic solution to death is always alluded to only to be exposed as inadequate. We have already seen the aged Capulets and Montagues, and are therefore already subliminally aware of what Romeo would decline to even if he lived to exercise the comic solution; and the rest of the play expands upon and reinforces the limits of the comic denouement in relation to death.

Romeo winds up his flood of conceits with (among other images) a reference to his own "death" from unrequited love: "She hath forsworn to love, and in that vow/ Do I live dead that live to tell it now" (I.i. 226-7). For Romeo, his death is still a mere verbal convention. But we are aware that in the world of feud with which the play opens, conceits of death may — as they do — become actual.

As Romeo's Petrarchan-style poeticizing reminds us, the conventional claim of dying for love is conventionally directed to unrequited love; whereas mutual love, fulfilled in marriage, is associated rather with life, with pleasure and with offspring. But in this play the deep connections are between married love and death, not between unrequited love and death. Romeo's Petrarchan conceits of death are directed to his relationship with Rosaline. But as soon as Juliet enters the picture, married love and death are linked, in the imagery and, also, through the action.

The play's first direct linking of married love and death occurs just after Romeo and Juliet's first meeting, when Juliet sends the Nurse to find out Romeo's name, declaring, "If he is married,/ My grave is like to be my wedding bed" (I.v.136-7). In II.vi, Romeo and Juliet are joined in marriage; and in the scene immediately following (III.i), Romeo, now Juliet's husband, slays Tybalt. Thus marriage and death are linked at the level of action; and after these scenes, they are linked at the level of language as well, as passages associating marriage with death (and love with hate, joy with sorrow, pleasure in the beloved with grief at his/her absence) proliferate. For example, hearing of Romeo's banishment, Juliet declares, "I'll to my wedding bed;/ And death, not Romeo, take my maidenhead!" (III.iii. 136-7). The Friar tells Romeo, "Thou art wedded to calamity" (III.iii.3). Paris links "woe" (for Tybalt's death) and "woo" (III.iv.8). Juliet, whose mother believes she is weeping for Tybalt's death (not, as she is, for Romeo's absence), links revenge-murder with the sexual act, declaring her wish "To wreak [*i.e.* "avenge," and "give expression to," Signet note] the love I bore my cousin/ Upon his body that hath slaughtered him" (III.v.102-3), by which Lady Capulet understands Juliet to mean murder, whereas Juliet means the sexual act. Lady Capulet, furious at Juliet's refusal to marry Paris, exclaims, "I would the fool were married to her grave!" (III.v.141); and Juliet, begging her parents to delay marriage to Paris, declares, "Or if you do not, make the bridal bed/ In that dim monument where Tybalt lies" (III.v.202-3).

The fourth act continues and intensifies the connections between married love and death, at the level of both imagery and action. On the level of action, the act consists of alternating scenes of marriage and death, wedding festivity and funeral: the planning of the mock-death, with its charnel-house imagery (IV.i); preparations for the proposed wedding (IV.ii); Juliet's taking of the drug, preceded by her terrified imagining of awakening in the tomb (IV.iii); further preparations of feasting and festivity (IV.iv); and the discovery of, and lament for, Juliet's "death" (IV.v). And on the level of imagery the language linking marriage and death reaches new heights in IV.v, in the laments which follow the discovery of Juliet's death. The Nurse opens the scene by coming in to wake Juliet with a characteristic reminder of what, for the Nurse, is the heart of marriage, the sexual act.

> Sleep for a week; for the next night, I warrant,
> The County Paris hath set up his rest
> That you shall rest but little.
> (IV.v.5-7)

But her sexual allusion is followed instantly by the discovery that Juliet is "dead"; and in the ensuing laments, marriage and death are repeatedly linked, as in the following examples.

> *Friar.* Come is the bride ready to go to church?
> *Capulet.* Ready to go, but never to return.
> O son, the night before thy wedding day
> Hath Death lain with thy wife. There she lies,
> Flower as she was, deflowered by him.
> Death is my son-in-law, Death is my heir;
> My daughter he hath wedded. I will die
> And leave him all. Life, living, all is Death's.
> (IV.v.33-40)

> Capulet. All things that were ordained festival
> Turn from their office to black funeral—
> Our instruments to melancholy bells,
> Our wedding cheer to a sad burial feast;
> Our solemn hymns to sullen dirges change;
> Our bridal flowers serve for a buried corpse;
> (IV.v.84-89)

But it is in the fifth act that the links between married love and death reach their ultimate intensity, culminating in the scene of the lovers' deaths where, at the level of both action and language, the act of love and the act of suicide, sexual union in marriage and union in death, become completely, and finally, indistinguishable. The blurring of the distinction between sexual union in marriage, and death, is further reinforced in our minds in this scene because the lovers, who were last seen together immediately after they consummated their marriage (III.v), are seen together again only in the tomb, in death—a juxtaposition giving substance to the many preceding images speaking of the marriage bed as a tomb, but also, of the tomb as a marriage bed.[35]

The link between married love and death is at the heart of the play's language and action. One function that association serves is to remind us that the comic solution to death, which appears so desirable, is also radically inadequate; for married love, like the mortal individuals who create it, is not exempt from the death taint inherent in every aspect of mortal existence.[36] In *A Midsummer Night's Dream, The Merchant of Venice, Twelfth Night, As You Like It*, no long-married couples exist; but the existence in this play of the Montagues and Capulets allow us to follow requited, married love—love which produces children—into the future (the future the comic conclusion stops short of fully visualizing), where we find that that it, too, ends in death: in individual death (the aging Capulets and Montagues, hastening towards the grave); in the death of youthful passion; and in the death of the family line (at the end of the play the Montague and Capulet direct lines are both extinct). The failure of the family lines underscores the fact that children, a crucial element in the comic solution to death, are themselves mortal, and therefore represent not only a limited, but also an uncertain means of achieving mastery over death. Moreover, married love, unlike sonnet-style love, is ineluctably sexual—therefore linked with the perishable body. Accordingly, on one level the association of married love with death simply expresses the reality of death's inescapability—thus, of the very thing this play, and Shakespearean tragedy in general, is designed to confront and overcome. For these reasons, the passages linking married love and death more and more urgently push us more and more strongly to seek a solution to the death inherent in all aspects of bodily-based existence, including love itself.

At the opening of the play death immediately threatens (the references to death in the Prologue; the feud-prompted brawl). And throughout the play pleasure, joy, love attempt to outrun suffering, grief, hatred and death. From the moment Romeo kills Tybalt, the pace of that contest increases dramatically, as the lovers try more and more frantically to outrun death. But the faster the lovers hasten, the faster death presses, until finally death catches up, as Romeo drinks the poison only a moment before the Friar, whose presence would have forestalled Romeo's death, appears. The sequence of events has the appearance of accident. But in a very real sense life is just such a race, with suffering and death continually threatening, and human beings hastening to seize their moments of life and pleasure before the inevitable end. Thus the action of the play—the sequence of wedding bed to grave—is a telescoped version of the course of mortal life, revealing to us the movement of even the longest and happiest of lives.[37] For like the young lovers, all human beings are pitted against death in its many forms: time, passion, aggression, accident, age, disease, implacable law, human limit; and those forms are not external to them, but are inherent in the nature of physical and social being. The question then is what, if anything, mortal beings can oppose to the fact of death's inevitable victory. And it is to this question that the denouement of this tragedy—and of every Shakespearean tragedy—addresses itself.

Denouement

The denouement begins in V.i., when Romeo receives the (mistaken) news of Juliet's death. Immediately the tone of his language changes, signifying a change in attitude. As Romeo declares his intention of dying, he delivers that declaration neither in the shallow Petrarchan conceits of the opening scenes, nor in the impassioned poetic lyricism which characterizes his exchanges with Juliet (*e.g.*, II.ii.1 ff.; III.v.1 ff.), but rather with an unadorned simplicity and power which expresses forgetfulness of self, and unhesitating commitment to the contemplated action: "Well, Juliet, I will lie with thee tonight" (V.i.35).[38] The words "lie with" also perfectly fuse the acts of sexual union and union in death, preparing us to see the final deaths as consummation as well as conclusion.

Romeo's reaction contrasts markedly with that of Paris in both the preceding and the ensuing scenes; and in fact, Paris' function is chiefly as a foil for Romeo, to show more clearly, by contrast, what Romeo represents. In the lament following Juliet's fourth-act "death," Paris, the Capulets and the Nurse mourn Juliet in terms of her role: intended bride, daughter, foster daughter; but they do not mourn for Juliet herself, as a unique individual, and the formal, stylized, highly rhetorical nature of their lament reflects that fact. Juliet could be any pretty young woman, daughter or bride, no more individual than the flowers of the field she is compared with: "Death lies on her like an untimely frost/ Upon the sweetest flower of all the field" (*Capulet*, IV.v.28-9). In V.iii Paris reveals the same attitude towards Juliet's death, expressed through the same kind of conventional highly stylized rhetoric, when he comes to strew flowers on Juliet's grave.

> Sweet flower, with flowers thy bridal bed I strew
> (O woe! thy canopy is dust and stones)
> Which with sweet water nightly I will dew;
> Or, wanting that, with tears distilled by moans.
> (V.iii.12-15)

And significantly, Paris' imagery is totally free of sexual overtones; for Paris' love is akin to sonnet love, which does not recognize—thus cannot confront or transcend—the sexual (death-tainted) nature of love itself.[39] The difference in attitude expressed in the contrast between Romeo's and Paris' style is confirmed by the actions of the two young men. Paris is prepared to strew flowers on Juliet's grave, and to journey nightly to the grave to do so; but Romeo is prepared to join her there. In short, Paris' love is real so far as it goes, but unlike Romeo's love, it does not go beyond nature, to accept and defy death itself.

Romeo's final speech (V.iii.74 ff.) reaches a height of impassioned intensity, made the more striking by contrast to the flowery little speech of Paris's which precedes it. The speech, the culmination of all of the love/death associations, is filled with fevered sexual imagery linking love and death.[40] Death is imagined as a sexual rival who has "sucked the honey of thy breath"—"amorous," a "lean, abhorred monster" keeping Juliet "here in the dark to be his paramour" (V. iii.103-5). And Romeo's final words, "Thus with a kiss I die" (V.iii.120), perfectly sum up all of the preceding love/death allusions, since "die" in Elizabethan English meant both to reach sexual climax and actually to die.

The same effect recurs in Juliet's death scene. She kisses Romeo's lips, hoping "some poison yet doth hang on them/ To make me die with a restorative" (V.iii.165-66),[41] and then, hearing the watchman, exclaims, "O happy dagger!/ This is thy sheath [her body]; there rust, and let me die" (V.iii.169-70), and stabs herself (the stabbing action also has sexual overtones). Thus, both death speeches end with "die," and both employ imagery which makes it clear that the word is being used in its double sense, to reach sexual climax, and actually to die. This effect is echoed and underscored in the line (from Romeo's letter) describing how Romeo came to the tomb "to die and lie with Juliet" (V.iii.290), where both "die" and "lie" have each the same double meanings. Thus, the passages on the lovers' deaths give final expression to what the play has insisted upon throughout, the inseparability of sexual union in marriage, and death. The death implicit in, and inseparable from, sexually-based love is made powerfully manifest in the imagery and, above all, in the suicides, which constitute the simultaneous embrace of love and of death. The moment of the lovers' deaths is also the moment at which the strategies against death of the other characters in the play fail, for those strategies consisted of attempts to avert, rather than to confront, the coming of death.

The lovers have dealt with death by choosing to die.[42] But the living are now faced with their deaths, and with the need to confront and master the irrefutable fact of death's reality. And that confrontation is what is depicted in the play's closing moments. The conclusion of *Romeo and Juliet* amounts to a replay of the resurrection drama of earlier times. But in Shakespeare's play, the witnesses gathered at the tomb—the Prince, the Friar, the two sets of parents, the Chief Watchman and the other onlookers, on stage and in the theater—see not the empty tomb of earlier resurrection plays, giving proof that the mortal body can be overcome, nor the still-living bodies the Friar (and the audience) hoped and wished to see, but three forever-dead bodies—proof that the death-aspect of the body cannot be escaped, on earth, within time. This demonstration also constitutes the definitive exposure of the limits of the comic solution to death.[43] What is needed is neither the mock-resurrection of the Friar's plot, in which death is to be averted rather than directly dealt with, nor the future resurrection the Friar, as the spokesman for orthodox religion, promises in the hereafter, but a way of mastering death which we, embodied creatures, can enact in the here and now. Yet because this victory over death is to occur on earth, it must be one which fully acknowledges the real fact of death—a triumph over death which includes, even rests upon, the irrefutable fact of human mortality. And this is precisely what the play provides. The authorities who should have been sources of life to Romeo and Juliet—the Prince, head of the body politic; the Friar, representative of religion; and the two sets of parents, author of Romeo and Juliet's bodily being—stand beside the grave, powerless to undo the deaths which they in part have helped to bring about. But at the very moment death's inescapability is most strongly felt, we see also that the lovers, in embracing death, have demonstrated a partial solution to it. For their action revalues, even as it accepts death, demonstrating that something in human beings is stronger than, and apart from, the animal self which fears death and values life above all else. Earlier in the play, immediately before they are married, Romeo claims that one moment with Juliet is equal in joy to the greatest sorrow life may bring.

> Come what sorrow can,
> It cannot countervail the exchange of joy
> That one short minute gives me in her sight.
> (III.vi.3-5)

And he then casts a defiant challenge to "love-devouring death".

> Do thou but close our hands with holy words,
> Then love-devouring death do what he dare—
> It is enough I may but call her mine.
> (II.vi.6-8)

Romeo means the phrase "love-devouring death" to signify that death devours love, but we hear it also as meaning that love devours death (an echo of the biblical assertion, "For love is stronger than death," *Song of Songs*, 8:6); and the ambiguity of the phrase "love-devouring death" is evoked again in the imagery of the concluding scene, in which death is shown both as devouring Juliet ("thou detestable maw. . ./ gorged with the dearest morsel of the earth," V.iii.45-6), and as destroyed by love, as in the passage where Romeo lays Paris in Juliet's grave.

> I'll bury thee in a triumphant grave.
> A grave? O, no, a lanthorn, slaughtered youth,
> For here lies Juliet, and her beauty makes
> This vault a feasting presence full of light.
> Death, lie thou there, by a dead man interred.
> (V.iii.83-87)

The feasts in the play—the masque, the wedding—have led directly to this grave; but the grave now becomes a "feasting presence full of light." The body of Paris, addressed as "Death" (87), is both a youth destroyed by death and a figure of Death itself, now buried ("Death, lie thou there . . .

interred"). And Romeo, looking on Juliet's grave, declares it "a triumphant grave" (another biblical echo—"O grave, where is thy victory? O death, where is thy sting?" *1 Cor.* 15:55). But like "love-devouring death," the phrase "a triumphant grave" is irresolvably ambiguous. The grave is a scene of a triumph over death, for the power of Juliet's beauty has converted the "vault" to "a feasting presence full of light"; but the grave has also triumphed, for as Romeo cried out only moments ago, it has swallowed Juliet.

For the lovers, the creation of love's religion, begun in the sonnet they create when they first meet (with its references to the lovers as pilgrims), and continued in the speeches in which they mythologize one another (for example II.ii.1 ff.; III.ii.1 ff.), is now complete. It is a religion tested against actual death, and therefore a universe away from the conventional, merely verbal, sonnet-style religion of love which Romeo invokes at the play's beginning. Moreover, from the lovers' point of view it has succeeded where the Friar's religion has failed. But the lovers' revaluation of death is not, or not wholly, the playwright's. For in the play two views of death are directly juxtaposed; both are tested at the play's conclusion; and neither is completely, or finally, victorious.[44]

The characters who compose the communal body all acknowledge death's power: the Montagues, the Capulets, the Nurse, the servants, the young aristocrats, including Mercutio, the apothecary, and even the Friar, the spokesman for religion, who in his frightened flight from the graveyard implicitly acknowledges the power of the bodily self, the self which fears death above all things. That fear finds echo in each member of the audience, for at a basic level we also fear death and value life above all things. Only the lovers declare otherwise. But if Romeo and Juliet's impassioned speeches assert what their suicides prove—that for them, love is stronger than death—those same speeches are replete with images evoking the reality of bodily corruption and death, images strong enough to stand comparison with the most powerful of the late-medieval graveyard homilies.

Juliet's most important pre-death speech is actually not the comparatively brief speech which precedes her real death

(V.iii.160 ff.), but the speech which precedes her mock-death (IV.iii.14 ff.), in which she imagines awakening in the tomb—a Lazarus-like vision of living death, filled with powerful images of mortal corruptibility.[45] These include images of the corruptibility of the physical body: "the bones/ Of all my buried ancestors"; "bloody Tybalt, yet but green in earth/ . . . festering"; "loathsome smells"; "the mangled Tybalt". They also include images of another form of mortal corruptibility, madness—the decay of human reason, of the soul, or the personality—of all that we feel distinguishes us from mere animals.[46] Thus, Juliet's vision evokes a more terrifying form of death than merely physical death, for it projects not oblivion, but a fully conscious confrontation with the worst horrors of mortal corruptibility. Accordingly, it is the full horror of death which Juliet confronts and overcomes as she drinks the poison in order to be united with Romeo; but she evokes even as she confronts and conquers death's horror; and the demonstration of her conquest of death is not separable from the evocation of its power. And in Romeo's comparable pre-death speeches (his speeches in V.iii), death's power is also evoked even as it is denied, as, for example, in his dwelling on the strange fact of Juliet's still uncorrupted flesh, which (among other effects) reminds the audience, who knows she is still alive, of the bodily decay her actual death will bring.[47] Thus the lovers' last words remind us powerfully of what the body we inhabit must come to. At the same time, the characters— and our—awareness of death's reality and horror is at the heart of the depiction of death-transcendence, for it is what is overcome in the choice to die.[48]

In Shakespeare's complete vision, then, neither of the two realities—death-devouring love, or love-devouring death—is finally stronger, for the demonstration that something exists which transcends death is directly dependent upon the demonstration of death's reality and power. This effect extends beyond the lovers' deaths, to the play's close. As the play ends, the Capulets and Montagues, reconciled, vow to put up golden statues to commemorate their children. But that offer intensifies our sense of loss, making us feel the immeasurable difference between the cold metal statues which have never lived and can therefore never die, and the still warm bodies ("warm and new-killed," V.iii.197) of the lovers who, being once alive, can and and have died forever.[49] Our sense of loss is reinforced visually as we gaze at a stage empty of the lovers' living presence, and it is also reinforced aurally, by the absence of the lovers' soaring romantic lyricism and the vision it expresses and reflects. Their lyricism is silenced now, replaced by the prosaic voices of the community: the stern and legalistic Prince, the sententious Friar, (whose account of the play's events is strikingly flat), the grieving but uncomprehending parents, the equally uncomprehending onlookers, who together represent order and continuity, yet also a greatly diminished reality. Yet our very consciousness of loss testifies to the reality and power of what was lost. For something real, though non-material, goes out of the play-world at the lovers' deaths — something we experience directly as we watch the play; and the extinction of that non-material reality gives irrefutable proof of its existence and value, as we see, hear, feel the universe of difference between a world that contains the lovers and the flat, colorless world they leave behind. This is also the explanation of why in this play — and at the conclusion of every Shakespearean tragedy — the dead bodies are prominently in view. Those silent bodies speak, for they tell us that death is real and irreversible, but also, that the questioning, passionate, sentient beings whose actions we have witnessed are not reducible to the bodies we now look upon.

The effect produced by the denouement of *Romeo and Juliet* is characteristic of the later tragedies as well. If the deaths of tragic protagonists confirm what we know to be true — that on earth, human beings do not survive the deaths of their bodies — those deaths also demonstrate that human beings are more than their perishable bodies; and, characteristically, the assertion of death-transcendence is made most strongly in the concluding death scene, thus, at the very moment that death's actuality is most powerfully confirmed. The resultant effect is never one of balance, for the reality of the existence of death, and the reality of the existence of something which transcends death, are wholly and inextricably fused, the demonstration of one in fact depending on the demonstration of the other.[50]

Accordingly, we feel at the same time both sadness and satisfaction: sadness that we are inescapably tied to our bodies, thus, to death; and satisfaction because we witness the existence of something which transcends the bodily self. Moreover, the fact that something uniquely human is demonstrated at the very moment of its snuffing out increases our feeling of sadness in exact proportion to the measure it accords of satisfaction, for it is the death of what is most fully human that occasions the deepest grief.

The need to depict what is most fully human explains why the character of a Shakespearean tragic protagonist is more fully developed both in relation to comedy, and to the other characters in the tragedy in which he appears. Thus, comedy (as numerous critics have noted) stresses what characters have in common with the rest of humanity—for example, lovers, whatever their individual differences, are viewed at one level simply as variations on a theme ("as all is mortal in nature, so is all nature in love mortal in folly," *As You Like It*, II.iv.52-54); and this reinforces our sense of the interchangeability of human beings, which lends weight and power to the comic solution to death. Tragedy, in contrast, stresses what is unique in the tragic protagonist, for tragedy addresses our awareness of our own and other's individuality—of exactly that part of the self which dies, irredeemably.[51] Thus Hamlet, Macbeth, Othello, Lear, are particularized beyond any character in comedy, or in the plays in which they appear, as they live out their highly individualized versions of the common mortal destiny. If Romeo and Juliet seem less individualized than do other tragic protagonists, it is because this tragedy depicts the process of individuation itself—the moment at which individuals, separating themselves from the community, accept and embrace their own and one another's unique individuality,[52] which is to say, accept and embrace death.

It should be repeated that in *Romeo and Juliet*, as in other Shakespearean tragedies, effort is directed to mastery of death in the here and now—a depiction of death-transcendence enacted by and for time- and flesh-bound human beings. In this, Shakespearean tragedy occupies a point midway between the absolute victory over death enacted in medieval drama, and the absolute victory of death enacted in some modern drama. Shakespearean tragedy does offer a hope of ultimate death-transcendence, for in the demonstrated existence of something non-material and uniquely human lies the possibility—not the certainty—that the promises of religion could prove true. If this contrasts sharply with the enacted certainties of earlier drama, it also contrasts sharply with, say, the Beckettian dramatic universe, for the latter construes our present reality in such a way as to preclude the possibility that anything more, or other, might exist.

Conclusion

In Shakespearean drama, as in its medieval predecessors, death is confronted in order to be overcome; and the ability of the drama to master death is tested most powerfully in Shakespearean tragedy, where death is most fully confronted. In *Romeo and Juliet*, as in all Shakespearean tragedy, the inescapable death taint in both the physical and the social bodies is fully revealed. That revelation exposes the limits of comedy, preparing us to accept another way of mastering mortality—the enactment of a form of death-transcendence which is inseparable from the demonstration of death's reality and power. The acknowledgement of the limits of comedy, and the consequent need to devise a solution to death based on the full embrace of death, are implicit starting points of all Shakespearean tragedy; but in *Romeo and Juliet* they are enacted within the play itself.

At the start of this work I discussed the *Quem quaeritis* plays as paradigmatic of the medieval-Renaissance dramatic tradition (see above, pp. 6 ff.). If we compare *Romeo and Juliet* to that earlier drama we can see, distilled, both continuities and essential distinctions between the handling of death in Shakespearean drama and in the dramatic tradition preceding his work. In the *Quem quaeritis* play examined in the Introduction (the *Visitatio Sepulchri* contained in the *Regularis Concordia*), the grieving Marys approach Christ's tomb. The angels announce resurrection, the overcoming of death; and the curtain of the sepulchre is drawn aside to reveal the absence of a body—the total overthrow of the dead, corruptible flesh. The Marys who witness this demonstration experience a turn from grief at death to joy at its overthrow; and the larger audience to the action, the congregation, who see and hear precisely what the Marys do, experience the same emotion. At the conclusion of *Romeo and Juliet* the witnesses on stage and in the theater gaze at the outcome of the Friar's failed resurrection plot: not, as in the *Quem quaeritis* play, an empty tomb—proof of the literal and absolute conquest of the corruptible body—but rather a tomb containing three forever-dead bodies—proof that the death aspect of bodily-based life cannot be wholly escaped on earth, within time. But here, the experience of those on and off stage diverge; for what the characters and the audience are witness to is no longer identical either throughout the play or at its denouement. Throughout Shakespeare's play we see the lovers' creation of a love which includes, yet transcends and finally defies, its own bodily (therefore death-tainted) basis—a counter to death whose strengths and limits are illustrated at one and the same time in the lovers' decision to die. And at the denouement of the play the effort to master death moves outward, from stage to theater, from the characters to the audience, as we evaluate the deaths at the conclusion in the light of the enacted whole—a whole to which we alone (in contrast to any of the characters who remain on stage) have been privy. In the naturalized Shakespearean theater (as in the actual world that theater represents) the overthrow of death is not, and cannot be, literal or absolute; and the action of resurrection is now completed, if at all, only in the minds of the audience, who are moved to reassess the meaning of what they have seen.

Notes

1 Marjorie Garber, "'Wild Laughter in the Throat of Death': Darker Purposes in Shakespearean Comedy," in *Shakespearean Comedy*, ed. Maurice Charney (N.Y.: New York Literary Forum, 1980), also sees the overcoming of a threat of death as central to Shakespearean comedy. Cf. also Susan Snyder, *The Comic Matrix of Shakespeare's Tragedies*: Romeo and Juliet, Hamlet, Othello *and* King Lear (Princeton U. Press, 1979), who comments on the "generic refusal of mortality" common not only to Shakespearean comedy, but to romantic comedy of the late 1580's and early 1590's, in general (p. 20).

2 Many critics, among them Northrop Frye, *Anatomy of Criticism: Four Essays* (Princeton U. Press, 1957), Sherman Hawkins, "The Two Worlds of Shakespearean Comedy," *Shak. Studies*, 3 (1968 for 1967), 62-80, and C. L. Barber, *Shakespeare's Festive Comedy: A Study of Dramatic Form and its Relation to Social Custom* (Princeton U. Press, 1959), see a three-part movement as fundamental to Shakespearean comedy, whether they describe that movement as from an overly rigid society controlled by the old, through chaos and confusion, back to a society integrated with and centered around the next generation (Frye); from city world to green world and back again (Hawkins); or from everyday to holiday and back again (Barber).

3 For an extended discussion of the connection between comedy and tragedy in *Romeo and Juliet*, see Susan Snyder, *Comic Matrix*. Snyder examines the conventions of romantic comedy of the late 1580's and the 1590's in order to discover what an audience would have expected, and then explores how Shakespeare uses those expectations, and how they contribute to shaping structure and meanings in his tragedies.

4 A persistent critical concern in discussions of *Romeo and Juliet* is the issue of what kind of tragedy the play is, and the related issue of whether the play is different in kind from later Shakespearean tragedy. Critics who believe it is tend to judge the play as somehow flawed or inferior, either by comparison to Shakespeare's own later works, or in relation to something they believe the play intends, but fails, to do. For example, H. A. Mason, *Shakespeare's Tragedies of Love: An Examination of the Possibility of Common Readings of* Romeo and Juliet, Othello, King Lear *and* Anthony and Cleopatra (Barnes & Noble, Inc., 1970), takes the position that it is the business "of serious drama to relate love and death in significant wholes" (p. 55), and feels that while the play succeeds incomparably in moments (such as the balcony scene) in imbuing us with a sense of the

power and transcendent value of their love, we do not "see this unique value in a contrasting context of all the great values that depend on man entering into multiple relations with other men" (p. 54). T.J. Cribb, "The Unity of 'Romeo and Juliet,'" *Shak. Survey*, 34 (1981), believes that the play illustrates a Renaissance Platonic (in particular, a Ficinian) vision of love in which the lovers are led through physical love towards an appreciation of divine love, but that the play can embody such an idea only imperfectly: "Both in overall design and local detail," the play is shaped by the Ficinian view of love; but to "say this is to accept the play on its intellectual, ideal and poetic level. In the physical medium of the theatre concreted in the personalities of actors and responding to an audience in all of its humanity, the Ficinian aspirations may well fade in the light of common day, or haunt the play with a sense of the strained and unachieved" (p. 104). Kenneth Muir, *Shakespeare's Tragic Sequence* (London: Hutchinson U. Library, 1972), in common with many other critics, regards *Romeo and Juliet* as apprentice work, among other reasons, because it relies too much on accident (a common charge). Ruth Nevo, *Tragic Form in Shakespeare* (Princeton, N.J.: Princeton U. Press, 1972), remarks that *Romeo and Juliet* "is less tragic than the major tragedies, not because it is different in kind—a 'tragedy of chance' rather than a 'tragedy of character'—but because the possibilities of the medium are not yet fully exploited, perhaps not yet fully understood" (p. 35). She does believe, as I do, that the play contains the essential elements of the later tragedies, but thinks those elements are "not fully mastered" (p. 36). Other critics, while addressing the issue of the play's supposed differences from (inferiority to) other, later Shakespearean tragedies, insist that we view the play on its own terms, assuming that what is there is there because Shakespeare intended it to be. For example, John Lawlor, "Romeo and Juliet," in *Early Shakespeare*, Stratford-upon-Avon Studies 3 (London: Arnold, 1961; rpt. with modifications, 1967; rpt. 1976), discusses the common criticism that the play is a lesser work because its events spring from fortune rather than from character. He concludes, "If we can lay aside our preconceived notions alike of the 'tragedy of character' and the 'tragedy of fortune,' we may see that *Romeo and Juliet* is profoundly consistent with the longer run of the Shakespearean imagination" (p. 143). However, Lawlor sees the play as more closely related to the late comedies: "If we seek the line of development from *Romeo and Juliet*, we may find it not in the later tragedies but in the antitype of *tragedie* [Lawlor's term for medieval tragedy, tragedy centered on reversal of fortune], those last plays of Shakespeare where the scope of accident includes the truth of fortunate accident, so that ancient wrongs are righted and the old make way for the newness of life in the young; where fulfillment is achieved in this world and not in a region beyond the stars, even death itself being cancelled and the exile returned to his native land; where all, in fine, is subject to a Time which is not envious or calumniating but, joining with mortal designs, 'Goes upright with his carriage'" (p. 141). Norman Rabkin, *Shakespeare and the Common Understanding* (N.Y.: The Free Press; London: Collier-Macmillan Ltd., 1967), in discussing the mixture of styles in *Romeo and Juliet* (a mixture sometimes cited as evidence of Shakespeare's incomplete mastery of his medium), comments, "Surely it is not bardolatry to suggest that in a play whose every line reflects an intense concern with language Shakespeare knew that he was making Mercutio's language very different from Capulet's, and the Nurse's from Paris' . . ." (p. 167). And Derick R. C. Marsh, *Passion Lends Them Power: A Study of Shakespeare's Love Tragedies* (Manchester University Press, 1976), sums up the issue at the beginning of his perceptive analysis of the play: "Too rigid a definition of what tragedy ought to be is one important reason it seems to me, why a good deal of adverse criticism has been directed at *Romeo and Juliet*: it has been attacked primarily for being an immature or defective tragedy" (p. 46). Although Marsh does succumb to the temptation of ranking the tragedy ("it is not as great a play as *Hamlet* or *King Lear*"), he sensibly insists that we view the play "on its own terms" (p. 48), for, as he points out, "By asking the wrong questions, some able critics have blinded themselves to those qualities that are really there" (p. 46).

5 This and all subsequent quotations from the play are taken from the Signet paperback edition of *Romeo and Juliet*, ed. J. A. Bryant, Jr., The Signet Classic Shakespeare, ed. Sylvan Barnet (N.Y.: New American Library, 1964).

6 Cf. Irving Ribner, *Patterns in Shakespearian Tragedy* (London: Methuen & Co., Ltd., 1960; rpt. 1960): "He [Romeo] has come willingly to embrace the necessary end of life's journey" (p. 34).

7 Cf. James L. Calderwood, *Shakespeare and the Denial of Death*, who says that the play sets up a situation in which either retaining collective identity (which he defines as identification with patriarchy), or denying it and creating a different identity, entails a risk of death. But Calderwood thinks that this is so only because "in *Romeo and Juliet* the immortality that normally attends patriarchy is compromised by the deadliness of the family feud which the lovers also inherit from their fathers" (p. 108). He does not, as I do, see the feud—and "plague-and feud-ridden Verona"—as merely a special instance of the universal fact that all collective bodies entail a death-aspect *vis-à-vis* their individual members.

Kirby Farrell, *Play, Death, and Heroism in Shakespeare*, focuses closely on the relation in *Romeo and Juliet* between love and death, and contemporary concepts of patriarchy. He argues that the meaning of the lovers' actions, and of the play itself, can be understood only in the context of a patriarchy which "like religion . . . systematized heroic fantasies of immortality" (p. 131). See the whole of Chapter 11 (pp. 131-71).

8 Although now classified as histories, the First Folio classifies *Richard II* and *Richard III* as tragedies; but the chief protagonists there are kings, and so fit the pattern. Timon is the only other exception; but while his life is not linked with that of the state in any official capacity, neither is it familial.

9 Actually, the social level is somewhere between upper middle and lower upper class; we do not have an exact social equivalent of the leisured young men who are a little less than aristocrats, but a little more than bourgeois gentlemen. In any event, as Marion Bodwell Smith, *Dualities in Shakespeare* (U. of Toronto Press, 1966), notes (as do other critics), the characters are the kind usually associated with comedy rather than tragedy: "Shakespeare sets out in *Romeo and Juliet* to write a new kind of tragedy . . . involving not royal or politically important figures but the upper and upper-middle class lovers he had used in comedy" (p. 109).

10 Cf. G. K. Hunter, "Shakespeare's Earliest Tragedies: *Titus Andronicus* and *Romeo and Juliet*," *Shak. Survey*, 27 (1974), who describes the Verona of the play as a place of ". . . domestic luxury and homely social display, a cosy familiarity of masters and servants, a world poised between the bourgeois and the aristocrats" (p. 5); and T. J. Cribb, "The Unity of 'Romeo and Juliet,'" who also notes the domestic, familiar atmosphere: "An important part of the play's tone and atmosphere is determined by domestic arrangements, bedrooms, adolescent joking, potmen, nurses, orchard walls, truckle beds, people sitting up late talking or returning from parties, cooks, parental tantrums and family scenes, worms pricked from the lazy fingers of maids. Proverbs are ready for every occasion and the busy surface of domestic normality is confidently maintained, supported in turn by the novella elements of the plot" (p. 101).

11 The fact that a Shakespearean protagonist can be understood only in relation to the way the society of the play is depicted is of course true in all Shakespearean drama. Cf. Michael Long, *The Unnatural Scene: A Study in Shakespearean Tragedy* (London: Methuen & Co., Ltd., 1978), who stresses that while character is important, it cannot be understood apart from the highly specific way in which the social world of a given play is created. " . . . these plays [certain tragedies and so-called problem plays, *e.g., Hamlet* and *Measure for Measure*] present not just individuals moving in a 'universe' or 'world' but men seen in social situations of highly specific kinds, social milieux which receive the highest degree of social/psychological documentation" (pp. 3-4).

12 Whatever contemporary authorities have to say on the subject of daughterly disobedience, Shakespeare has dramatized this father-daughter interchange in a way which shifts our sympathies to Juliet; and Capulet appears culpable even to characters within the play, not only to the Nurse, but to the colder Lady Capulet as well ("Fie, fie! What, are you mad?" III.v.158).

13 For a view of the Nurse which accords with mine, see Barbara Everett, "*Romeo and Juliet*: The Nurse's Story," *Critical Q.*, 14 (1972): " . . . from the beginning what the Nurse has is more than personality: it is function; and by function she is a 'natural'" (p. 131). This article offers a subtle and suggestive analysis of how the Nurse's speeches operate in

the play "to provide a *natural* context for the motif of 'death-marked love' which governs the play" (p. 132).

14 Cf. Gordon Ross Smith, "The Balance of Themes in *Romeo and Juliet*," in *Essays on Shakespeare*, ed. Gordon Ross Smith (University Park & London: The Pennsylvania State U. Press, 1985). Smith points out that two reactions to Romeo's behavior in this scene are possible, sympathetic, or condemnatory; and indeed, critical views on how we are to take this scene diverge (as do views on the Friar in general). While critics usually take one or the other position (adolescent excess— understandable grief), Ruth Nevo notes the ambivalent effect of the scene. However, she thinks that effect is due to a deficiency in dramatic technique (the apprentice theory again): "Romeo's transports here are a regrettable lapse, an outburst of immature extravagance. But I believe we should learn to see them as fully expressive—to Shakespeare's capacity at this stage—of the poignance and complexity of his anguish ... " (p. 48).

15 For a close analysis of this scene, see Norman Rabkin, *Shakespeare and the Common Understanding*, esp. pp. 188 ff. Rabkin points out that the scene moves from lovely, though formal, expressions of grief at death, to increasingly banal, and finally, bathetic, formulations of grief and loss.

16 Cf. Phyllis Rackin, *Shakespeare's Tragedies* (N.Y.: Frederick Ungar Publishing Co., 1978), who also sees the Friar's running away as symbolically significant: the Friar "underestimates the quality of their love, which transcends death as well as sexual appetite and social prosperity; and it is significant that he finally fails them by running from the place of death, the Capulet's tomb. He repeatedly counsels, 'wisely and slow; they stumble that run fast,' but it is he who runs at the crucial moment" (pp. 30-31).
   Gerry Brenner, "Shakespeare's Politically Ambitious Friar," *Shak. Studies*, 13 (1980), sums up the two most common (and opposing) views of the Friar. "He can be characterized, as is customary, to be a representative of moderation and wisdom. But his stratagems and their aborted results also make it tempting to characterize him as a bungling priest, a hand-me-down from medieval fabliaux and *commedia erudita*" (p. 48). However, Brenner himself argues that the Friar is neither, but rather "a duplicitous and ambitious man whose benevolent manner masks the political objectives of his deeds" (p. 48)—a totally self-interested character, concerned mainly with power politics, especially with the wish to "assert his superiority over domestic and civil authorities [Capulet, the father; Escalus, the ruler] ..." (p. 52). Brenner's view of the Friar seems extreme, for the text stresses his inadequacy, rather than any positively evil qualities. However, if the Friar is not evil, neither is he (as some critics believe) morally normative. I agree with Derick R. C. Marsh, *Passion Lends Them Power*, that "the play's authority" is "not vested in Friar Lawrence's demands for caution and a more deliberate pace" (p. 65). For while the characters within the play never

question the Friar's wisdom or the quality of his sanctity ("We still have known thee for a holy man," Escalus declares, V.iii.270), the play itself certainly does so (see my discussion).

17 Although I do not, some critics see *Romeo and Juliet* as ultimately reflective of an orthodox Christian perspective. These include Fredson Bowers, "Death in Victory: Shakespeare's Tragic Reconciliations," in *Studies in Honor of DeWitt T. Starnes*, ed. Thomas P. Harrison, Archibald A. Hill, Ernest C. Mossner, James Sledd (Austin: The U. of Texas, 1987); Irving Ribner, *Patterns in Shakespearian Tragedy*; Paul N. Siegel, *Shakespeare in His Time and Ours* (Notre Dame, Indiana: U. of Notre Dame Press, 1968); and Harry Morris, Last *Things in Shakespeare* (Tallahassee, Florida: University Presses of Florida, Florida State U. Press, 1985). Although Bowers deals mainly with *Hamlet*, and does not specifically address *Romeo and Juliet*, he believes that Shakespearean tragedy in general derives from, and evokes, a Christian vision of reconciliation between Justice and Mercy, the Old Law and the New Law. "Thus punishment, though still required as payment for tragic error, is not the end-all of the larger idea of equity that permeates the Shakespearean tragic drama. In Christian terms, the one resembles the Old Law of punishment without hope. The other stems from the New Law, which by joining Mercy to Justice establishes a dispensation in which Hope is one of the triad of intermediaries" (p. 61). Irving Ribner believes that "A Christian view of man's position in the universe provides a design for tragedy in this early play" (p. 34). Paul Siegel, who discusses the relationship in *Romeo and Juliet* between "Christianity and the Religion of Love . . ." (his chapter heading), sees the two as sometimes conflicting, but ultimately working together to produce a unified vision in which contemporary ideas of the religion of love are harmonized with an overriding Christian vision: "*Romeo and Juliet* dramatizes this concept of a cosmic love manifesting itself through sexual love and working against strife and disorder in society" (p. 95). Harry Morris, who identifies and discusses the abundance of *memento-mori* material in *Romeo and Juliet*, believes Shakespeare uses that material for a traditional religious purpose: to direct the audience's thoughts to the Last Judgement and, specifically, to the problem of whether a basically good human being with one sin can be damned (a problem Morris believes is considered "profoundly" in *Hamlet* and *Othello*) (p. 231). In my view, while *Romeo and Juliet* is not ultimately incompatible with Christian orthodoxy, that is not what the play dramatizes.

18 Harry Morris, *Last Things in Shakespeare*, also sees Escalus's pronouncements as evoking images of the Last Judgement. But Morris believes Shakespeare intends the scene as a foreshadowing of God's judgement, not as a comment on the inadequacy of human rulers in the face of death: "Surely God is no more severe than a merciful Renaissance prince. Surely God, as the Prince, is struck with woe by the story of these tragic children; and in heaven above as on earth below, although some shall be punished, surely 'Some shall be pardon'd (V.iii.308)'" (p.231).

19 Cf. Norman N. Holland, "Mercutio, Mine Own Son the Dentist," in *Essays on Shakespeare*, ed. Gordon Ross Smith (University Park & London: The Pennsylvania State U. Press, 1965), who claims we regard Mercutio as both "symbolic, and not detachable from the specific (literary) work in which [he] appear[s], and also as naturalistic, or realistic"—a character whose psyche we construe in our own minds, from our own experience, as we would a personage in life. Holland's chief concern is to establish the validity of applying psychoanalytic concepts to a literary character.

20 Many critics relate Mercutio and the Nurse to one another, and associate both with the element of comedy in the play; and they, as do I, see those characters' shared viewpoint as that against which the lovers' values are defined. For example Barbara Everett, "*Romeo and Juliet*: The Nurse's Story," comments, "Something important is contributed to *Romeo and Juliet* by the fact that she [the Nurse] and her counterpoise Mercutio are each, in their opposed ways, exceptionally funny. She is a 'natural' and he is a 'fool', and this fact makes a good deal of difference to the way we respond to their two 'straight men', the hero and heroine of the play. Romeo and Juliet are two romantic children, but we take them—or should take them—absolutely straight; and we might fail to do so were it not for the obliquity, or folly, that characterises their constant companions" (p. 132). And Norman Rabkin, *Shakespeare and the Common Understanding*, comments on "the tone of earthy commonplace present whenever she or Mercutio is on stage" (p. 170).

21 For a comparison of the Queen Mab speech as it appears in Q1 and Q2, see Sidney Thomas, "The Queen Mab Speech in 'Romeo and Juliet,'" *Shak. Survey*, 25 (1972), 73-80. Thomas argues that "the Q1 text of the Queen Mab speech" is "perhaps less corrupt and closer to Shakespeare's intentions than the Q2 text" (p. 80). However, even if this were so it does not change my reading, since both the Q1 and the Q2 versions show the same reduction of dreams to animal desires.

For a suggestive and illuminating comparison between Mercutio's Queen Mab speech and Juliet's "Gallop apace, you fiery-footed steeds" speech, see Nicholas Brooke, *Shakespeare's Early Tragedies* (London: Methuen and Co. Ltd., 1968). Brooke comments, "The emblems are the same, and their significance is similar: Phaethon's coach of day is driven into the night of Juliet's desire. Queen Mab's coach is driven through the night of dreams to fulfill the real ambitions of men and women, greed and lust. But the scale of the two waggons is radically different, in fact sheer opposite. Queen Mab is infinitely small, trivial, insignificant, malicious and contemptible (however gossamer-charming); Phaethon's chariot is the Sun, its region the whole sky, vast, and in its regular motion, irresistible.... Their relationship is ... [like] successive emblem pictures ... radically *different* views of the *same* thing. In the case of Queen Mab, reduced to minimum, as Mercutio sees it; and with Phaethon, in Juliet's view on her clandestine wedding night, at maximum extension, translated from the absurd to the magnificent" (p. 85).

22 Shakespearean successors to the doubter figures appear in all three genres, and include figures as diverse as Falstaff, Shylock, Jacques, Hamlet, Othello, Lear (for a discussion of these figures see Chapter One, p. 32). Critics sense that Mercutio is of central importance in the play, yet disagree on how or why (this feeling has given rise to the absurd notion that Shakespeare kills off Mercutio because he is stealing the show). Marsh, *Passion Lends Them Power*, describes Mercutio in terms which concur with my view of Mercutio as a doubter figure. "It does not seem to me too far-fetched to see in him a similarity to Enobarbus, and even, though of course in a strictly limited way that precludes any suggestion of a share in villainy, to Iago. Each of these characters operates by a sort of cynical intelligence, each priding himself on his ability to see through the romantic illusions that may deceive other men, yet neither seems to find in this operation of the intelligence an attitude to life that will reveal a rewarding purpose. Iago can only destroy, with a lack of satisfactory motive that is almost proverbial; in the end he destroys himself, while the love whose reality he denies is proved real. Enobarbus too, thinks he can see Antony's infatuation for what it is, and by contrast sees reason as indicating that his own most profitable course of action lies in deserting to Caesar. He finds that his cynical assessment of Antony has missed the quality of the man, and that his betrayal has left him with no reason to live. Mercutio, seeing everything from which men fashion a purpose as illusion, perhaps sees no reason for living at all...." (p. 69).

23 For an explication of some of the puns revolving around sexuality and aggression in this scene, see Frank Fabry, "Shakespeare's Witty Musician: *Romeo and Juliet*, IV.v.114-17," *Sh. Q.* 33 (1982), 182-83.

24 The Signet edition identifies this song as "from Richard Edwards' 'In Commendation of Music,' in *The Paradise of Dainty Devices*, 1578."

25 Harry Levin, "Form and Formality in 'Romeo and Juliet,'" in *Modern Shakespearean Criticism: Essays on Style, Dramaturgy, and the Major Plays*, ed. Alvin B. Kernan (N.Y.: Harcourt Brace Jovanovich, Inc., 1970), also relates the musicians' scene to Romeo's "How silver sweet sound lovers' tongues by night,/ Like softest music ..." (for his discussion of this scene, see pp. 389-90).

26 For many critics, Mercutio's death is the most powerfully affecting death in the play. For example Mason, *Shakespeare's Tragedies of Love*, comments, "The moment remains so powerful that the deaths at the end of the play seem by contrast merely parts of a story" (p. 30); and Brooke, *Shakespeare's Early Tragedies*, asserts, "The most moving scene in the play, in a sense, is the death of Mercutio ..." (p. 82). As I see it, these critics are reacting to the shock of a death to which no counter is offered. Mercutio's death is the thing itself, the raw unaccommodated fact of animal death, the manner of the death underlining our creaturely vulnerability; whereas meaningless animal death is the very thing which the deaths of Romeo and Juliet are designed to revalue.

27 Many critics see the death of Mercutio as the point at which the play passes from comedy to tragedy. For example, Snyder, *Comic Matrix*, states that "if we divide the play at Mercutio's death, the death that generates all those that follow, it becomes apparent that the play's movement up to this point is essentially comic" (p. 59). Raymond Utterback, "The Death of Mercutio," *Shak. Q*, 24 (1973), 105-116, points out that "Mercutio's death affects the action critically and thoroughly alters the tone of the play. In the midst of the story of romantic love which has occupied the stage, and in spite of the general atmosphere of danger and the predictions of doom, this actual death comes as a shock. It introduces the crucial fact, irrevocable and damaging, that shifts the play into the tragic mode" (p. 107). And Brooke, *Shakespeare's Early Tragedies*, comments, "The whole play is challenged and re-directed by this scene [*i.e.*, Mercutio's death]. The genre in which it is conceived is set sharply against a sense of actuality as Mercutio dies the way men do die—accidentally, irrelevantly, ridiculously; in a word, prosaically ... The shock of this scene is used to precipitate a change of key in the play: it becomes immediately more serious, and decisively tragic where before it had been predominantly comic" (p. 83). Later, Brooke associates the death of Mercutio—rightly, I think—with the entrance of Marcade in *Love's Labors Lost*: "Mercutio's minimally stated, prosaic death makes a powerful impact in the courtly-comic world of love and acts as a catalyst projecting a freshly serious perception," just as "Mercade's entrance in Act V, as a silent figure dressed in black, has a startling effect of invalidating the courtly games to which the play seems to have become committed for its finale" (p. 87). The point is, in both cases it is the reality of death which has entered the play, forcing a shift from the comic to the tragic mode.

28 Cf. Snyder, *Comic Matrix*, who links the death of Mercutio to Juliet's rejection of the Nurse, and sees both as a rejection of the comic strategy: "Like the slaying of Mercutio, Juliet's [and the audience's] rejection" of the Nurse "has symbolic overtones. The possibilities of comedy have again been presented only to be discarded" (p. 66).

29 However differently they describe them, many critics see, as I do, two contrasting components (viewpoints, value systems), embodied respectively in the lovers and in the community, as the basic building blocks of *Romeo and Juliet* (or, in some critics' views, of Shakespearean tragedy in general); however, none sees those components as centrally related to the problem of death. Critics who discuss two opposing elements include Cribb, "The Unity of 'Romeo and Juliet'"; James Calderwood, *Shakespearean Metadrama: The Argument of the Play* in Titus Andronicus, Love's Labour's Lost, Romeo and Juliet, A Midsummer Night's Dream, and Richard II (Minneapolis, Minn.: U. of Minnesota Press, 1971); Brooke, *Shakespeare's Early Tragedies*; Maynard Mack, "The Jacobean Shakespeare: Some Observations on the Construction of the Tragedies," in *Modern Shakespearean Criticism: Essays on Style, Dramaturgy, and the Major Plays*, ed. Alvin B. Kernan (N.Y.: Harcourt, Brace Jovanovich, Inc., 1970); Rene E. Fortin, "Desolation and the Better

Life: The Two Voices of Shakespearean Tragedy," *Shak. Q.*, 32 (1981), 80-94; Robert Grudin, *Mighty Opposites: Shakespeare and Renaissance Contrariety* (Berkeley/Los Angeles/London: U. of Calif. Press, 1979); Nevo, *Tragic Form*; Mason, *Shakespeare's Tragedies of Love*; Harry Levin, "Form and Formality ...". Cribb comments on the fact that the Nurse, Mercutio, Capulet and the servants are comic, and that the Nurse and Mercutio "supply the mixture of simple earthiness and cynical obscenity for which the play is well known" (p. 109); and he points out that "Each of the two romantic lovers is pointedly coupled with a satiric counterpart embodying an attitude remote indeed from lyricism ..." (p. 101) (Cribb regards the presence of these two elements as a problem, since they have to be reconciled with the Ficinian tradition he believes the play illustrates). Calderwood locates the conflicting elements as a private and a public dimension—love as private, and the public world (for him, the dramatic dilemma is, crucially, a linguistic, or stylistic, dilemma as well). Brooke stresses the vitality of the characters other than Romeo and Juliet, and he contrasts the lovers to those characters, commenting on the presence in the play of "an extra-ordinary vitality ..., a sense of life which is manifest in all the roles most alien to Romeo and Juliet themselves, that is to say the nurse, Mercutio, and the old Capulets. In all of these the stuff of life is earthy, bawdy, comic, certainly thoughtless, and impatient; and it has the conditions for continuance, the instinct for self-preservation and fertility. ... All of these have a warmth that is reassuring, but which is also utterly in contrast to the glory of Romeo and Juliet ..." (p. 102). Maynard Mack's discussion of Jacobean tragedy obviously does not include *Romeo and Juliet*, but his description of the two voices he sees as essential components of the later tragedies fits *Romeo and Juliet* as well, and accords with my view of the two basic elements of which the earlier tragedy is composed:

> If it is true, as can be argued, that the Greek chorus functions in large measure as spokesman for the values of the community, and the first actor, in large measure, for the passionate life of the individual, we can perhaps see a philosophical basis for the long succession of opposing voices. What matters to the community is obviously accommodation—all those adjustments and resiliences that enable it to survive; whereas what matters to the individual, at least in his heroic mood, is just as obviously integrity—all that enables him to remain an *individual*, one thing not many.
> (p. 331)

Fortin elaborates on Mack's observations, speaking of "the interplay of antiphonal voices [heroic and anti-heroic] within the tragic hero himself," and pointing out that "These antiphonal voices give expression to the hero's dilemma, his urgent need to choose between the heroic and the anti-heroic in a world wherein neither response seems wholly adequate" (pp. 80, 81). Fortin's description of the two voices differs from mine (for him, the anti-heroic or "kenotic" voice embodies an essentially Christian outlook, associated with the "feminine" and including the virtues of humility, selflessness, patience, compassion); but his view of the impossibility of definitively choosing between the two voices accords exactly with my view: "... the kenotic voice does not replace the heroic voice" (p. 84). Both are heard throughout a given play, and neither is finally, or unambivalently, espoused; for the "conflict of the two ideals, the secular heroic and the religious kenotic, is expressive finally of the human condition itself" (p. 84) (following Mack, Fortin deals with later tragedy, and therefore does not discuss *Romeo and Juliet* directly). Grudin sees the exploration of contrarieties as fundamental to Shakespearean drama, and views those contrarieties not so much as problems to be depicted and examined, but rather, as elements of meaning and technique, and as structuring principles of whole plays as well. Nevo refers to "the conflict between the autonomous dictates of an imaginative passion and the socially sanctified codes of conventional behavior" (p. 47), and she sees the development of the play as in part a movement of the lovers away from one, to a full development of the other. Mason understands such figures as the Nurse and Mercutio to be representative of the community, but feels the lovers, and therefore the play, fail to some degree, because the two (individual and community) are not brought into full relationship. Harry Levin discusses the "tendency toward reduplication, both stylistic and structural," in *Romeo and Juliet* (p. 286), and comments, "against this insistence upon polarity at every level, the mutuality of the lovers stands out, the one organic relation amid an overplus of stylized expressions and attitudes" (p. 287).

30 For a discussion of the degree to which the effect of the lovers' poetry depends upon the surrounding linguistic context, see Robert Penn Warren, "Pure and Impure Poetry," in *Selected Essays* (N.Y.: Random House, N.D.).

31 For a discussion of the linking of love and death in the wordplay (and action) of the tragedy, see M. M. Mahood's *Shakespeare's Wordplay* (London: Methuen & Co., Ltd., 1957), especially Chapter Two, "Romeo and Juliet," pp. 56-72.

32 Cf. Roger Stilling, *Love and Death in Renaissance Tragedy* (Baton Rouge, La.: Louisiana State U. Press, 1976), who, in discussing the sonnet Romeo and Juliet create at their first meeting, comments, "One sees here the beginnings of the Shakespearean attempt to fuse body with soul and to unite them in one union, one couple. The effort here and the success of it makes this sonnet a radical contrast to those of Shakespeare's non-dramatic sequence, where bodily desire and spiritual love are so completely separated that they must house themselves in totally different beloveds, of different sex" (p. 78).

33 Many critics stress the conjugal, and strongly sexual, nature of Romeo and Juliet's love. Nevo notes that "... marriage forms their view of their relations with each other from the very first balcony scene ..." (p. 57). Stilling points out that literary history offers numerous images

of both "sexual love as lust" and "of the totally non-physical love usually called Platonic love" (p. 79), but that Shakespeare wants to combine both in "the love-marriage, as opposed to both the courtly liaison and the marriage arranged by outsiders" (p. 79). However, in contrast to my view, Stilling sees death as external to, rather than as inseparable from the lovers and their love: "Still, death remains an external force pressing in on them, or else it becomes something they make use of and welcome—as at the end . . ." (p. 80). Philip J. Traci, "Suggestions About the Bawdry in *Romeo and Juliet*," *South Atlantic Q.*, 71 (1972), 573-86, explicates some of the sexual allusions in *Romeo and Juliet* to show how great an emphasis is placed on the sexual nature of Romeo and Juliet's relationship (Traci's point is not mine, for he is interested in following "the growing sexual maturity of the protagonists in their search for identity through sexual union," p. 573). Brooke stresses the sexual quality of Romeo and Juliet's love, pointing out that the three great love scenes are all sexually charged (the orchard scene, stressing Romeo's body rather than his name; Juliet's "Gallop apace" speech, conveying her desire for sexual fulfillment; the post-consummation aubade); and in his discussion of the play, Brooke specifically relates the stress on the sexual nature of their love to Shakespeare's qualification of the sonnet tradition: the play is in part "a dramatic exploration of the world of the love-sonnet" (p. 80), in which the "formal structure is strongly emphasized; but it is also continually questioned, and penetrated—so that we are made to . . . grasp the movements of experience which lie beneath the formal surface" (p. 82). Brooke does see the play as constituting, "ultimately . . . a highly perceptive exploration of the love-death embrace of the sonneteering tradition, which regards both its superiority and inferiority to the world of common day" (p. 106); but he does not, as I do, see both elements (the poetic/tragic and the realistic/comic) as related to the problem of death.

34 See, for example, sonnets 1 - 7.

35 Brooke comments, of the bedroom and the tomb scenes, "If both are located, as I suppose, on the inner stage, then the parallelism will be the more obvious. Between them, these two sequences fulfill precisely the Prologue's anticipation of a 'death-marked love' . . ." (p. 82).

36 Cf. Marsh: "They are defeated, as all who love must ultimately be defeated, by their own mortality" (p. 51).

37 Many critics note the speeded-up quality of the action, which is such a salient feature of the play; and some relate it, as I do, to the telescoping of the universal human destiny. Marsh, for example, comments, "It is thus the common fate that Romeo and Juliet endure, but it is given terrible dramatic emphasis by the swiftness with which they are destroyed" (p. 49). And Ribner believes that Romeo and Juliet epitomize a universal fate, "for every human being is born into a world where evil [the feud] already waits to destroy him, and he marches steadily towards an inexorable death . . . . It is this universality which

gives the play its stature as a tragedy, for Romeo and Juliet emerge as prototypes of everyman and everywoman" (p. 27). Ribner's ultimate emphasis differs from mine, for he goes on to relate Romeo and Juliet's destiny to a Christian vision of evil contained within a providential universe.

38 Cf. Rabkin: "Linked to an unblinking resolve really to die, it is more moving than all the protestations of Juliet's family circle that their lives are finished when in fact it is quite clear that their grief has not driven them to the death they apostrophize so repetitiously" (p. 176).

39 Cf. Navarre and his lords in *Love's Labor's Lost*, in whose company Paris belongs; like them, he has not accepted the related realities of sexuality and death.

40 Mahood discusses the wordplay in this scene.

41 Romeo dies by poison, and he dies for passionate love. Cf. *Measure for Measure*, in which sex is actually lethal (because of Viennese law, which decrees death for fornication), and is also imaged as a lethal poison which our animal self makes us vulnerable to: "Our natures do pursue,/ Like rats that ravin down their proper bane,/ A thirsty evil, and when we drink, we die" (I.ii.131-33). That whole play grapples directly with the death aspect of sexually based love.

42 We should note that this is different from a *Liebestod*. Denis de Rougemont, *Love in the Western World*, trans. Montgomery Belgion (N.Y.: Pantheon Books, Inc., 1956; rpt. N.Y.: Harper & Row Publishers, 1974), speaks of the Western literary tradition in which love seeks its fulfillment in death; and Rabkin places *Romeo and Juliet* in this tradition when he says that Romeo knows that his love for Juliet "can find its ultimate satisfaction not in the vigorous life that Mercutio so poignantly embodies, but only in death" (p. 180). But Romeo and Juliet, it must be stressed, seek love and life. Death is not an end in itself for them, but chosen only because life without one another is a form of death worse than death itself. Nevo points out that "It is not true to say that [Romeo and Juliet] are married only in death, for their marriage is consummated before Romeo leaves for Mantua" (p. 57). And Mahood notes that *Romeo and Juliet* departs from the classic *Liebestod* myth in several respects, including the fact that "tragic love is always adulterous," but "Romeo and Juliet marry, and Juliet's agony of mind at the prospect of being married to Paris is in part a concern for her marriage vows" (p. 58).

43 Cf. Snyder: "The play's last scene shows how completely the comic movement has been reversed. It is inherent in that movement, as we have seen, that the young get their way at the expense of the old. The final tableau of comedy features young couples joined in love; parents and authority figures are there, if at all, to rectify with more or less good grace what has been accomplished against their wills. But here, the stage is strikingly full of elders—the Friar, the Prince, Capulet, Lady

Capulet, Montague. Their power is not passed on. Indeed, there are no young to take over" (pp. 63-4).

44 Although the denouement is usually spoken of as if it constituted an unambiguous triumph over death, some critics do note the qualified nature of the triumph. Marsh, for example, offers an analysis in which the positive and negative elements of the concluding passages are given full weight, and he comments, ". . . if throughout my account of these final scenes, I have come down heavily against a reading that sees death as an unequivocal triumph for the lovers it is only because I want to redress a critical imbalance that seems to me to have inclined too far towards a comfortably romantic view of this play, either in order to praise it or to dismiss it. The play is the stronger because it does not flinch from showing the physical extinction of the love by the same act that testifies to its unique value. . . . The love cannot exist without the lovers . . ." (p. 88). Rabkin comments, "Were love simple—were it not . . . the cursed mingling of two unreconcilable worlds, and two kinds of experience, two opposed drives—we could find Romeo and his bride either right or wrong. But in a universe whose values are always complementary, there is no such single judgement to be made" (p. 183). Brooke, in describing what I refer to as the communal values, remarks that "this sense of life is utterly alien to the romantic vision; and . . . each criticizes the other. The ecstatic love-death becomes unreal, fantasy-type experience set against this; but this becomes tawdry set against beauty's ensign and death's pale flag" (pp. 102-03).

45 According to medieval tradition, what Lazarus saw in death was so terrible that he never again smiled.

46 Cf. *Hamlet*, in which madness is seen in just this way: "O heavens, is't possible a young maid's wits/ Should be as mortal as an old man's life?" (IV.v.159-60); and "poor Ophelia/ Divided from herself and her fair judgement,/ Without the which we are pictures or mere beasts" (IV.v.84-6).

47 Cf. Marsh, who discusses the images of death preying sexually on Juliet and comments, "The finality and horror of these images of death surely make us realise that of the physical being of the lovers nothing will remain" (p. 86).

See also Morris, *Last Things in Shakespeare*, who singles out for discussion some of the same elements as I do; for example, the linking of grave and wedding bed throughout the play, the images of bodily corruption in Juliet's speech before her mock death, and allusions to the Last Judgement and to resurrection. However, Morris believes these and other elements are designed to compel the audience to consider the Last Judgement and "retributive justice" (p. 208). See Chapter 5, "*Romeo and Juliet*: Some Shall be Pardoned," pp. 205-231.

48 Cf. Marsh, who points out that Romeo and Juliet's death is meaningful just because they see death as "ugly," not as desirable, but choose to die anyway (pp. 83-4).

49 Cf. the statue scene in *The Winter's Tale*, in which a similar contrast is exploited as Leontes comments on the difference between a statue and a living body.

50 In this respect the strategy repeats the strategy seen in medieval dramatizations of the Raising of Lazarus (see above, pp. 27-29). Of course, in contrast to medieval drama, the "resurrection" in *Romeo and Juliet*—the enactment of victory over death—occurs on a plane other than the literal. Norman Rabkin's idea of complementarity—irreconcilable opposites which co-exist without canceling one another out—is also relevant here. See *Shakespeare and the Common Understanding*; and *Shakespeare and the Problem of Meaning* (Chicago and London: The U. of Chicago Press, 1981). Cf. also Mahood, who remarks, "It is the prerogative of poetry to give effect and value to incompatible meanings.... Shakespeare ensures that our final emotion is neither the satisfaction we should feel in the lovers' death if the play were a simple expression of the *Liebestod* theme, nor the dismay of seeing two lives thwarted and destroyed by vicious fates, but a tragic equilibrium which includes and transcends both those feelings" (p. 72).

51 Cf. Harry Levin, "Form and Formality...": "Tragedy tends to isolate where comedy brings together, to reveal the uniqueness of individuals rather than what they have in common with others" (p. 288).

52 This accounts for the emphasis on Romeo and Juliet as young adolescents; for adolescence is the stage of sexual awakening, and of the greatest psychological individuation (both of which entail a death as well as a life aspect).

Conclusion

Death, by which Shakespeare means not merely the end of life, but rather the inseparability of life and death in all aspects of existence, is the condition that Shakespearean drama addresses itself to. The characteristic Shakespearean formulation of this condition is that man is locked into a physical and social body, each of which is simultaneously a basis of life and a source of death. In plays from all periods of Shakespeare's life and from all three basic Shakespearean genres (history, comedy, tragedy) death is confronted—by characters within plays and by plays as a whole—in order to be overcome; and each play is therefore best understood in kinetic terms, as a strategy for encompassing and mastering the basic Shakespearean situation of the oneness of life and death.

Each play confronts death in its own unique way. However, generic similarities also exist, for certain ways of handling death are specific to each of the genres, and it is in fact those characteristic ways of meeting death which define Shakespearean genre.

In history, the strategy depends upon the submergence of individual identity in group identity; for the community continues, the individual dies. The flaw in this strategy is the reality of the irreducibly individual self, and the inability of the body politic to confer immortality on that self. This flaw necessitates the comic and tragic strategies.

The comic strategy has affinities with the strategy of history, for it too depends upon identification with an ongoing community. But the community is not, as in the histories, insistently envisioned as the nominalistic abstraction England, but rather as a collection of flesh-and-blood individuals, to be continued through the offspring of the marriage with which comedy concludes. And accordingly, the premier identity in comedy is that of lover and parent-to-be, not that of ruler or subject. As a given comedy unfolds, the death aspect of the communal body is overcome, allowing individuals to secure life and pleasure within the larger society. However, the comic solution to death, while offering the possibility of individual pleasure and satisfaction, is still flawed; for the problem of individual mortality is deflected rather than directly dealt with. Our children live, but we die; and victory over death in a comedy is brought about only by stopping the action of the play at a certain point in time. Moreover, like individual death, the death aspect of the community is deflected for the moment only.

In tragedy, the reality of individuality is fully affirmed, and with it, the concomitant reality of individual death. The death aspect of society and of the body is directly confronted, as various forms of death are enacted within the playing space, and we see what mortal men counterpose to the fact of their mortality.

In both comedies and tragedies, the ways of meeting death are not separable from the particular way in which the death aspect of physical, social and spiritual being is formulated (that is, from the entire play world); and each play, therefore, offers a unique variant of the comic or tragic solution to death. In *A Midsummer Night's Dream*, for example, the related powers of art and love, given dramatic embodiment in the fairies, are shown as able to transform the death side of human nature and of society. In *The Merchant of Venice*, the partial nature of the transformation achieved is more in evidence. The play presents a world with death at its heart, embodied in the figure of Shylock, whose house and presence are at the center of Venetian society. Shylock's house, the larger Venetian society, and Belmont are all simply successively purified versions of the same law-bound, money-based world, the world depicted in detail in the second history tetralogy. Each version is at one further remove from the taint of death, but none wholly escapes it. In *As You Like It*, the death side of human nature and of society is presented in the bad Duke's realm, a place of brotherly hatred, suspicion, usurpation, violence and murder; and the death side of nature is imaged in the Forest of Arden, where cold winter winds blow, thorns prick, animal sexuality threatens human love (the constant allusions to animal mating and to cuckoldry), and the living sustain themselves through the murder of the hapless deer. The solution recommended is simply the adoption of an attitude: the decision to rejoice and affirm, rather than to analyze, rail and satirize; and to to join in the flow of life, deliberately choosing love, in full knowledge of every ill mortal man is subject to. Thus, Orlando transforms the abundant "briers" of the "working-day world"—made literal in the Forest of Arden—by hanging love poems on them; Rosalind loves, knowing the fragility of both love and life ("Sell when you can, you are not for all markets"; "Men are April when they woo, December when they wed"); Touchstone presses in "amongst the rest of the country copulatives"; and the good Duke creates a larger community of love, in which all are welcome at the feast. "Be truly welcome hither," he declares, characteristically, to Adam and Orlando, only a moment before we hear the bad Duke's equally characteristic "Push him out of doors." The stress in *Measure for Measure*, in contrast, is on the death side of the physical and social body, rather than on possible solutions to it; and the solutions depicted are as tainted as the reality those solutions are designed to deal with. The action unfolds as a search for a "remedy" for death: on one level, the death sentence imposed on Claudio, but on another level, the death taint inherent in society and in the body (the death penalty imposed by the Viennese law is a figure for the inexorable law of nature, which decrees that we must die). At the literal and figurative center of the play is the prison where a young man is brought close to death by his sexuality; and he is released only into the larger prison of society and of his own body, both tainted by the related realities of sexuality and death—a reprieve, not a pardon.

    The degree to which a given comedy exposes the death side of life is the degree to which we will experience it as a dark, or "problem," comedy (*The Merchant of Venice*, *Measure for Measure*); but in all the comedies, that death taint is present, even when (as in *A Midsummer Night's Dream*) it is successfully submerged and/or transformed. In tragedy, death is explicitly at the fore. *Hamlet* is a tragic variant of *As You Like It*, in which attitude offers the only way of countering the death-tainted prison of human existence. Hamlet is trapped in a physical and social body poisoned by all the ills of mortality; and therefore the ghost's warning—"howsomever thou pursues this act/ Taint not thy mind"—proves impossible to heed. Like the limed bird whose struggles to free itself only entrap it further, Hamlet's attempts to escape his circumstance only entangle him the more. But the most pernicious trap is not death itself, but the death of the spirit, the fall into bitterness, cruelty and negation; and from this trap, Hamlet does in part rescue himself, in the only way possible—by a kind of spiritual restoration, a partial return from self-absorbed, nihilistic despair. In *As You Like It*, Jacques and the Jacques attitude must be confronted and overcome. In *Hamlet*, the doubter figure is within the tragic protagonist himself, and his partial victory over his own bitter nihilism offers such conquest of death as the play affords.

The construction of *Hamlet* imitates entrapment within a single, death-tainted body. We see almost always through Hamlet's eyes; for part of what the play is depicting is what is entailed in existence within an irreducibly individual self: isolation; limit (of knowledge, of efficacy); death. In *Kinq Lear*, in contrast, the angle of vision shifts. It is as if we are looking downward, like the spectators in Rembrandt's *Anatomy Lesson*, onto an amphitheater in which the body of the world is anatomized in order to discover the source of the ills that lie about its "hard heart." *King Lear* is the darkest of the tragedies, for in it we confront the worst of the death side of nature, human nature and society: cold, vicious cruelty, unbearable suffering, mutilation, death, and, worst of all, the possibility that such suffering and death may be completely meaningless. In Acts I - III we witness a swift stripping away of all of the illusions which protect against the "cold night" of pitiless actuality; and we are left on the bare, featureless heath, the world as it appears to the unillusioned eye, devoid of innate meaning or value. In Acts IV and V we watch as various characters, attempting to put the world back together, endow it with such meaning and value as they themselves can create.

With *Antony and Cleopatra*, we are at the far side of a movement beginning with the early comedies. In *A Midsummer Night's Dream*, mortality is held outside the charmed circle of the playing space, a space akin to the space the fairy attendants create around their sleeping Queen, from which ugly and lethal aspects of physical and mental life are banished: "spotted snakes" (the death side of physical nature); human cruelty and faithlessness (Demetrius is called a "spotted and inconstant man," and a "serpent" and an "adder"). And for the duration of the play we, like the Fairy Queen, sleep within a charmed circle, dreaming the dream Shakespeare has created for us: a dream in which the death aspects of human nature are banished or transformed into something beautiful and pleasing. But while we watch, time is passing, for us, as well as for the lovers whose pleasure we witness; and as they depart for their marriage beds the "iron tongue of midnight" is tolling, a reminder that their brief night of love and pleasure is passing, bringing them inexorably closer to the neverending night of death. The image of that midnight bell recurs at a crucial point in the late tragedy *Antony and Cleopatra*. Throughout that play, two sets of values are depicted through the contrasting worlds of Rome and Egypt: one, headed by the boy Octavius, associated with power politics, order, restraint, coldness, sterility; and the other, presided over by the middle-aged Cleopatra, associated with love, flux, excess, liberty and expansion, passion and fertility. Each world has both a life and a death aspect; but only the lovers' world is associated with the possibility of death-transcendence (as well as with death). After a series of continuous reversals, in which our view of the lovers shifts violently and irresolvably between the positive and the negative, Antony reaches a nadir of defeat and self-defeat: loss of the battle — thus literally of the world — through willfulness, weakness, failure of judgement; and loss of his ideal self, and of all transcendent ideals and values, as he denies the love he has asserted when he rails on Cleopatra. But he rises from this nadir to become the ultimate champion of humanity, a warrior against mortality itself. The movement from comedy, through dark comedy and mature tragedy, to late comedy is reaching completion, as Antony, echoing Theseus' invocation of the midnight bell, calls his followers to rejoice in the darkness of defeat and death: "call to me/ All my sad captains; fill our bowls once more:/ Let's mock the midnight bell." From here it is a short step, dramatically and psychologically as well as chronologically, to a late comedy such as *Winter's Tale*, in which death is successfully integrated within a comic whole.

Works Consulted

Adams, Barry B. "The Prudence of Prince Escalus." *ELH*, 35 (1968), 32-50.

Allman, Eileen Jorge. *Player-King and Adversary: Two Faces of Play in Shakespeare*. Baton Rouge & Louisiana State U. Press, 1980.

Altman, Joel B. *The Tudor Play of Mind: Rhetorical Inquiry and the Development of Elizabeth Drama*. Berkeley & Los Angeles, Calif.: U. of California Press, 1978.

Ariès, Philippe. *The Hour of Our Death*. Trans. Helen Weaver. N.Y.: Alfred A. Knopf, 1981.

___. *Western Attitudes Toward Death: From the Middle Ages to the Present*. Trans. Patricia Ranum. Baltimore & London: The Johns Hopkins U. Press, 1974.

Auden, W.H. *The Dyer's Hand*. 1948; rpt. London: Faber & Faber, 1962.

Bale, John. *Kynge Johan*. In *Specimens of the Pre-Shakespearean Drama*. Vol. I. Ed. John Matthews Manly. 1897; rpt. N.Y.: Dover Publications, Inc., 1967.

Barber, C.L. *Shakespeare's Festive Comedy: A Study of Dramatic Form and its Relation to Social Custom*. Princeton, N.J.: Princeton U. Press, 1959.

Barber, C.L. and Richard Wheeler. *The Whole Journey: Shakespeare's Power of Development*. Berkeley/Los Angeles/London: U. of California Press, 1986.

Barry, Patricia S. *The King in Tudor Drama.* Salzburg Studies in English Literature. Elizabethan & Renaissance Studies, No. 58. Ed. James Hogg. Salzburg, Austria: Institut fur Englische Sprache und Literatur, Universitat Salzburg, 1977.

Barton, Anne. "Shakespeare and the Limits of Language." *Shak. Survey,* 24 (1971), 19-30.

Becker, Ernest. *The Denial of Death.* N.Y.: The Free Press, Macmillan Publishing Co., Inc., 1973.

___. *Escape From Evil.* N.Y.: The Free Press, Macmillan Publishing Co., Inc., 1975.

Berlin, Norman. *The Base String: The Underworld in Elizabethan Drama.* Rutherford/Madison/Teaneck, N.J.: Fairleigh Dickinson U. Press, 1968.

Berry Ralph. *The Shakespearean Metaphor.* Totowa, N.J.: Rowman & Littlefield, 1978.

___. "The Words of Mercury. *Shak. Survey,* 22 (1969), 69-77.

Bevington, David M. *From Mankind to Marlowe: Growth of Structure in the Popular Drama of Tudor England.* Cambridge, Mass.: Harvard U Press, 1962.

___. *Medieval Drama.* Boston: Houghton Mifflin Company, 1975.

___. *Tudor Drama and Politics: A Critical Approach to Topical Meaning.* Cambridge, Mass.: Harvard U. Press, 1968.

Bishop's Bible. Ann Arbor, Michigan: U. Microfilms, Inc.

Blanpied, John W. *Time and the Artist in Shakespeare's English Histories.* Newark: U. of Delaware Press; London & Toronto: Associated U. Presses, 1983.

Boas, Frederick S. *Shakespeare and Elizabethan Culture: An Anthropological View*. N.Y.: Schocken Books, 1984.

The Book of the Craft of Dying and Other Early English Tracts Concerning Death. Ed. Frances M. M. Comper. London: 1917; rpt. Arno Press, Inc., 1977.

A Booke of Christian Prayers. London: Richard Yardley & Peter Short, 1590.

Booth, Stephen. King Lear, Macbeth, *Indefinition, and Tragedy*. New Haven & London: Yale U. Press, 1983.

Bowers, Fredson. "Death in Victory: Shakespeare's Tragic Reconciliations." In *Studies in Honor of DeWitt T. Starnes*. Ed. Thomas P. Harrison, Archibald A. Hill, Ernest C. Mossner, James Sledd. Austin: the U. of Texas, 1967, pp. 53-75.

Brenner, Gerry. "Shakespeare's Politically Ambitious Friar." *Shak. Studies*, 13 (1980), 47-58.

Brooke, Nicholas. *Shakespeare's Early Tragedies*. London: Methuen & Co. Ltd., 1968.

Bryant, James C. "The Problematic Friar in *Romeo and Juliet*." *English Studies*, 55 (1974), 340-350.

Burckhardt, Sigurd. *Shakespearean Meanings*. Princeton, N.J.: Princeton U. Press, 1968.

Burke, Kenneth. *The Philosophy of Literary Form: Studies in Symbolic Action*. Berkeley & Los Angeles, Calif.: U. of Calif. Press, 1941; rev. 1973.

Calderwood, James L. *Metadrama in Shakespeare's Henriad: Richard II to Henry V*. Berkeley/Los Angeles/London: U. of Calif. Press 1979.

___. *Shakespeare and the Denial of Death.* Amherst, Mass.: U. of Massachusetts Press, 1987.

___. *Shakespearean Metadrama: The Argument of the Play in* Titus Andronicus, Love's Labour's Lost, Romeo and Juliet, A Midsummer's Night's Dream, *and* Richard II. Minneapolis, Minn.: U. of Minnesota Press, 1971.

Campbell, Lily B. *Shakespeare's "Histories": Mirrors of Elizabethan Policy.* San Marino, Calif.: Huntington Library, 1947; rpt. 1968.

Carroll, William C. *The Great Feast of Language in Love's Labor's Lost.* Princeton, N.J.: Princeton U. Press, 1976.

The Castle of Perseverance. In *Medieval Drama.* Ed. David Bevington. Boston: Houghton Mifflin Company, 1975.

Certaine Sermons or Homilies Appointed to be Read in Churches in the Time of Queen Elizabeth I (1547-1571). Intro. Ellen Rickey & Thomas Stroup. Gainesville, Fla.: Scholars' Facsimiles & Reprints, 1968.

Chambers, E. K. *The English Folk-Play.* 1933; rpt. N.Y.: Russell & Russell, Inc. 1964.

The Chester Mystery Cycle. Vol. I. Ed. R. M. Lumiansky & David Mills. EETS, S.S. 3, 1974. London/N.Y./Toronto: Oxford U. Press, 1974.

Chesterton, G. K. *Chesterton on Shakespeare.* Ed. Dorothy Collins. Henley-on-Thames, Oxon.: Darwen Finlayson Ltd., 1971.

Clarkson, Paul S. and Clyde T. Warren. *The Law of Property in Shakespeare and the Elizabethan Drama.* 1942; rpt. N.Y.: Gordian Press, 1968.

Clemen, Wolfgang. *English Tragedy Before Shakespeare: The Development of Dramatic Speech.* Trans. T.S. Dorsch. 1961; rpt. London: Methuen & Co. Ltd., 1966.

Cohen, Kathleen. *Metamorphosis of a Death Symbol: The Transi Tomb in the Late Middle Ages and the Renaissance.* Berkeley/Los Angeles/London: U. of California Press, 1973.

Coursen, H.R. *The Leasing Out of England: Shakespeare's Second Henriad.* Wash. D.C.: U. Press of America, Inc., 1982.

Craig, Hardin. *English Religious Drama of the Middle Ages.* Oxford U. Press, 1955.

Craik, T.W. *The Tudor Interlude: Stage, Costume, and Acting.* Leicester U. Press, 1958.

Creeth, Edmund. *Mankynde in Shakespeare.* Athens, Georgia: The U. of Georgia Press, 1976.

Cribb, T. J. "The Unity of 'Romeo and Juliet.'" *Shak. Survey,* 22 (1981).

Cunningham, J. V. "Woe or Wonder: The Emotional Effect of Shakespearean Tragedy." In his *Tradition and Poetic Structure: Essays in Literary History and Criticism.* Denver: Alan Swallow, 1960.

Danby, John F. *Poets on Fortune's Hill.* London: Faber, 1952.

Danson, Lawrence. *The Harmonies of the Merchant of Venice.* New Haven & London: Yale U. Press, 1978.

___. "*Henry V*: King, Chorus, and Critics." *Shak. Q.,* 34 (1983), 27-43.

Dash, Irene G. *Wooing, Wedding and Power: Women in Shakespeare's Plays.* N.Y.: Columbia U. Press, 1981.

Delaney, Paul. "*King Lear* and the Decline of Feudalism." *PMLA*, 82 (May 1977).

Dollimore, Jonathan. *Radical Tragedy: Religion, Ideology and Power in the Drama of Shakespeare and His Contemporaries.* Chicago, Illinois: U. of Chicago Press, 1984.

Elizabethan Theatre. Stratford-upon-Avon Studies 9. Ed. John Russell Brown and Bernard Harris. London: Edward Arnold (Publishers) Ltd., 1966.

Evans, Robert O. *The Osier Cage: Rhetorical Devices in Romeo and Juliet.* Lexington, Kentucky: U. of Kentucky Press, 1966.

Everett, Barbara. "*Romeo and Juliet*: The Nurse's Story." *Critical Q.*, 14 (1972), 129-39.

Fabry, Frank. "Shakespeare's Witty Musician: *Romeo and Juliet*, IV.v.114-17." *Shak. Q.*, 33 (1982), 182-83.

Farnham, Willard. *The Medieval Heritage of Elizabethan Tragedy.* 1936; rpt. Oxford, England: Basil Blackwell, 1963.

Farrell, Kirby. *Play, Death, and Heroism in Shakespeare.* Chapel Hill and London: The U. of North Carolina Press, 1989.

Felperin, Howard. *Shakespearean Romance.* Princeton, N.J. Princeton U. Press, 1972.

Fortin, Rene E. "Desolation and the Better Life: The Two Voices of Shakespearean Tragedy." *Shak. Q.*, 32 (1981), 80-94.

Frazer, James George. *The New Golden Bough: A New Abridgement of the Classical Work.* Ed. Theodor H. Gaster. N.Y.: Criterion Books, Inc., 1959.

Frye, Northrop. *Anatomy of Criticism: Four Essays.* Princeton, N.J.: Princeton U. Press, 1957.

Garber, Marjorie. *Coming of Age in Shakespeare*. London & N.Y.: Methuen & Co. Ltd., 1981.

___. "'Remember Me': *Memento Mori* Figures in Shakespeare's Plays." *Renaissance Drama*, 12 (1981), 3-25.

___. "'Wild Laughter in the Throat of Death': Darker Purposes in Shakespearean Comedy." In *Shakespearean Comedy*. Ed. Maurice Charney. N.Y.: New York Literary Forum, 1980.

Gardiner, Harold C., S.J. *Mysteries' End: An Investigation of the Last Days of the Medieval Religious Stage*. 1946; rpt. Archon Books, 1967.

Geertz, Clifford. *The Interpretation of Cultures*. Basic Books, Inc., 1973.

Godly Queen Hester. In *Early English Dramatists: Six Anonymous Plays* (second ser.). Ed. John S. Farmer. London: EEDS, 1906; facsim. rpt. N.Y.: Barnes & Noble, Inc., 1966.

Goldman, Michael. *Shakespeare and the Energies of Drama*. Princeton, N.J.: Princeton U. Press, 1972.

Greenblatt, Stephen. *Renaissance Self-Fashioning: From More to Shakespeare*. Chicago & London: U. of Chicago Press, 1980.

___. *Shakespearean Negotiations: The Circulation of Social Energy in Renaissance England*. Berkeley/Los Angeles: U. of California Press, 1988.

Grudin, Robert. *Mighty Opposites: Shakespeare and Renaissance Contrariety*. Berkeley/Los Angeles/London: U. of Calif. Press, 1979.

Hamilton, Donna B. "The State of Law in *Richard II*." *Shak. Q.*, 34 (1983), pp. 5-17.

Hapgood, Robert. "Shakespeare and the Ritualists." *Shak. Survey,* 15 (1962), 111-124.

Hardison, O.B., Jr. *Christian Rite and Christian Drama in the Middle Ages: Essays in the Origin and Early History of Modern Drama.* Baltimore, Maryland: The Johns Hopkins U. Press, 1965.

Hawkins, Sherman. "The Two Worlds of Shakespearean Comedy." *Shak. Studies,* 3 (1968 for 1967), 62-80.

Heninger, S.K. Jr. "The Pattern of Love's Labour's Lost." *Shak. Studies,* 7 (1974), 25-53.

"Herod the Great." In *Medieval Drama.* Ed. David Bevington. Boston: Houghton Mifflin Company, 1975.

Hill, Christopher. *Reformation to Industrial Revolution: The Making of Modern English Society, Vol. I, 1530-1780.* N.Y.: Pantheon Books, 1967.

Holderness, Graham. *Shakespeare's History.* Dublin: Gill and Macmillan; N.Y.: St. Martin's Press, 1985.

Holland, Norman N. "Mercutio, Mine Own Son the Dentist." In *Essays on Shakespeare.* Ed. Gordon Ross Smith. University Park, London: The Pennsylvania State U. Press, 1965, pp. 3-14.

Hoy, Cyrus. "*Love's Labour's Lost* and the Nature of Comedy." *Shak. Q.,* 13 (1962), 31-40.

Hunter, G.K. "Shakespeare's Early Tragedies: *Titus Andronicus* and *Romeo and Juliet.*" *Shak. Survey,* 27 (1974), 1-9.

Hunter, Robert G. "The Function of the Songs at the End of *Love's Labour's Lost.*" *Shak. Studies,* 7 (1974), 55-64.

Jeffrey, David L. "English Saints' Plays." In *Medieval Drama*, Stratford-upon-Avon Studies 16. Ed. Neville Denny. London: Edward Arnold (Publishers) Ltd., 1973.

Kantorowicz, Ernst H. *The King's Two Bodies: A Study in Medieval Political Theology*. Princeton, N.J.: Princeton U. Press, 1957.

Kastan, David Scott. "Proud Majesty Made a Subject: Shakespeare and the Spectacle of Rule." *Shak. Q.*, 37 (1986), 459-475.

___. *Shakespeare and the Shapes of Time*. Hanover, New Hampshire: U. Press of New England, 1982.

Kernan, Alvin B. "The Henriad: Shakespeare's Major History Plays." In *Modern Shakespearean Criticism: Essays on Style, Dramaturgy, and the Major Plays*. Ed. Alvin B. Kernan. N.Y./Chicago/San Francisco/Atlanta: Harcourt Brace Jovanovich, Inc., 1970.

___. *The Playwright as Magician: Shakespeare's Image of the Poet in the English Public Theater*. New Haven & London: Yale U. Press, 1979.

King Darius. In *Early English Dramatists: Anonymous Plays* (3nd ser.). Ed. John S. Farmer. London: EEDS, 1906; facsim. rpt. N.Y.: Barnes & Noble, Inc., 1966.

Klein, David. *Milestones to Shakespeare: A Study of the Dramatic Forms and Pageantry that were the Prelude to Shakespeare*. N.Y.: Twayne Publishers, Inc., 1970.

Knight, W. Nicholas. *Shakespeare's Hidden Life: Shakespeare at the Law, 1585-1595*. N.Y.: Mason & Lipscombe, 1973.

Kokeritz, Helge. *Shakespeare's Pronunciation*. 1953; rpt. New Haven & London: Yale U. Press, 1966.

Kolve, V.A. *The Play Called Corpus Christi.* Stanford, Calif.: Stanford U. Press, 1966.

Kott, Jan. *Shakespeare Our Contemporary.* Trans. Boleslaw Taborski. N.Y.: W.W. Norton & Company, Inc., 1964.

Langer, Suzanne. *Feeling and Form: A Theory of Art.* N.Y.: Charles' Scribner's Sons, 1953.

Lawlor, John. "*Romeo and Juliet.*" In *Early Shakespeare.* Stratford-upon-Avon Studies 3. 1961; modified 1967; rpt. London: Arnold, 1976, pp. 123-43.

Levin, Harry. "Form and Formality in 'Romeo and Juliet.'" *Shak. Q.*, 11 (1960). Rpt. in *Modern Shakespearean Criticism: Essays on Style, Dramaturgy, and the Major Plays.* Ed. Alvin B. Kernan. N.Y.: Harcourt Brace Jovanovich, Inc., 1970.

Levin, Richard. *New Readings vs. Old Plays: Recent Trends in the Reinterpretation of English Renaissance Drama.* Chicago and London: U. of Chicago Press, 1979.

Lifton, Robert J. *The Broken Connection: On Death and the Continuity of Life.* N.Y.: Simon & Schuster, Inc., 1979.

Liturgical Services: Liturgies and Occasional Forms of Prayer Set Forth in the Reign of Queen Elizabeth. Ed. William Keatinge Clay. Vol. XXX. Cambridge U. Press, 1847.

The Liturgy of the Church of England Before and After the Reformation. Ed. Stephen A. Hurlbut. Washington, D.C.: The St. Albans Press.

Long, Michael. *The Unnatural Scene: A Study in Shakespearean Tragedy.* London: Methuen & Co., Ltd., 1976.

Mack, Maynard. "The Jacobean Shakespeare: Some Observations on the Construction of the Tragedies." In *Jacobean Theatre.* Stratford-upon-Avon Studies. Vol. I. Ed. John Russell Brown and Bernard Harris. Rpt. in *Modern Shake-*

speare Criticism: Essays on Style, Dramaturgy, and the Major Plays. Ed. Alvin B. Kernan. N.Y.: Harcourt Brace Jovanovich, Inc., 1970.

___. *Killing the King: Three Studies in Shakespeare's Tragic Structure.* Yale Studies in English, 180. New Haven and London: Yale U. Press, 1973.

___. *King Lear in Our Time.* Berkeley & Los Angeles: Univ. of Calif. Press, 1965.

Mahood, M.M. *Shakespeare's Wordplay.* London: Methuen & Co., Ltd., 1957.

Manheim, Michael. *The Weak King in the Shakespearean History Play.* Syracuse, N.Y.: Syracuse U. Press, 1973.

Marsh, Derick R.C. *Passion Lends Them Power: A Study of Shakespeare's Love Tragedies.* Manchester U. Press, 1976.

Mason, H.A. *Shakespeare's Tragedies of Love: An Examination of the Possibility of Common Readings of* Romeo and Juliet, Othello, King Lear, *and* Anthony and Cleopatra. N.Y.: Barnes & Noble, Inc. 1970.

McFarland, Thomas. *Shakespeare's Pastoral Comedy.* Chapel Hill: U. of North Carolina Press, 1972.

___. *Tragic Meanings in Shakespeare.* N.Y.: Random House, Inc., 1966.

McLay, Catherine M. "The Dialogues of Spring and Winter: A Key to the Unity of *Love's Labour's Lost.*" *Shak. Q.,* 18 (1967), 119-27.

Montrose, Louis Adrian. *"Curious-Knotted Garden": the Form, Themes, and Contexts of Shakespeare's* Love's Labour's Lost. Salzburg Studies in English Literature. Elizabethan and Renaissance Studies, No. 56. Ed. James Hogg. Salzburg,

Austria: Institut fur Englische Sprache und Literatur, Universitat Salzburg, 1977.

Morris, Harry. *Last Things in Shakespeare*. Tallahassee, Florida: U. Presses of Florida, Florida State U. Press, 1985.

Muir, Kenneth. *Shakespeare's Tragic Sequence*. London: Hutchinson U. Library, 1972.

Mundus et Infans. In *Specimens of the Pre-Shakespearean Drama*. Vol. I. Ed. John Matthews Manly. 1897; rpt. N.Y.: Dover Publications, Inc., 1967.

Nelson, Alan H. *The Medieval English Stage: Corpus Christi Pageants and Plays*. Chicago & London: U. of Chicago Press, 1974.

Nevo, Ruth. *Tragic Form in Shakespeare*. Princeton, N.J.: Princeton U. Press, 1972.

Ornstein, Robert. *A Kingdom for a Stage: The Achievement of Shakespeare's History Plays*. Cambridge, Mass.: Harvard U. Press, 1972.

Owst, G.R. *Literature and Pulpit in Medieval England*. 1933; rpt. London: Oxford U. Press, 1961.

Oxford English Dictionary (Compact Edition). Oxford U. Press, 1971.

Partridge, Eric. *Shakespeare's Bawdy: A Literary & Psychological Essay and a Comprehensive Glossary*. 1948; revised, N.Y.: E.P. Dutton & Co., Inc., 1969.

Penn Warren, Robert. "Pure and Impure Poetry." In *Selected Essays*. N.Y.: Random House, n.d.

Pierce, Robert B. *Shakespeare's History Plays: The Family and the State*. Ohio State U. Press, 1971.

Potter, Robert. *English Morality Play: Origins, History and Influence of a Dramatic Tradition.* London & Boston: Routledge & Kegan Paul, 1975.

The Pride of Life. In *Tudor Interludes.* Ed. Peter Happe. Middlesex, England: Penguin Books Ltd., 1972.

Prior, Moody E. *The Drama of Power: Studies in Shakespeare's History Plays.* Evanston, Illinois: Northwestern U. Press, 1973.

Prosser, Eleanor. *Drama and Religion in the English Mystery Plays: A Re-evaluation.* Stanford Studies in Language and Literature, 23. Stanford, Calif.: Stanford U. Press, 1961.

Rabkin, Norman. *Shakespeare and the Common Understanding.* N.Y.: The Free Press: London: Collier-Macmillan Ltd., 1967.

___. *Shakespeare and the Problem of Meaning.* Chicago & London: The U. of Chicago Press, 1981.

Rackin, Phyllis. "The Role of the Audience in Shakespeare's *Richard II*." *Shak. Q.*, 36 (1985), 262-281.

___. *Shakespeare's Tragedies.* N.Y.: Frederick Ungar Publishing Co., 1978.

Reed, A.W. *Early Tudor Drama: Medwall, the Rastells, Heywood, and the More Circle.* 1926; rpt. N.Y.: Octagon Books, Farrar, Straus & Giroux, Inc., 1969.

Reese, M.M. *The Cease of Majesty: A Study of Shakespeare's History Plays.* London: Edward Arnold (Publishers) Ltd., 1961.

Respublica. In *"Lost" Tudor Plays with Some Others.* Ed. John S. Farmer. EEDS, 1907; facsim. rpt. N.Y.: Barnes & Noble, Inc., 1966.

Ribner, Irving. *The English History Play in the Age of Shakespeare.* 1957; rpt. & revised, London: Methuen & Co., Ltd., 1965.

___. *Patterns in Shakespearian Tragedy.* 1960; rpt. London: Methuen and Co., Ltd., 1969.

Righter, Anne. *Shakespeare and the Idea of the Play.* N.Y.: Barnes & Noble, Inc., 1962.

Roddy, K.P. "Epic Qualities in the Cycle Plays." In *Medieval Drama.* Stratford-upon-Avon Studies 16. Ed. Neville Denny. London: Edward Arnold (Publishers) Ltd., 1973.

Roesen [Anne Barton], Bobbyann. "*Love's Labor's Lost.*" *Shak. Q.*, 4 (1953), 411-26.

Rosen, William. *Shakespeare and the Craft of Tragedies.* Cambridge, Mass.: Harvard U. Press, 1967.

Rossiter, A.P. *Angel with Horns and other Shakespearean Lectures.* Ed. Graham Storey. N.Y.: Theatre Arts Books; Longmans, Green & Co., Ltd., 1961.

___. *English Drama from Early Times to the Elizabethans: Background, Origins and Developments.* London: Hutchinson's U. Library, 1950.

Roston, Murray. *Biblical Drama in England: From the Middle Ages to the Present.* Evanston, Illinois: Northwestern U. Press, 1973.

de Rougemont, Denis. *Love in the Western World.* Trans. Montgomery Belgion. 1956; rpt. N.Y. Harper & Row, Publishers, 1974.

Saccio, Peter. *Shakespeare's English Kings: History, Chronicle, and Drama.* Oxford U. Press, 1977.

Salingar, Leo S. *Traditions of Comedy.* London & N.Y.: Cambridge U Press, 1974.

Sanders, Wilbur. *The Dramatist and the Received Idea: Studies in the Plays of Marlowe and Shakespeare.* Cambridge: Cambridge U. Press, 1968.

Schwartz, Murray M. and Coppelia Kahn, ed. *Representing Shakespeare: New Psychoanalytic Essays.* Baltimore, Maryland.: The Johns Hopkins U. Press, 1980.

Shakespeare, William. *The Complete Signet Classic Shakespeare*, ed. Sylvan Barnet. N.Y.: Harcourt Brace Jovanovich, Inc., 1963.

___. *The Riverside Shakespeare.* Textual ed., G. Blakemore Evans. Boston: Houghton Mifflin Company, 1975.

Sidney, Sir Philip. "*The Defense of Poesy.*" In *Sir Philip Sidney: Selected Prose and Poetry.* Ed. Robert Kimbrough, N.Y.: Holt, Rinehart & Winston, Inc., 1969.

Siegel, Paul N. *Shakespeare in His Time and Ours.* Notre Dame, Indiana: U. of Notre Dame Press, 1968.

Siemon, James R. *Shakespearean Iconoclasm.* Berkeley/Los Angeles/Calif.: U. of Calif. Press, 1985.

Skelton, John. "*Magnificence.*" In *The Complete Poems of John Skelton*, Ed. Philip Henderson. 1931; revised 1948; rpt. London: Jim Dent & Sons Ltd., 1966.

Smidt, Kristian. *Unconformities in Shakespeare's History Plays.* Atlantic Highlands, N.J.: Humanities Press, 1982.

Smith, Gordon Ross. "The Balance of Themes in *Romeo and Juliet.*" In *Essays on Shakespeare.* Ed. Gordon Ross Smith. University Park & London: The Pennsylvania State U. Press, 1965.

Smith, Marion Bodwell. *Dualities in Shakespeare.* Toronto: Toronto Press, 1966.

Snyder, Susan. *The Comic Matrix of Shakespeare's Tragedies: Romeo and Juliet, Hamlet, Othello, and King Lear.* Princeton, N.J.: Princeton U. Press, 1979.

Specimens of the Pre-Shaksperean Drama. Ed. John Matthews Manly. Vol. I. 1897; rpt. N.Y.: Dover Publications, Inc., 1967.

Spencer, Theodore. *Death and Elizabethan Tragedy: A Study of Convention and Opinion in the Elizabethan Drama.* Cambridge, Mass.: Harvard U. Press, 1936.

Spivack, Bernard. *Shakespeare and the Allegory of Evil: The History of a Metaphor in Relation to Shakespeare's Major Villains.* N.Y.: Columbia U. Press, 1958.

Spivack, Charlotte. *The Comedy of Evil on Shakespeare's Stage.* Cranbury, New Jersey: Associated University Presses, Inc., 1978.

Stilling, Roger. *Love and Death in Renaissance Tragedy.* Baton Rouge, La.: Louisiana State U. Press, 1976.

Stone, Lawrence. *The Crisis of the Aristocracy, 1558-1641*, abridged edition. London/Oxford/N.Y.: Oxford U. Press, 1967.

Sundelson, David. *Shakespeare's Restorations of the Father.* New Brunswick, N. J.: Rutgers U. Press, 1983.

Taylor, Jerome. "The Dramatic Structure of the Middle English Corpus Christi, or Cycle, Plays." In *Medieval English Drama: Essays Critical and Contextual.* Ed. Jerome Taylor and Alan H. Nelson. Chicago & London: U. of Chicago Press, 1972.

Taylor, Mark. *Shakespeare's Darker Purpose: A Question of Incest.* N.Y.: AMS Press, 1982.

Thomas, Sidney. "The Queen Mab Speech In 'Romeo and Juliet'." *Shak. Survey*, 25 (1972), 73-80.

Tillyard, E.M.W. *Shakespeare's History Plays*. N.Y.: The Macmillan Company, 1946.

Traci, Philip J. "Suggestions About the Bawdry in *Romeo and Juliet*." *South Atlantic Q.*, 71 (1972), 573-86.

Traversi, Derek. *Shakespeare: The Last Phase*. 1955; rpt. Stanford, Calif.: Stanford U. Press, 1969.

___. *Shakespeare From* Richard II *to* Henry V. Stanford, Calif.: Stanford U. Press, 1957.

Tucker, Brooke, C.F. *The Tudor Drama: A History of English National Drama to the Retirement of Shakespeare*. 1911; rpt. Hamden, Conn./London: Archon Books, 1964.

The Two Liturgies, A.D. 1549 and A.D. 1552, with Other Documents Set Forth by Authority in the Reign of King Edward VI. Ed. Joseph Ketley. Vol. XXIX. Cambridge U. Press, 1844.

Udall, Nicholas. *Respublica*. In *"Lost" Tudor Plays With Some Others*. Ed. John S. Farmer. London, 1907; facsim. rpt. N.Y.: Barnes & Noble, Inc., 1966.

Utterback, Raymond V. "The Death of Mercutio." *Shak. Q.*, 24 (1973), 105-116.

Vickers, Brian. *The Artistry of Shakespeare's Prose*. London: Methuen & Co., Ltd., 1968.

The Wakefield Mystery Plays. Ed. Martial Rose. London: Evans Brothers Limited, 1961.

Weimann, Robert. *Shakespeare and Popular Tradition in the Theater: Studies in the Social Dimension of Dramatic Form and Function*. Ed. Robert Schwartz. Baltimore and London: The Johns Hopkins U. Press, 1978.

Welsh, Alexander. "The Task of Hamlet." *The Yale Review*, 69 (1980), 481-502.

Westlund, Joseph. "Fancy & Achievement in *Love's Labour's Lost*." *Shak. Q.*, 18 (1967), 37-46.

Wheeler, Richard P. *Shakespeare's Development and the Problem Comedies: Turn and Counter-Turn*. Berkeley/Los Angeles/London: U. of Calif. Press, 1979.

Wickham, Glynne, ed. *English Moral Interludes*. London: J.M. Dent & Sons Ltd., 1976.

___. *Shakespeare's Dramatic Heritage: Collected Studies in Medieval, Tudor and Shakespearean Drama*. N.Y.: Barnes & Noble, Inc., 1969.

___. "Stage and Drama till 1660." In *Sphere History of Literature in the English Language*. Vol. III, *English Drama to 1710*. Ed. Christopher Ricks. London: Sphere Books Limited, 1971.

Wilders, John. *The Lost Garden: A View of Shakespeare's English and Roman History Plays*. Totowa, N.J.: Rowman & Littlefield, 1978.

Wilders, John. "The Unresolved Conflicts of *Love's Labour's Lost*." *Essays in Criticism*, 27 (1977), 20-33.

Wilson, F.P. *The English Drama 1485-1585*. Ed. G.K. Hunter. Oxford History of English Literature. Ed. Bonamy Dobree and Norman Davis. N.Y. & London: Oxford U. Press, 1968.

___. "Illustrations of Social Life IV: the Plague. "*Shak. Survey*, 15 (1962), 125-129.

Winny, James. *The Player King: A Theme of Shakespeare's Histories*. London: Chatto & Windus, 1968.

Woolf, Rosemary. *The English Mystery Plays*. Berkeley & Los Angeles: U. of Calif. Press, 1972.

Yates, Frances *A Study of Love's Labour's Lost*. 1936; rpt. Folcroft, Pa.; Folcroft Library Editions, 1973.

Yeats, William Butler. "Sailing to Byzantium." In *The Collected Poems of W.B. Yeats*. N.Y.: The Macmillan Company, 1956.

The York Plays. Ed. Richard Beadle. York Medieval Texts, 2nd ser. Ed. Elizabeth Salter and Derek Pearsall. London: Edward Arnold (Publishers) Ltd., 1982.

York Plays: The Plays Performed by the Crafts or Mysteries of York on the Day of Corpus Christi in the 14th, 15th and 16th Centuries. Ed. Lucy Toulmin Smith. 1885; rpt. N.Y.: Russell & Russell, 1963.

Index

A

actions, wholeness of in drama, 10
Aethelwold, Saint, 8
Antony and Cleopatra,
    death aspect of human nature in, 223-224
    as means to overcome death, 123-135, 146n.20, 220
As You Like It,
    death aspect of human nature in, 220-221

B

Bale, John
    as supporter of Tudor absolutism, 41-42
    See also Kynge Johan
Becker, Ernest, 2
Berry, Ralph, on *Love's Labor's Lost*, 109-110
birth, as source of death, 153
body politic, 56
    See also nation-state
Burke, Kenneth, 3

C

Castle of Perserverance, The
    death and resurrection in, 19-20, 21
Chester Octavian, 26-27
Church, the
    in *Henry V*, 82, 83
    nation-state, supremacy over, 82-83, 101n.34
comedy
    See death, dealing with in Shakespearean drama
    See death, genre and
communal body,
    as source of death in *Romeo and Juliet*, 154-155, 157-183
    death and resurrection of, 94-95
    in *Henry V*, 91
    separation from as form of death, 94, 151-152
Conversion of Saint Paul, The, 31
Corpus Christi, *See* mystical body
crucifixion, 7
cycle plays, 6
    See drama, Corpus Christi

D

death,
    art as means to overcome, 123-135, 146n.20, 220
    as dramatic character, 19
    birth, as source of, 153
    dealing with in Shakespearean drama,
        in comedy, 142-143, 151-152, 204n.1, 219-220
        in history plays, 219
        in tragedy, 5, 152-53, 220, 222
        See also 1 Henry IV, 2 Henry IV, Henry V, Love's Labor's Lost, Richard II, Romeo and Juliet
    denial of, 12n.1 & 2
    dying as a means to deal with, 196
    genre and, 4-5, 93-95, 151-152, 200-202, 219-220
    individuality and, 153-154, 156, 186, 201, 218n.52
    joy and rebirth aspect of, 7

kings/rulers as figures of, 25-27, 35-36, 45, 87-88, 89-90, 104n.40, 177-179
mastery of (i.e., oneness with life), 1, 3
mastery of in here and now, 196-198, 201-202, 217n.44
mortal corruptibility and, 28-29, 199, 217n.47
nation-state as source of, 80, 86, 102n.38
permanence of, 79
resurrection and, 10, 11, 17-22, 23-29, 30-36, 93, 94-95
separation from communal body as form of, 94, 151-52
sexuality and, 108, 111-112, 118-21, 122, 131, 132, 135, 139, 141, 145n.6, 8, 187-193, 196-203, 214n.31, 33, 221
suffering and, 7, 112
war and, in *Henry V*, 85
See also mortality
death-transcendence, 2-3, 9, 10, 11, 18-25
absence of in nation-state, 57, 93, 94
absence of in *Richard II*, 88
conversion as, 30, 32
doubters of, 32-33, 72, 182, 211n.22
in *Mary Magdalene*, 33-36
in *The Play of the Sacrament*, 31-32
in *Romeo and Juliet*, 154, 155, 157, 171, 187, 199, 200-202
See also death, genre and drama,
Corpus Christi,
death and resurrection in, 23-29, 93
episodes in, 24
extrascriptural material in, 31
history of, 22
Lazarus, raising of, 27-29
Mystical Body in, 22-23
Greek, 6
medieval, 11, 17, 94
death, overcoming in, 151

rulers, earthly in, 25-27, 33, 35-36
See also morality plays
See also Quem Quaeritis texts
morality,
death and resurrection in, 18-22
mankind as character in, 18, 20
Renaissance, 8, 11
See also Quem Quaeritis texts
Roman, 6
Tudor morality, 6
king as identified with nation-state in, 36-37
Dunstan, Saint, 8

E

Elizabeth,
English population's perspective of, 81
England,
economy in, 62-63
God and Elizabethan, 56-57
historical change in, as depicted by the history tetralogy, 56-58, 93, 96n.2, 97n.3, 98n.4
land, perspective of in Elizabethan, 59-62
law, changed perspective of, 80-81, 82-84, 86-87
restoration of a unified, 79
See also history tetralogy, second
Eve, 112
Everyman,
death and resurrection in, 20-21

F

fate, transcendence of in,
2 Henry IV, 20
Measure for Measure, 20
Merchant of Venice, 20
feudalism, 60
Four Daughters of God, allegory of, 20

G

genre,
  See death, genre and
God,
  as determiner of history, 82
  Elizabethan England and, 56-57
  Justice and, 82

H

Hamlet,
  death aspect of human nature in, 222
1 Henry IV, 4, 55, 56
  Falstaff, as representative of life/death, 72-75
  Glendower as representative of magic/romantic love/art, 71-72
  Hotspur as representative of personal honor, 68-70
  land, treatment of, 59
  money, puns on, 66-67, 76, 100n.18
  Welsh in, 72
2 Henry IV, 20, 55
  Falstaff, as representative of life/death, 72-75
  land, treatment of, 59
  law, perspective of, 80-81
  Justices of the Peace in, 84
  redemption, as defined by Hal, 76
Henry V, 4, 55
  audience in, 92, 93, 104n.43, 105n.45
  chorus in, 91, 104n.44
  church relations in, 82, 83
  communal body in, 91
  death in, 85, 88-89, 90, 151
  England, changing perspective of, 56, 57, 58
  Justice of the Peace in, 84
  land, treatment of, 59
  law in, 82-84, 86-87
  nation-state in, 79-80, 85
Henry V (ruler),
  as absolute ruler, 90-91
  as hero-king, 79-80
  critics' views of, 102n.39
  death, as associated with, 89-90
  in medieval ruler tradition, 89
Henry VIII, 55
Herod, 26
history,
  as determined by God, 82
  linear conception of, 79
  medieval conception of, 93, 105n.46
history tetralogy, second, 56-106
  debt/currency/counterfeiting in, 62-79
  land in, 58-62
  law/justice/warfare in, 79-93

I

immortality
  through children, 114, 115-116, 123, 126, 136, 139-140, 145n.13, 146n.15
  within the community, 153
Imperial Majesty
  as dramatic figure, 40
  in *Kynge Johan*, 40-41
  Mystical Body, as associated with, 36-37, 40-41, 42-45, 55, 56
  nation-state, as synonym of, 36-37, 40
  See also King
  See also ruler, earthly

J

Justices of the Peace, 84

K

Kantorowicz, Ernst
  "The King's Two Bodies", 42, 44
  See also Plowden, Edmund
king
  as death figure, 35-36, 87-88, 104n.40
  as dramatic figure, 18-19
  as representative of divine power, 81-82

counterfeit, 67
land and, 59
nation-state, as identified with, 36-37
Tudor legal and political conception of, 42-43
See also Imperial Majesty
See also Kantorowicz, Ernst
See also rulers, earthly
king, divine, 36, 87
King Lear, 10
death aspect of human nature in, 222
Kynge Johan,
as transition between morality and history plays, 39
Imperial Majesty in, 40-41
kingship, changed role in, 37
nation-state resurrection of in, 40
See also Bale, John

L

land
treatment of, in Second History Tetralogy, 58-62
law
changed view in *2 Henry IV*, 80-81
Salic, 83
view in *Henry V*, 82-84, 86-87
view in *Richard II*, 81-82
See also Justices of the Peace
Lazarus, raising of in Corpus Christi drama, 27-29
Lifton, Robert Jay, 2-3
literature, creation of, as means to counter death, 123-135, 146n.20, 220
Love's Labor Lost, 3, 4
death,
art as means to overcome, 123-135, 146n.20, 220
Marcade as messenger of, 109, 132, 141
sexuality and, 108, 111-112, 118-121, 122, 131, 132, 135, 139, 141, 145n.6, 8

wordplay as a means to cope with, 108-110, 123, 126, 132, 135, 144n.5
of Armado, 121-122
of the Courtiers, 115-121
of the Ladies, 122-123
of Moth and Costard, 110-113
of the Pedants, 113-115
immortality through children, 114, 115-116, 123, 126, 136, 139-140, 145n.13, 146n.15
mortality,
absence of solution to, 109, 123, 124, 125-126, 132
action against, 108-109, 135-142
individual, problem in, 107-109, 151
resurrection in, 131-132

M

Marx, Karl, 78
Mary Magdalene, 31
death, transcendence in, 33-36
dramatic themes, medieval in, 33-35
See also Saint's plays
Measure for Measure, 20
sexuality and death, link between, 111-112, 221
Merchant of Venice, 20
death aspect of human nature in, 220
Midsummer's Night's Dream, 139
death aspect of human nature in, 220, 223
military, in the history tetralogy, 85
morality plays, 6
death and resurrection in, 17-22
mortality, 1
of man, 37-39
See also Love's Labor's Lost, mortality
Mundus et Infans,
mortality of man in, 37-39

Mystical Body,
   Corpus Christi and, 22-23
   Imperial Majesty, as associated with, 36-37, 40-41, 42-45, 55, 56
   Saints and, 30, 31

N

nation-state
   as depicted in *Henry V*, 79-80, 85
   as source of life/death, 80, 86, 102n.38
   Church, control of, by, 82-83, 101n.34
   death-transcendence, absence of individual in, 57, 93, 94
   immortality of, 42
   Imperial Majesty, as synonym for, 37, 40
   in Elizabethan England, 57
   king, as identified with, 36-37, 40
   resurrection of, 40, 55, 56
   See also body politic

P

Play of the Sacrament, The
   death, transcendence of in, 31-32
   doubters, conversion of, 32
   See also Saint's plays
plays, folk, 13n.11
Plowden, Edmund
   king, Tudor legal and political conception of, 42, 43
Pride of Life,
   death and resurrection in, 18-19

Q

Quem quaeritis texts, 6-11, 14n.16, 17, 21, 24, 28, 34, 178, 202-203

R

redemption
   as defined by Hal, 76

Regularis Concordia,
   See Visitatio sepulchri
Respublica, 42
resurrection, 5
   death and, 10, 11, 17-22, 23-29, 30-36, 93, 94-95
   in *Love's Labor's Lost*, 131-132
   in *Romeo and Juliet*, 167, 168-169, 196, 218n.50
   in *The Tempest*, 124
   Lazarus-like version of, 112, 202-203
   of Christ, 6, 7, 8-9, 24
   of Lazarus, in Corpus Christi drama, 27-29
   of the nation-state, 40, 55, 56
Richard II, 4, 55
   death-transcendence, absence of, 88
   England, changing view of, 56, 57, 58
   land, treatment of, 59
   law, view of, 81-82
   money, puns on, 64-65
Richard II (king)
   as death figure, 87-88
Ripoll Resurrection Play, 32
Romeo and Juliet,
   as aborted comedy, 152, 204n.3
   as tragedy, 204n.4
   death,
     comic solution to, 152-153, 154
     inadequacy of, 185, 189, 192, 193, 196, 202, 212n.27 & 28, 216n.43
     communal body as source of, 154-155, 206n.7
       aristocrats as, 182-183
       Escalus as, 174-179
       Mercutio as, 179-182
       parental figures as, 154-174, 208n.16
       servants as, 183
     confrontation with, as means of mastery of, 202
     dying as way to deal with, 196-203, 216n.42
     Escalus as associated with, 177-179

fear of, by communal body, 198
individuality and, 153-154, 156, 186, 201, 218n.52
irreversibility of, 200
love, sexuality and, 187-193, 196-203, 214n.31 &33
mastery of, in here and now, 196-198, 201-202, 217n.44
mock, 167-168
Nurse's view of, 154
death-transcendence in, 154, 155, 157, 171, 187, 199, 200-202
denouement in, 194-202
Doomsday, images of, 177-178
lovers,
    pre-death speeches of, 198-199
    role of, 186-188, 193, 212n.29
Mercutio,
    as doubter figure, 182, 211n.22
    Conjuring speech of, 180-181
    death of, 185-186, 211n.26
    Queen Mab speech of, 180, 181, 210n.21
mortal corruptibility in, 199, 217n.47
resurrection in, 167, 168-169, 196, 218n.50
wordplay in, 181
rulers, earthly
    in medieval drama, 25-27, 33, 35-36
    in Tudor drama, 42, 55
    See also king
    See also Imperial Majesty

S

Saint's plays, 6, 16n.32
    death and resurrection in, 30-36
    See also Mary Magdalene and *The Play of the Sacrament*
sexual reproduction, 114

T

Tempest, The, 124
tragedy
    See death, dealing with in Shakespearean drama
    See death, genre and
treason, 81, 101n.32

U

Udall, Nicholas, 42

V

Visitatio Sepulchri, 8-10

W

Welsh, the
    in *1 Henry IV*, 72
Winter's Tale, The, 10
wordplay,
    in *Henry IV*, 66-67, 76, 100n.18
    in *Love's Labor Lost*, 108-123, 126, 132, 135, 144n.5
    in *Richard II*, 64-65
    in *Romeo and Juliet*, 181

Studies in Shakespeare

This series deals with all aspects of Shakespearean drama and poetry. Studies of dramatic structure, verse and prose style, major themes, stage or performance history, and film treatments are welcomed. The editor is particularly interested in manuscripts that examine Shakespeare's work in its American setting–in the academy, on stage, and in popular culture. Inquiries and manuscripts should be sent to the series editor:

> Robert F. Willson, Jr.
> Dept. of English
> University of Missouri–Kansas City
> College of Arts & Sciences
> 106 Cockefair Hall
> Kansas City, MO 64110-2499